The Eastern Establishment and the Western Experience

AMERICAN STUDIES SERIES
William H. Goetzmann, Editor

THE EASTERN ESTABLISHMENT AND THE WESTERN EXPERIENCE

The West of Frederic Remington, Theodore Roosevelt, and Owen Wister

by G. Edward White

 UNIVERSITY OF TEXAS PRESS, AUSTIN

First University of Texas Press Paperback Edition, 1989

LIBRARY OF CONGRESS CATALOGING-IN-PUBLICATION DATA
White, G. Edward.
    The Eastern establishment and the western experience : the West of
Frederic Remington, Theodore Roosevelt, and Owen Wister / by G.
Edward White. — 1st University of Texas Press pbk. ed.
      p. cm. — (American studies series)
    Reprint. Originally published: New Haven : Yale University Press,
1968.
    Originally presented as the author's thesis (Ph. D.—Yale
University, 1967).
    Bibliography: p.
    Includes index.
    ISBN 0-292-72065-3 (alk. paper)
    1. West (U.S.)—Civilization.   2. United States—
Civilization—1865–1918.   3. Remington, Frederic, 1861–1909.
4. Roosevelt, Theodore, 1858–1918.   5. Wister, Owen, 1860–1938.
I. Title. II. Series.
F595.W6   1989
978'.02—dc 19   89-31095
                                    CIP

For F. McC. W., G. L. W., and S. D. W.

It is my great happiness that, twenty-one years after the original dedication page, its designees are still at the center of our extended family. May they long remain there.

Contents

Preface

In the course of my attempt to find a connection between such disparate events as the Johnson County War in Wyoming in 1892 and the Bradley-Martin ball in New York City five years later, I have profited from the assistance of a number of people who were willing to enlighten me on various aspects of the East and the West, regardless of whether they thought that the twain had ever met. Mrs. Robin McKown has filled a void in my research on Frederic Remington by allowing me to make use of her voluminous notes and patiently responding to queries. Mrs. Frances Kemble Wister Stokes and Owen J. Wister, Jr., have cheerfully discussed their father at length. Mrs. Sheila K. Hart and the reference staff of the Harvard College Library have placed the Theodore Roosevelt Collection of papers at my disposal and answered questions with kindness and dispatch.

Profitable discussions with E. Digby Baltzell, Michael H. Cowan, Lewis L. Gould, William Lilley, III, and Orm Overland have opened new areas of investigation and helped to clarify some of my own notions. Mrs. Catherine W. Taggert, Curator of the Remington Art Memorial at Ogdensburg, New York; David C. Mearns, Chief of the Manuscripts Division at the Library of Congress; and the staffs of the Rare Manuscripts Division of the New York Public Library and the Western History Research Center of the University of Wyoming have guided the direction of my research. Mrs. Anne Granger has performed a range of editorial and typing services in several stages of the manuscript. A. N. Kaul, Kenneth Keniston, and Edwin Fussell have read the entire manuscript in preliminary form and made valuable critical suggestions.

I am especially indebted to Howard Roberts Lamar, who inspired and directed the work in its original form, and to Wayland Schmitt, who has labored hard to made it readable. To them and to the above my thanks and gratitude.

Washington, D.C.   **G. E. W.**
September 1967

Preface to the Paperback Edition

It is always a pleasure for an author to be asked to introduce an additional edition of one of his works, in this case for William Goetzmann's distinguished American studies series. On this occasion my pleasure has been enhanced by the unusual circumstances of the reissue. *The Eastern Establishment and the Western Experience* originally appeared in 1968, having been a doctoral dissertation that I submitted to the Department of American Studies at Yale the previous year. The book was in a tradition of American studies literature on the relationship between symbolic figures and images in America and the culture in which they had appeared. Shortly after the book appeared that sort of methodology became less compelling in academic circles, quantitative studies became more in vogue, and a genre of works that had their origin with Henry Nash Smith's *Virgin Land* and R. W. B. Lewis' *The American Adam* became encapsulated in time. I would not like to think there was any causal relationship between the appearance of my book and the end of the genre, but the fact was that by the early 1970s American studies work of that sort was not being produced and *The Eastern Establishment and the Western Experience* was out of print.

One reviewer of the first edition had noted that I was attending Harvard Law School at the time of its appearance and surmised that I might "write no more."[1] For a time I did not, and when my next book appeared, in 1976, it was in legal history and I was a law professor. Since then I have not done any more western history, although I have been fortunate enough to have a chance to apply some of the techniques I used in the first edition of *The Eastern Establishment* to some legal history topics. In my most recent book, for example, a cultural history of the Marshall Court, I revisit the writings of James Fenimore Cooper, whom I treat with a different

---

1. Earl Pomeroy, *Journal of American History*, 55 (1969), 660.

substantive emphasis but a similar methodological perspective.[2] For the most part, however, I have been working on strikingly different issues from the ones addressed in this volume and have regarded myself as occupying a scholarly position far removed from that of the persons I was addressing in *The Eastern Establishment*. That is one reason why it is a particular pleasure to revisit the subject matter of this volume and to imagine that its themes are still germane.

The most satisfying feature of this reissue for me, however, is neither its nostalgic dimensions nor its opportunity to concern myself once again with western history. It is the reemergence of cultural studies as an area of significance in current scholarship. Just as it was no accident that the first edition went out of print in the early 1970s, it is no accident that interest has recently surfaced in bringing it back into print. *The Eastern Establishment* represents a historiographical approach that places an emphasis on the relationship between products of the literary and artistic imagination and their cultural setting; a methodology that is qualitative in its orientation; an effort to fuse the insights of several disciplines in a cultural history; an emphasis on biography as a source of cultural data; and an exercise in recovering "lost" attitudes and assumptions that were once regarded as "beyond dispute" by previous generations of Americans and now seem problematic or distasteful to moderns. In short, the work's emphasis is not dissimilar from that employed by current work on the cultural setting of politics, language, and ideology. It is a work of cultural studies.

Looking back over a twenty-year period and imagining how one might have written a book differently can be daunting, especially when one has changed fields. I have not attempted any revisions or additions to the text, although I have attempted to ascertain if any scholarship in the interval has called my findings or conclusions into question. In that brief survey I have come upon a number of fine works: Edmund Morris's biography of Theodore Roosevelt's early life, Ben Vorpahl's volumes on Frederic Remington and his friendship with Owen Wister, Darwin Payne's biography of Wister, Ray Billington's *Land of Savagery/Land of Promise* on the image

2. See G. Edward White, *The Marshall Court and Cultural Change, 1815–35* (New York, 1988), pp. 12–48.

of the West in the nineteenth century, and Lee Mitchell's study of similar themes from a more rigorously anthropological perspective, *Witnesses to a Vanishing America.*[3] It is clear to me that some of these works represent an advance from mine in methodological sophistication, and some address issues, such as the cultural subjugation of Native Americans that accompanied the impulse to romanticize the "Wild West" in the period I survey, that I might have fruitfully explored. But on the whole I do not find that recent scholarship has seriously questioned the conclusions I advance in *The Eastern Establishment.*

A final word before offering this edition to perhaps a less gentle reading public than originally received it. In the preface to the first edition I mention the contributions of Howard Roberts Lamar, who had directed the original dissertation. That reference significantly understated his impact. Howard Lamar, on being confronted with a graduate student who was actively resisting professionalization and maturity, not only endured the prospect but also was somehow able to suggest that the student's entire identity was not at stake in conforming to the ordinary rites of passage in the academic world. As a result Howard was rewarded, after both he and the graduate student had survived the dissertation experience, by the student's jumping ship for the legal profession, which at least saved Howard the prospect of having to write him recommendations for teaching positions. Many years later the episode still strikes me as a model for dissertation directors. May Howard's future students be exemplars of maturity and quiescence.

G. E. W.

Charlottesville, Virginia
December 27, 1988

---

3. Edmund Morris, *The Rise of Theodore Roosevelt* (New York, 1980); Ben Vorpahl, *Frederic Remington and the West: With the Eye of the Mind* (Austin, Tex., 1978) and *Frederic Remington and Owen Wister: The Story of a Friendship* (New York, 1978); Darwin Payne, *Owen Wister: Chronicler of the West, Gentleman of the East* (Dallas, 1985); Ray Billington, *Land of Savagery/Land of Promise: The European Image of the American Frontier* (Norman, Okla., 1981); Lee Mitchell, *Witnesses to a Vanishing America: The Nineteenth-Century Response* (Princeton, N.J., 1987).

The Eastern Establishment and the Western Experience

Introduction

Of the three regions broadly conceived as subdividing the continental United States, the West has had the most dramatic impact upon the American imagination. For although the East has been the fountainhead of many of the energies which have directed the course of the nation's history, and the South has had its own powerful and poignant relationship with the nation, the West, far more than the other regions, has tended to elicit imaginative responses, which stress the distinctiveness of its regional heritage while closely identifying that heritage with the intrinsic "Americanness" of American civilization. A development in twentieth-century mass culture will serve to demonstrate this. The term "western" has come to mean a story, moving picture, comic strip, or television show which depicts "life in the West, especially cowboy life," and few Americans have difficulty in extrapolating from the term an image of what that life entails. The terms "southern" and "eastern" are meaningless when used in the same manner. Countless Europeans, Asians, Africans, and Latin Americans have come to identify the western as representative of a mode of life peculiar not only to the American West but to the whole of the United States, whereas the same claim could hardly be made for an "eastern" novel such as *Ethan Frome* or a portrait of the American South such as *Gone with the Wind*.

Given this dramatic interaction between the American West and American civilization, it is no surprise that historians of the West have made numerous attempts to link the region with the nation, and students of American culture have tried to formulate generalizations about the nation which encompass yet preserve the identity of the region. Frederick Jackson Turner, for example, saw in the moving frontier a rationale for both a nativist and a regionalist view of American history: the frontier experience was at once "American" and "western." Walter Prescott Webb, who claimed to view the American experience from deep in the heart of Texas, first documented the distinctiveness of a barbed-wire, six-gun, range-cattle civilization which grew up on the western plains and then contended that the social and economic patterns which had evolved in the American hinterland could be seen represented in various stages throughout the whole of the civilized world.[1]

Recent scholarship dealing with the relation of the West to American culture has tended to reject the regionally oriented views of Turner and Webb for analyses which stress the complex interactions between national and regional cultures. These studies have not come to any agreement on whether the role of the West in American cultural history can be best studied as a support for meaningful generalizations about the national culture or as a focus in itself; indeed, out of them have emerged at least two contrasting viewpoints.

The first is "western centered," being associated with a number of recent historical studies which have measured detailed observations of various aspects of the western experience against preconceived notions of American development. Such works as Earl Pomeroy's *The Territories and the United States* (1947) and *The Pacific Slope* (1965) and Howard Lamar's *Dakota Territory* (1956) and *The Far Southwest* (1966) have examined the spread of democratic institutions and the role of individualism, states' rights, and the frontier in shifting western contexts, while Henry Nash Smith's *Virgin Land* (1950) and Arthur Moore's *The Frontier Mind* (1957) have delineated the relation between the development of the West and imaginative constructs of that development. Although Pomeroy, Lamar, Smith, and Moore discuss different Wests and come to differing conclusions about interactions between the region and the nation, their efforts center debates about the role of the West in American civilization in the geographic context of the region itself. The first task of each of their studies may be seen as an acute understanding of the differing territorial versions of western life.

The second set of investigations of the West shifts the focus of the discussion to the interworkings of American culture itself. These "American-centered" studies, primarily by men of a literary rather

1. See Frederick Jackson Turner, "The Significance of the Frontier in American History," American Historical Association *Annual Report for 1893* (Washington, 1894), pp. 199–227; Walter Prescott Webb, *The Great Plains* (New York, 1931), and *The Great Frontier* (New York, 1952), passim.

than a historical persuasion, tend to view the western experience in the context of a preconceived American cultural framework. Such interpretations as R. W. B. Lewis' *The American Adam* (1955), Richard Chase's *The American Novel and Its Tradition* (1957), Charles Sanford's *The Quest for Paradise* (1961), Leo Marx's *The Machine in the Garden* (1964), and Edwin Fussell's *Frontier: American Literature and the American West* (1965) begin with the premise that "a culture is not a flow, nor even a confluence; the form of its existence is struggle, or at least debate—it is nothing if not a dialectic."[2] Only Fussell's study has as its direct focus the relation between the American West and American civilization, but in each of the other works the West is identified with what Chase calls "extreme ranges of experience," from which spring the contradictions that mark American culture.

Particularly in those studies which deal with early nineteenth-century writers, the West is associated with the terms "nature" and "wilderness," which have been adjudged to have had profound effects upon the American mind and which form for Sanford and Marx one pole of the American dialectic. Fussell makes this interpretation explicit. "Without the real and imagined experiences of actual pioneering to serve as informing principle and guiding light," he writes, "nineteenth-century American literature as we know it would never have come into being. Insofar as it resulted from a series of aesthetic transformations . . . American literature may in its origins fairly be called an effect of the frontier." Whereas in the western-centered studies "West" is associated with a collection of observable pioneer experiences, Fussell finds these experiences "intrinsically meaningless" unless "elevated to the status of ideas and forms." The frontier, which Turner termed a process as indigenously western as it was American, has become for Fussell a "figure of speech," a "basic metaphor" for "reconciling opposites through interpenetration and transcendence."

Fussell's use of "frontier metaphor" as an all-inclusive term for relating the West to nineteenth-century American culture is characteristic of American-centered studies. The region is considered as symbolic of one of the polarities which frame American civilization; the western experience, conceived metaphorically, is seen as rein-

2. Lionel Trilling, *The Liberal Imagination* (New York, 1950), p. 9.

forcing the central notion of American culture as a composite of paired contradictions. Since the frontier is acknowledged to be the meeting ground between nature and civilization, it proves a particularly apt metaphor to express the duality of American civilization. In the American-centered studies "West," like "nature," is read as one segment of the opposing pairs in which this duality is manifested.

Of the two viewpoints from which America and the West have repeatedly been examined, there can be little doubt that that which stresses the dialectical character of American civilization offers a wider range of interpretive possibilities: one can call to mind endless examples of paired alternative possibilities in American life. But the application of such an approach to the relationship between the West and America also contains certain limitations. Although Fussell claims that *Frontier* is "a short history . . . of the American West impinging upon the American mind, and to a considerable extent, forming it,"[3] he is forced to substitute for West the term "frontier," which refers not to the West per se but to a metaphoric expression of the meeting of "West" (nature, wilderness) with the advance guard of civilization. Lost in Fussell's analysis is the sense of the West as a civilization in itself, with its unique geography, social structure, economic patterns, and political institutions. And yet as one follows American history through the latter portions of the nineteenth century, one is struck by the emergence of such a civilization in the western portions of the continent. Indeed, the various forms that this civilization took constitute the focus, as previously noted, of several of the major historical treatments of the West in nineteenth-century America.

It is also significant that while the western-centered studies pursue their analyses beyond the Civil War to the 1880s, 1890s, and 1900s, the American-centered studies primarily deal with the first portions of the nineteenth century, when the sparseness of western settlement enabled the region to be better characterized as a vast wilderness. Of the five American-centered works already mentioned, only that of Marx discusses in any detail American culture after the Civil War, and such discussion is largely in the form of an epilogue. This is not surprising, for not only does the kind of civilization

3. Edwin Fussell, *Frontier* (Princeton, N.J., 1965), pp. viii, 12.

which flowered in mid-nineteenth-century America present an admirable example of a culture whose central focus seems to be the exploration of a wide range of alternative possibilities, but the trans-Mississippi West at mid-century had barely developed a regional identity. Perhaps the most observable duality in the mid-century American experience was that of eastern civilization and western space, and the inclusion of the pre-Civil-War West in an American context has in this sense an inherent consistency.

The continuation of the dialectical view of the relation between the West and American civilization into the latter portions of the nineteenth century poses special problems, however. In the first place, the kinds of alternatives available to Americans at mid-century were drastically modified by the impetus of industrialization, which changed the focus of American civilization, introduced new experiences, and posited new alternatives. Secondly, the emergence of the West as a separate regional entity, albeit with varying geographic shadings, necessitated its being considered on more than a metaphoric level. Moreover, the late nineteenth century saw, along with the development of a unique, identifiable West, the beginnings of the identification of that West with the past and future history of the nation; these twin occurrences resulted in the peculiarly privileged status the West has held in the twentieth century.

Such occurrences mark profound changes both in the composition of the region and in its interaction with the nation. At the heart of an understanding of the unique place occupied by the West in twentieth-century American culture is a consideration of the civilization which emerged west of the Mississippi in the last half of the nineteenth century, not only in terms of its inner workings (which has been done in admirable detail by the western-centered works listed above) but in terms of a dialectical theory of American culture. In the broadest sense such will be the task of this study.

The dialectic of postbellum American civilization most clearly manifests itself in contradictory attitudes toward industrialization: the simultaneous embracing and rejecting of the industrializing process. In regional terms the impetus of nineteenth-century industrialism came from the East, whereas the West remained in a pre-industrial state. One can therefore convey the dualistic character of postbellum responses to the industrialization of American culture through the symbolic pairing of regions—"East" standing for those portions of the continent which had assumed an industrialist, metropolitan character, and "West" representing those portions which remained nonindustrial and nonmetropolitan or, on another level, anti-industrial and antimetropolitan.

Both "eastern" and "western" civilization as they are construed in this study will be still more narrowly defined in its course, but a concept relating to the East needs explication at this point. The phrase Eastern Establishment may bring to mind a sinister collection of mysterious potentates manipulating the lives of millions from the very apex of the "power structure," but as used here it is an imaginative construct employed in connection with an interrelated group of institutions which developed in response to the pressures of late nineteenth-century industrialism. These institutions—the boarding school, the Ivy League university, the college club, the metropolitan men's club, and the *Social Register*—were either formed in the last quarter of the nineteenth century, or they changed their shape to meet the demands of industrialism. They were affiliated with two "classes" of individuals that inhabited the postbellum East: the preindustrial eastern upper class—families of established wealth and long-standing social prominence who traced their ascendancy to a period before the dawn of industrialism—and the "new rich"—families of less distinguished origins to whom the industrial era had brought great wealth.

In the last quarter of the nineteenth century such institutions preserved status in the hands of a preindustrial upper class by helping to maintain a system of artificial but exclusive standards through which individuals were evaluated on a social basis, and they also consolidated power in the hands of a relatively small number of individuals and families by equating social success with occupational success. Moreover, by enabling certain influential families to maintain their close contact with certain powerful and prestigious occupations, they guaranteed that the most influential segments of the late nineteenth-century East—the great industrial enterprises, the massive financial concerns, the most revered professions—would be dominated to a great extent by individuals from the same social background.

The late nineteenth-century formation of an Eastern Establishment was by no means the only manifestation of the sweeping status changes that accompanied the advent of industrialism, but it was the most identifiable and the most important. It has been chosen to illustrate the distinctiveness of postbellum eastern civilization not only for these reasons but for its effect upon twentieth-century America. A significant number of Americans who came to positions of national prominence in the early years of the twentieth century had had their nineteenth-century training, as it were, in the schools of the Establishment. If the course of a civilization is most influenced by publicly prominent individuals, the special response of these individuals to their heritage in an industrializing East is of particular interest.

Of equal significance, in terms of this study, is the response of the same individuals to the West. What follows is in turn a history of the response of three men to the East and West, which emerged in the course of their lifetimes. Frederic Remington, Theodore Roosevelt, and Owen Wister were born within three years of each other in the decade of the Civil War, products of an East whose accelerating economic situation paralleled their own growth to maturity. In their adolescence each man forsook his heritage for a thoroughgoing exploration of the western experience, and each publicized that exploration to his eastern contemporaries. In later life each man became identified with powerful and prestigious elements in eastern society but retained his reputation as an exponent of western life. In the first decade of the twentieth century each man had reached the top of his profession and was among those individuals most influential in American life: Remington as the nation's leading illustrator and one of its most popular painters; Wister as author of the most widely read work of fiction in the decade of the 1900s; Roosevelt as President and "moral leader of all the people." The relationship of each of the three men to East and West in the last three decades of the nineteenth century and the first of the twentieth serves as a guide to an understanding of the regions and the areas in which they intersected and interacted.

Part I: The East

1. The Formation of an Eastern Establishment

The last thirty years of the nineteenth century bore witness to remarkable changes in the social structure of America. Before 1870 the nation was dotted with small communities, which had little communication with one another, making for a relative diffusion of wealth and status. But by 1901, according to one social historian, "a class of Protestant patricians . . . led the nation and dominated its traditions . . . held the vast majority of positions at the very heart of the national power, and set the styles in arts and letters, in the universities, in sports, and in the more popular culture which governs the aspirations and values of the masses."[1] The emergence of a "primary group of prestige and power" which came to exert influence in virtually all aspects of American culture had its origin in the soil of pre-1870 America, with its diversification of wealth, power, and status, and the triumph of industrialism in the late nineteenth century influenced all phases of American life, even the supposedly intuitive organization of social life at the highest levels. An analysis of the changes in social stratification in the metropolitan Northeast for the thirty-odd years after 1870 should give some attention to the state of eastern social organization as the 1870s opened and to the relation between that organization and the demands of industrial enterprise.

At the outset of the Civil War the United States was in effect "an 'undeveloped' country," relying upon "imports of manufactured articles, and . . . investments, immigrant workers, and ideas from overseas." Moreover, prior to the Civil War, American civilization was primarily agricultural: "the value of farm lands, livestock, farm machinery, and tools in 1860 was still roughly seven times the capital in manufacturing." Although developments in transportation had paved the way for the growth of a nationwide economic

1. E. Digby Baltzell, *The Protestant Establishment* (New York, 1964), pp. 11–12.

system by 1860, America at that time still retained two important factors of her colonial economy: the presence of vast quantities of free land and an access to Europe through seaports on the Atlantic coast. As late as 1860 foreign trade and land speculation were the prime means of acquiring wealth in America: nearly three-fourths of the early nineteenth-century magnates listed in Gustavus Myers' *History of the Great American Fortunes* founded their fortunes in shipping or landholding.[2]

The acquisition of wealth in America before 1870 was limited to a handful of occupations, and its distribution was of a diffuse nature and on a relatively small scale. Although 137 individuals were reported to be worth at least $250,000 each in New York in 1846, the city contained only 14 millionaires, and in 1858 the total number of millionaires in Boston, New York, and Philadelphia was approximately 70.[3] By 1850 John Jacob Astor, anticipating techniques which were to prove successful in a later age, had combined fur trading with land speculation to accumulate over 20 million dollars, but he appears to be the rare exception; although statistical evidence remains inconclusive, one may assume that his American Fur Company, which built its own forts and owned a fleet of ships, was one of the few examples of a full-scale corporate enterprise operating out of the Northeast prior to the Civil War. Diffuse wealth, as exemplified by family landholdings, a successful mercantile practice, or a budding manufacturing concern was consistent with America's status as an "undeveloped" nation in the decade of the sixties.

Power, as well as wealth, was of a diversified and localized nature in the Northeast as the Civil War ended. New York had almost a million and a half inhabitants by 1870, but was to add another million more in the next twenty years.[4] Even the largest cities were mostly residential, with poor communication between the different districts: to Edith Wharton the New York of her girlhood was a "village," consisting of the area around Washington Square.

2. Edward Kirkland, *Industry Comes of Age* (New York, 1961), pp. 1–2; G. R. Taylor, *The Transportation Revolution* (New York, 1951), p. 395; Gustavus Myers, *History of the Great American Fortunes, 3* (3 vols. Chicago, 1910), 395–407.

3. M. Y. Beach, "Wealth and Wealthy Citizens of New York," reprinted in Henry W. Lanier, *A Century of Banking in New York* (New York, 1922), pp. 151–84; Taylor, *Transportation,* p. 395.

4. *World Almanac and Book of Facts* for 1924 (New York, 1924), p. 390.

The newness of intercontinental transportation and the infant state of many American industries mitigated against the concentration of economic power in eastern cities; the day when decisions in Wall Street quickened the nation's pulse was yet to come.

Status groupings of the sixties differed only slightly from those at the time of the War of 1812. Social life, to commentators on the times, was serene and simple: Henry Cabot Lodge recalled in his *Early Memories* that "Society was based on the old families . . . the families which had held high position in the colony, the province, and during the Revolution and the early decades of the United States. They represented several generations of education and standing in the community. . . . They had ancestors . . . who had won success as merchants, manufacturers, lawyers, or men of letters."[5] A success model of the times was the well-rounded gentleman; Nicholas Biddle, for example, in addition to his banking interests, edited a periodical, wrote sonnets, and published an edition of the journals of Lewis and Clark; Francis Parkman, the grandson of a merchant, devoted his life to the writings of history; James Russell Lowell of the Lowell shipping interests functioned as a "man of letters." A relatively stable system of social stratification furthered leisure and learning among those of accumulated wealth.

The difficulty of maintaining a diffuse status system which encouraged self-made men yet based "Society" upon the "old families" had become apparent even before the Civil War. The sons and grandsons of successful landowners and merchants, particularly in eastern cities, tended increasingly to devote their energy to recreational and intellectual pursuits, relying upon inherited wealth for financial independence: George Jones, Edith Wharton's father, spent a "busy day" duck hunting, boat racing, and reading material on Arctic exploration. The growth of certain "fashionable" communities within Boston, New York, and Philadelphia in the mid-nineteenth century furthered a growing self-consciousness and concern for form among the "old" families: Mrs. John King Van Rensselaer remembered that in the New York of the sixties "it was unthinkable that a young lady should venture into the business district and return home unescorted," that "the appearance of the women of a family, in any public place after dark, without the

5. Henry Cabot Lodge, *Early Memories,* quoted in Dixon Wecter, *The Saga of American Society* (New York, 1937), p. 206.

convoy of the head of their house, would have been a shock, almost amounting to scandal, to the social organization of that day," and that "appearances went for everything." The "real thing was never said or done or even thought," said Edith Wharton of her life in Washington Square, "but only represented by a set of arbitrary signs."[6]

Along with this clannishness and formality exhibited by certain of the "best families" in the sixties went a growing indifference toward changes in the America in which their fathers had so flourished. "The leading merchants of the colonial period," George R. Taylor writes, "had often been men of broad culture and superior education. Many took an interest in politics and held important governmental positions." Between 1815 and 1860 "this became less true . . . the direct participation of businessmen in politics declined sharply . . . position and success came to be measured more and more by a purely monetary standard. A number of the captains of industry had only an elementary education, and among some, at least, the feeling developed that it was hardly necessary for success." Not only were the sons of merchants less active in business as business success became "more than ever the prize sought by the able and ambitious," but the values prized by the "aristocracy of lineage, land, and learning" seemed less applicable to a nation enthralled with the cult of self-help.[7]

Changes in the distribution of wealth and the composition of urban centers after 1870 had a considerable effect on status groupings in the last quarter of the nineteenth century. The installment of stock tickers in Wall Street in 1867 and the completion of the first transcontinental railroad in 1868 crystallized two separate aspects of American economic development—technology and transportation. After major innovations in the processing of extractive industries, the production of iron, coal, and steel, as well as other natural resources, began to influence the economy substantially, and a burgeoning railroad network not only made the distribution of such products feasible on a nationwide basis but at the same time

6. Olivia Coolidge, *Edith Wharton* (New York, 1964), p. 18; Mrs. John King Van Rensselaer, *The Social Ladder* (New York, 1924), pp. 45–47; Edith Wharton, *The Age of Innocence* (New York, 1920), p. 4.

7. Taylor, *Transportation*, p. 395; Irvin Wyllie, *The Self-Made Man in America* (New Brunswick, N.J., 1954), p. 141.

gave Americans an exceptional geographic mobility. As a result, those eastern cities which enjoyed a commercial reputation and a favorable location grew tremendously after 1870: urban real estate boomed, fierce fights were waged for control of municipal transportation systems, and city housing construction went forward at a dizzy pace. Industries of all kinds dotted the metropolis, financiers arrived in their wake, and immigrants poured in by the thousands.[8]

A more ostensible effect of industrialization came in changes in the distribution of wealth. Using E. Digby Baltzell's survey of social stratification in the metropolitan Northeast as a guide, and dividing the nineteenth century into two periods at the year 1860, one can ascertain the nature of these changes. There are 69 eighteenth- and nineteenth-century magnates Baltzell deems "elite"; of these 26 acquired their wealth before 1860, and 43 afterward. Of the 26 members of the pre-1860 elite, 18 founded their fortunes through landholding or merchant shipping. Only 3 men became financially successful through railroading, and only one through finance. None acquired wealth through heavy industries or utilities. Of the 43 individuals who gained great wealth in the post-1860 period, 9 were associated with the railroad industry, 18 were engaged in heavy industries or utilities, and 10 were concerned with finance. None was strictly a landholder, only one was a merchant (department-store king John Wanamaker), and 3 were professional men. (The few remaining individuals in both groups were manufacturers of specific products such as matches, snuff, or sugar.)

A listing of the highest incomes in the city of Philadelphia for the year 1864 gives a further indication of the areas in which new fortunes were being made as the urban age dawned. Of the 50 persons listed with incomes of over $10,000, 20 were descendants of merchants or landholders. But, as Baltzell notes, only 2 of the 23 men in this group with incomes between $50,000 and $200,000 were descendants of merchants, while *all* were either bankers and industrialists or railroad magnates. And the sum total of the incomes of the 30 men of "new" wealth was approximately four times that of the 20 "old family" men.[9] Yet since two-fifths of the richest

8. See Allan Nevins, *The Emergence of Modern America* (New York, 1927), for a vivid description of urban life in the decade after the Civil War.

9. E. Digby Baltzell, *Philadelphia Gentlemen* (Glencoe, Ill., 1958), pp. 22–24, 108; *The Rich Men of Philadelphia, Income Tax of the Residents of Philadelphia and Bucks County* (Philadelphia, 1865).

men in Philadelphia in 1864 were "old family," it is clear that the growth of industrialization did not undermine old ways of making money so much as it created a myriad of new ones.

Few descendants of landowners and merchants suffered losses of income as the sixties passed into the seventies, although their fortunes may have paled in comparison with those of the "new rich." The landed gentry and princely merchants did lose power and status, however, as the supply of free land east of the Alleghenies dwindled. Merchant shipping and landholding, occupations at the very center of a colonial economy, became mere facets of an increasingly complicated national economic system. With the industrial age the railroad magnate came to replace the merchant as the chief profiteer of commerce and therefore achieved a greater degree of economic power. The influx of population into cities helped to break up the great estates, and the greatest profits in land after 1865 came from urban real estate, which was not always in the hands of the landed gentry.

Industrialism brought to the metropolitan Northeast an increasingly complicated social structure. The rise of the new rich upset the leisured world of the old families of high social standing, and an influx of immigrants threatened to destroy the ethnic and religious homogeneity which had been one of the stabilizing factors of colonial America. New figures of influence appeared in the cities—the political boss, himself often an immigrant; the "bull" and the "bear," speculators of an urban kind; and the "captain of industry," often a soldier of great fortune—but none of them represented the old families.

The status of "Society," representing the descendants of members of "acknowledged standing in the community" and their "fashionable" companions, appeared uncertain to both its members and others as eastern cities became the residence of fortune-hunters of all kinds in the 1870s and 80s. "Before [1874]," Mrs. John King Van Rensselaer noted, "one was either socially acceptable everywhere or one was not recognized anywhere. He was definitely within the pale or uncompromisingly out of it." But the later seventies had given rise to a "tide of wealthy aspirants for social honors rushing in from the North, South and West to fight for a place in New York Society." Frederick van de Water, himself "definitely within the pale," agreed with Mrs. Van Rensselaer that the onslaught of new wealth had destroyed the serene simplicity of Old New York. "Droughts in their homelands," he wrote, "brought the barbarian hordes down upon Rome"; similarly, "floods, inundations of gold brought against New York successive invasions of the climbers. These grew suddenly rich in their own cities and came up against New York; and, eventually, by weight of numbers, overthrew the established structure of Society." But Frederick Townsend Martin placed the blame for Society's disintegration elsewhere: "A few young men, sons of society, set up new idols in the ancient temples. They began to ape the habits and imitate the morals of that world which, while possessing wealth in plenty, had never possessed the refinement or the ethical standards of true society." In his eyes Society had lost what Edith Wharton called "the strict standard of uprightness in affairs," which was "the first duty of such a class." By 1883 Mrs. Wharton was noting that "New York social life had become more obviously based on money . . . the quiet entertainment of old friends was being succeeded by immense impersonal crushes where the conversation sank far below the level of quiet dullness which pervaded [the] earlier dinners."[10]

Whether barbarians with cash in their pockets had forced their way through the gates of the well-born or whether Society had succumbed to what Martin called the "madness of extravagance," accounts of eastern social life in the seventies and eighties were filled with allusions to hundred-dollar bills used to light cigars, expensive feasts, and costly costumes. Eventually the sumptuous Bradley-Martin ball, in the midst of the depression of the nineties, created such antagonism that Police Commissioner Theodore Roosevelt, who had been invited, took pains to explain that he would not be attending, merely prowling outside in his professional capacity.[11]

As industrialism brought about status changes at even the highest social levels in post-Civil-War America by imposing new demands upon individuals and relenting on ones previously imposed, the components of a successful man were altered. Oliver Wendell Holmes had defined Boston society in a preindustrial age in terms

10. Van Rensselaer, *The Social Ladder*, p. 194; Frederick van de Water, in Van Rensselaer, p. 201; Frederick Townsend Martin, *The Passing of the Idle Rich* (New York, 1911), p. 26; Edith Wharton, quoted in Coolidge, *Edith Wharton*, p. 47.

11. See Martin for the cigar story and Van Rensselaer for the Bradley-Martin incident.

of family position, education, and public service and had singled out merchants, lawyers, and men of letters as success models, but the men to whom wealth and power came in the first decades of urban America were generally not old family, had often not attended college, and "on the whole, avoided public office." The apologists of these men, such as Edward Bok, Edwin Freedley, and Elbert Hubbard, concluded that "a rudimentary education was sufficient unto success," that college training "was positively harmful in that it unfitted men for business," and that the political arena was unpredictable, unsound, and even immoral.[12]

While "book-learning" and public service did not necessarily fall in industrial America's scale of values, strength, self-discipline, and assertiveness certainly rose in importance. "Success," writes a student of the nineteenth-century business community, "demanded a strong will, persistence, ambition, good health, and self-discipline." Practicality surpassed erudition on the list of admirable traits, and one was expected to assert his wealth. Businessmen built large and sumptuous houses, and many reveled in the power their millions gave them. The half-educated financier, Daniel Drew, according to one account, "never allowed his educated employees to indulge in 'bookish airs' because he knew that he could buy them out ten times over." "Book learning is something," he reportedly said, "but thirteen million dollars is also something, and a mighty sight more."[13]

The descendants of eighteenth- and early nineteenth-century merchants, landholders, and public servants, on the other hand, had cultivated quite different values. While certain of them "did not doubt that humble men could rise from rags to riches, they doubted that it was possible for them to rise without subverting the true, the good, and the beautiful." They glorified "the serenities of a static agricultural age," favored "an elite that was born, not made," "doted" on the "vulgarity of wealth," and "constantly affirmed the superiority of non-business values and ways of life."[14]

A classic example of the conflict in values between new and old wealth appears in Edith Wharton's *The Custom of the Country.*

12. Baltzell, *Philadelphia Gentlemen*, p. 109; Wyllie, *The Self-Made Man in America*, pp. 101–02.

13. Wyllie, *The Self-Made Man*, pp. 102–03; Edward Kirkland, *Dream and Thought in the Business Community* (Ithaca, New York, 1956), passim.

14. Wyllie, p. 133.

Although Mrs. Wharton's sympathies are clearly on the side of the Marvells, one of the old mercantile families of New York in the 1870s, it is Undine Spragg, the daughter of a midwestern business magnate, who ultimately succeeds. At the novel's close she has married a "railroad king," while Ralph Marvell has killed himself. Earlier, although "struck by the singular coherence and respectability of the ideals of aboriginal New York as contrasted with the chaos of indiscriminated appetites which made up its modern tendencies," Ralph has had to "sell his brains to a firm" in order to support Undine's expensive tastes and has abandoned his hopes for a gentlemanly career as a man of letters to "conform to an environment" where "all the romantic values are reversed."[15] Edith Wharton was too keen an observer not to see that the direction in which urban and industrial America was moving favored the Undines at the expense of the Ralphs.

The vast changes industrialization brought to eastern America may have created a crisis of leadership in the growing metropolitan communities. "In periods of rapid social change, where new and quite different talents are needed for leadership," Baltzell notes, "the values and style of an upper class in one period often tend to inhibit its members from succeeding in a new type of function." A more complicated and specialized economy called for occupational professionalism, but descendants of the mercantile and landholding upper class had come to cultivate an amateurish well-roundedness. "Family position" was considered essential in evaluating one's contemporaries by metropolitan society in the seventies, but industrial wealth had blurred the lines of power and prestige between "old" and "new" families. Morever, the restless atmosphere of urban America was hardly conducive to an elevation of tradition for tradition's sake. Sons and daughters often moved to cities foreign to their parents, and the whole experience of past generations—in terms of occupational success models, accepted behavior patterns, status groupings, and distribution of power and prestige in the community—seemed related to a stable, agrarian, small-town way of life which eastern America no longer symbolized.

It is possible that in the East of the 1870s and 80s two "elites" simultaneously functioned and vied for power and prestige. The

15. Wharton, *The Custom of the Country*, pp. 74, 207.

descendants of successful individuals had long experience in positions of authority, which was perhaps the central factor reinforcing their social status, but the values held in esteem by the men who had acquired wealth and power in an industrial age, such as assertiveness and acquisitiveness, have been judged to be more consistent with a rapidly expanding industrial situation and therefore more popular with the majority of eastern Americans. Richard Hofstadter, building on this assumption, has claimed the existence of a "status revolution" in the 1880s and 90s which "displaced" old family professionals, intellectuals, and clerics from positions of prominence and eventually alienated them from the dominant order of industrial enterprise.[16]

Hofstadter has rightly characterized the last quarter of the nineteenth century as a period marked by a major shift in values, in which, in broadest terms, a preindustrialist ethos was replaced by an industrialist one. But the effect of this value shift upon status groupings, at least at the highest levels, did not take the form of a "revolution." The formation of an Eastern Establishment, which refers to the interaction of the elites of "new" and "old" wealth described in the remainder of this chapter, was an evolutionary, assimilative, conservative process rather than a revolutionary, fragmentative, radical one.

Four subprocesses marked the areas of interaction between old and new wealth, symbolized the ascription and achievement of upper-class status, and regulated the lives of the wealthy and the privileged in the metropolitan East after 1870. These were attended at one of a select group of New England boarding schools; matriculation at Harvard, Yale, Princeton, or the University of Pennsylvania and the joining of certain exclusive organizations while there; election to certain prestigious metropolitan men's clubs; and the listing of oneself and one's family in the unofficial status center of nineteenth-century America, the *Social Register*. The institutions associated with these processes grew rapidly both in terms of numbers and prestige throughout the period and functioned both as bailiwicks of tradition in the midst of swift social change and as assimilative associations which helped maintain prestige and power in the hands of select individuals. Within the upper class itself the

16. Richard Hofstadter, *The Age of Reform* (New York, 1955) esp. pp. 130–72.

boarding school, "Ivy League" university, exclusive men's clubs, and *Social Register* aided individuals in search for identity, providing them with a well-defined set of values. Within the metropolitan community, these institutions helped coalesce power in the hands of a set of successful families.

Evidence seems to indicate that the status upheavals of the 1870s, rather than displacing old family members from positions of prominence, actually cemented their relation to the established order. That order gradually changed and strengthened until it evolved at the highest levels into an Establishment, and the institutions furthering each phase in the process of status achievement were altered accordingly.

One major effect of nineteenth-century breakthroughs in technology and transportation, according to William R. Taylor, was the implantation of "a set of well-defined fears and misgivings" upon "the institution of the family." "Traditional modes of authority which had persisted within families during the colonial period had to be abandoned through the sheer impossibility of family councils and the difficulty of exercising patriarchal power on a shifting social scene. The nineteenth century was thus left to reckon with the dismembered family unit which it chose to call the Home and to accommodate itself to the changing roles of those within the Home—men, women, and children." Fathers, of course, were being called on to perform new functions by an industrial society, and the roles of motherhood, wifehood, and ultimately femininity were being reevaluated in accordance with the times.[17] Parents were faced with the dual problem of dispersing households and a lack of adequate experience with the contemporary urban and industrial situation.[18]

The importance that families of established wealth had come to place on position, lineage, and tradition by the 1870s was appar-

17. William R. Taylor, *Cavalier and Yankee* (New York, 1961), pp. 146–47; Walter E. Houghton, *The Victorian Frame of Mind* (New Haven, Conn., 1957), pp. 341–53.

18. Little is known of the internal structure of the nineteenth-century upper-class family, although it is generally agreed that it was "patriarchal." "From patrician personal literature centered upon the middle decades of the nineteenth century," writes Edward N. Saveth, "it is possible to know the patriarch as a real type." Yet Saveth admits that "the status of the patriarch under the last stages of industrial . . . capitalism" is "tentative" and "uncertain." For some suggestions for research in the area of upper-class family history, see Edward N. Saveth, "The American Patrician Class: A Field for Research," in Saveth, ed., *American History and the Social Sciences* (New York, 1964), pp. 202–14, esp. pp. 206–08.

ently reinforced by the threat that industrialism posed to these values, for the last quarter of the nineteenth century witnessed an important change in the conception of adolescent education among the upper class. Boys who had previously been tutored at home until college age left at thirteen or so to attend one of the fashionable New England boarding schools: Andover, Exeter, Groton, St. Paul's, and St. Mark's, to name only five. Of these, only Groton was actually founded in the 1870–1900 period, but the other four greatly increased in size. Exeter's enrollment rose from 200 to 600 in a forty-year span beginning in 1880, while the number of boys graduating from St. Paul's rose from 45 (in the 1870s) to 104 in the 1890s.[19] Girls' boarding schools also began to spring up in the last quarter of the nineteenth century, but reserved their period of greatest growth for the twentieth.

Sociologists have tended to see the New England boarding school as performing two functions. The first of these, according to Baltzell, is the "latent function of acculturating the members of a younger generation . . . into an upper-class style of life. As the educative role of the family declines . . . the private school [becomes] a kind of surrogate family." By transmitting upper-class values, the boarding school responds to the needs of an adolescent in an increasingly heterogeneous culture, helping him to identify with a particular set of standards. In addition to "upholding the higher standards among the children of families who have long been at the top," C. Wright Mills finds that "the private schools . . . perform the task of selecting and training newer members of a national upper stratum." "It is in 'the next generation,' " he notes, "that the tensions between new and upper classes are relaxed and even resolved. . . . The school—rather than the upper-class family—is perhaps the most important agency for transmitting the traditions of the upper social classes, and regulating the admission of new wealth and talent."[20]

The influence of an industrial age on the values of New England boarding schools is evident in their combining of traditional standards of behavior with new axioms of success in post-Civil-War

19. *Phillips Exeter Bulletin, 44* (March 1948); *Alumni Directory of St. Paul's School,* 1956.

20. Baltzell, *Philadelphia Gentlemen,* p. 293; C. Wright Mills, *The Power Elite* (New York, 1956) p. 64.

America. Groton, founded in the midst of a business age, balanced its "family" orientation (Endicott Peabody and his wife "said good night to every boy in the school every night they were there") with overtures to the "active work of life" and spoke of boys "standing on their own feet," developing "manly" attitudes, and learning to fend for themselves in the "rough and tumble" game of life. Phillips Andover, an ancient New England school which grew rapidly in the latter nineteenth century, while insisting that its graduates "conduct themselves like gentlemen at all times," instructed them that their major task was "to learn the great end and real business of living."[21]

Savage isolation was—and, in fact, still is—the keynote of many a term in New England, and such isolation in a period of high impressionability may create the peculiar closeness of boarding school friendships; indeed, Mills notes with some justice that "the clubs and cliques of college are usually composed of carry-overs of associations made in the lower levels at the proper schools; one's friends at Harvard are friends made at prep school."[22] In the nineteenth century, with its rapid fluctuations in status, the friendships formed in a spartan New England environment, with their propensity for persisting through later and more complicated environments, came to assume a certain communal significance.

In an age of flux Groton and the handful of other "exclusive" New England boarding schools gradually came to fulfill a much-needed role, which appealed to two kinds of families in urban America—one rich in status and poor by comparison in power and wealth; the other possessing great power and wealth and aspiring after status. The boarding school, with its rigid isolation, carefully defined standards, and elitist admission policies, formulated patterns of behavior among the sons of new and old wealth which were in the final analysis to have a considerable effect upon the world outside its gates.

The boarding school exerted a definite influence on the later educational careers of its graduates. From 1870 until 1900 approximately three-fourths of Phillips Exter graduates who went on to college attended Harvard; almost the same number of Andover boys attended Yale. This pattern continued through the twentieth

21. Frank D. Ashburn, *Peabody of Groton* (New York, 1944), p. 71; *Phillips Andover Blue Book,* 1955.
22. Mills, *Power Elite,* p. 67.

century: in 1934, 95 percent of the graduates of St. Paul's matriculated at Harvard, Yale, or Princeton, and 31 out of 32 Groton graduates went to one of those three institutions.[23]

Princeton, Harvard, Yale, and the University of Pennsylvania had existed long before industrial America but were by no means immune to some of the social changes brought by the increased matriculation of students from "fashionable" boarding schools after 1870. The inner social structure of these universities underwent a drastic shift, highlighted by the formation of exclusive social and eating clubs. The effects of this shift upon the atmosphere of the universities can be shown by a comparison of the Harvard of Francis Parkman with that of Theodore Roosevelt, both of whom came from families of established wealth and prominence. Parkman entered Harvard in 1840; Roosevelt in 1876. The "general frame" of the Harvard of Parkman's day, according to his most recent biographer, "made for cohesion rather than divisiveness, of which the young Brahmin seems to have rather gone out of his way to take advantage." Harvard in the 1840s was a small college with less than 500 members in all of its student body, including the schools of Divinity, Law, and Medicine, and the argument that "this very smallness of numbers, reinforced by the prescribed curriculum which every collegian followed, made membership in a class more or less equivalent to membership in a club, of itself conferring a certain equality of status" is persuasive. Samuel Eliot Morison, in discussing Parkman's Harvard, finds it "free of the abysmal cleavages that began to mark its social composition after the Civil War." Social clubs and societies abounded, to be sure, and Parkman was a member of several; but Morison notes that "it is difficult to see how any student, unless invincibly unsocial in temperament and tastes, could have been wholly unclubbed. Lack of money or social background was no bar."[24]

During the period from 1870 to 1890, however, the proportion of freshmen entering Harvard from private schools increased from 62 to 77 per cent, and, according to Morison, it was almost necessary for a Harvard student with social ambition "to enter from the 'right' sort of school and be popular there, to room on 'the Gold

23. Baltzell, *Philadelphia Gentlemen*, pp. 327–28; *Groton School Blue Book*, 1953.
24. Howard Doughty, *Francis Parkman* (New York, 1962), pp. 24–25; Samuel Eliot Morison, *Three Centuries of Harvard* (Cambridge, Mass., 1937), p. 203.

Coast' and be accepted by Boston Society his freshman year, in order to be on the right side of the social chasm." The "cleavage between Yard and Gold Coast," Morison writes, "was all the more unfortunate because it was financial as well as social: the rooms in the private dormitories were more comfortable and expensive than those provided by the College. . . . These factors of school, site, and the Boston hall-mark determined the socially eligible class." By Roosevelt's time the social structure of Harvard had begun to evolve into a system symbolized by the phrase "two Harvards": school affiliation had replaced family lineage as the chief manifestation of one's status; and graduates of "socially correct Eastern boarding schools" had begun their preoccupation with "the importance of . . . social success," especially in terms of the club system. The most prestigious of sophomore clubs, in Roosevelt's day, was the Hasty-Pudding-Institute of 1770, known as the "Institute," which had originally been a literary society but turned to social affairs exclusively in 1875. "Of those socially eligible," notes Morison, "it was a major catastrophe not to make . . . the Institute; whilst to be chosen . . . meant assured social success in college, a lion's role in Boston debutante society, prompt election to the best clubs of New York and Boston after graduation, and a job at Lee and Higginson's or a New York brokerage house."[25]

As the boarding school graduates at Harvard, Yale, and Princeton increased and those universities became more socially oriented, the social standards came to be set by graduates of Groton, St. Paul's, and the like. As George Biddle wrote of Harvard, "the standard . . . was established by the socially well born and those who were not socially well born sensed this standard . . . by the measure of undergraduate and graduate prestige—college activities far outweighed scholarship; athletics outweighed undergraduate activities; social standing—the importance of club life—outweighed them all." The elitist social hierarchy which had been formulated in New England perpetuated itself in college: one needed certain credentials to rise to the top of the Harvard club system, and boarding school background was perhaps the most important of these. Furthermore, the clubs at Harvard and at Princeton, the fraternities and senior societies at Yale, and the fraternities at the Univer-

25. Morison, *Three Centuries of Harvard*, pp. 420–24; George Biddle, *An American Artist's Story* (Boston, 1939), pp. 81, 82.

sity of Pennsylvania served not only to identify the undergraduate with a certain way of life and to reinforce that way of life by surrounding him with his boarding school friends and other men of the "right sort" but to measure an undergraduate's prestige within influential sectors of the metropolitan community. Boston papers took note of the club lists; New York, Boston, and Philadelphia brokerage houses and law firms hastened to recruit members of Porcellian, Skull and Bones, and Ivy; and "the prestige of a properly certified secondary education followed by a proper club in a proper Ivy League college" served as a "standard admission ticket to the world of urban clubs and parties in any major city of the nation."[26]

The transformation of the educational system in the years following the Civil War lay at the core of the formation of an Eastern Establishment. Boarding schools, perhaps subconsciously conceived in their early period of growth as substitutes for the dismembered family, had proven attractive as guardians of traditional values and training grounds for the sons of status-seeking men of recently acquired wealth; the patterns of behavior valued at these schools had come to dominate social life at prominent eastern universities; and a connection had been established between high-prestige social ranking at these universities and high-powered business enterprises in the metropolitan community. Since the boarding-school-university-club system recognized both family position and economic power, the sons of industrial magnates and the sons of landed gentry found within it a certain meeting ground. Boarding schools balanced gentlemanliness with self-reliance; clubs discriminated on financial as well as social terms; investment houses banked on the proposition that social success in college implied occupational success in later life. It was this proposition above all that enabled individuals of established social status to maintain positions of power in the industrial East. The economic and technological upheavals of the Civil War decade had created a status system based on new criteria; but these criteria were hardly revolutionary. Indeed, at its uppermost levels the system placed a premium on established status and thus enabled individuals of long-standing social prominence to have a hand in the shaping of a new prestige order.

26. Biddle, pp. 81–82; Mills, *Power Elite*, p. 67.

Like boarding schools and college clubs, metropolitan men's clubs, which served in a sense as the stairway to urban power and prestige, greatly increased in size and numbers in the last quarter of the nineteenth century. The Union and Somerset in Boston, the Union and Knickerbocker in New York, and the Philadelphia and Rittenhouse clubs in Philadelphia came to carry the most amount of prestige, but they were supported by countless others. By-products of a civilization whose basic concerns lay in the development of industrial enterprise, such clubs illustrated the close connection between social prominence and executive performance in the late nineteenth century.

The men's club, like the boarding school and campus club, was partially conceived of as an island of homogeneity in an ever-diversifying urban ocean. Within its walls, according to Dixon Wecter, a gentleman found "his peculiar asylum from the pandemonium of commerce and the bumptiousness of democracy." There were "the friends . . . with whom one grew up, saw through prep school and college, attended at their weddings—and whom the survivors will accompany decently in gloves to their long home in Mount Auburn or Sleepy Hollow." It was "comforting," Wecter notes, for upper-class businessmen "to think that one's sons and grandsons will sit in these same chairs, and firelight will flicker on the same steel engravings and oil portraits of past presidents."[27] The need within certain individuals to constantly identify themselves with institutions which perpetuated a particular set of values (suggested by the phrase "accompany decently in gloves") was one of the common bonds which united the Groton-Harvard-Porcellian-Somerset system.

Another less emphasized bond between the school and the college and the men's club was related to each member's desire to perform within an urban society to the best of his ability. Just as boarding schools were accessible to families of great wealth as well as to those of acknowledged position, and the cleavage between Yard and Gold Coast at Harvard was financial as well as social, so, as Baltzell points out, one could enter a prominent metropolitan men's club through familial antecedents or through business success. For example, a prime function of the Philadelphia Club for Baltzell, is "the ascrip-

27. Wecter, *The Saga of American Society*, pp. 253–55.

tion of upper-class status . . . business gentlemen of distinguished antecedents are continuously blended with men of distinguished achievement within its halls. . . . The circulation of elites of Philadelphia is stabilized in each generation by the assimilation of the descendants of newer family founders within this inner circle of Proper Philadelphians." This is the familiar Establishment pattern: blending men of high status with those of financial achievement to create, in Baltzell's terms, a "primary group of prestige and power."[28]

The privatist aspects of metropolitan men's clubs have contributed to their popular image as collections of white-mustached old gentlemen peering at the world from behind their newspapers, but their influence has long been determined by their relation to public life. By continually rewarding economic prominence with social acceptance and establishing a continuity of membership, they have embodied the philosophy of any institution whose central concern is the perpetuation of power. To be accepted into an exclusive men's club in the nineteenth century meant in many cases to have demonstrated the ability to survive and excel in industrial America.

Perhaps the clearest indication of the kind of status system that had developed with industrialization is the widespread success of a little book which first appeared in 1887, entitled the *Social Register*. Founded by an ex-gunsmith of Summit, New Jersey, named Louis Keller, the *Register* contained a "record of society, comprising an accurate and careful list of its members, with their addresses, many of the maiden names of the married women, the club addresses of the men, officers of the leading clubs and social organizations, and other useful social information." The *Social Register* spread from New York to Boston and Philadelphia by 1890, and by 1925 twenty-five other cities received little black books.[29]

There was no formal criterion for inclusion in the *Register;* eligibles were once described by the Social Register Association as "those families who by descent or by social standing or from other qualifications are naturally included in the best society of any particular city or cities." Persons who swore by the *Register* list had no idea how it was formulated or who formulated it. Even now the

28. Baltzell, *Philadelphia Gentlemen*, pp. 347–48, 354.
29. The *Social Register* (New York, 1888), Preface; Wecter, *Saga of American Society*, p. 233.

Social Register's unfashionable staff, ill-fitting address (381 Fourth Avenue in New York), and shroud of obscurity with which it surrounds itself have a comic quality, but since the late eighties it has represented the pinnacle of social aspiration for many metropolitan status-seekers: to have one's name listed in the *Register* meant, in a sense, that one had arrived. As Mills points out, "in any individual case, admission may be unpredictable or even arbitrary, but as a group, the people in the *Social Register* have been chosen for their money, their family, and their style of life."[30]

The initial popularity and subsequent prestige of the *Register* testify to the rise of new criteria for social success in the post-Civil-War East. The *Register* itself informally based selection of candidates on three grounds: "descent," "social standing," and "other qualifications." The first two of these retained a previous age's concern with family position in the community, but the last, deliberately vague, set the stage for the social rewarding of economic achievement. The kinds of questions asked on the *Social Register* application forms of the nineteenth century indicate the terms by which individuals were being evaluated. Full names of applicant, wife, and children were inquired after, and the *Register* was particularly anxious to know the maiden names of married women. Men's colleges and metropolitan clubs were listed, along with children's colleges and preparatory schools, and while the college of a married woman was of no interest, the boarding school of her daughter was. In other words, the nineteenth-century *Register* represented the public acceptance of a status system which, while retaining a certain concern for "lineage," placed an overwhelming value on the prestige of exclusive educational institutions and social clubs. It served to identify members of exclusive families with a set of high-prestige institutions and to testify to their acknowledged status. "I don't care to be listed in the *Social Register*," the mother of Proper Philadelphia novelist Owen Wister is reported to have said. "I know who my friends are."[31] But she was the exception: other individuals of her sort not only wanted to know who their friends were, they wanted everyone else to know as well.

This self-consciousness which the *Social Register* symbolized

30. Cleveland Amory, *Who Killed Society?* (New York, 1960), pp. 4–6; Mills, *The Power Elite*, p. 57.

31. Interview with Owen Wister, Jr., November 22, 1965.

perhaps marked the final consolidation of an Establishment in urban centers of the East. Eventually, individuals who had passed through the boarding-school-university-club route came to assume a "manner of simplicity and the easy dignity that can arise only out of an inner certainty that one's being is a definitely established fact of one's world, from which one cannot be excluded, ignored, snubbed, or paid off."[32] With the assurance that a self-perpetuating prestige order was upholding the traditions of their ancestors while exhibiting a sensitivity to contemporary changes in the distribution of power and wealth, men of social distinction set about to exercise leadership in the eastern metropolis. In the nineteenth century such leadership was largely directed toward the sphere of unregulated industrial enterprise. As the twentieth century dawned and business enterprises and status groupings began to coalesce, individuals who had received their training in the classrooms of the Establishment found themselves in a position to exert influence in the area of national affairs and returned, in an industrial setting, to the public service realm of their ancestors. Their conception of public service, as well as their larger conception of the direction in which twentieth-century America should move, was in part an outgrowth of their Establishment heritage.

32. Mills, *Power Elite*, p. 67.

2. Easterners and the Western Experience, 1835–1885

At the same time that the move to the city was changing the economic and social status of nineteenth-century Americans, the westward movement was exerting a profound influence upon the American imagination. Movement away from the city, crowds, and cliques to space and solitude became the theme of the American West. In a geographic sense, "West" refers to what Henry Nash Smith has called the "vacant continent beyond the frontier," and since the frontier moved toward the Pacific throughout the nineteenth century, it could be the Ohio Valley for Fenimore Cooper, the Oklahoma territory and Rocky Mountains for Washington Irving, the trail to Oregon for Francis Parkman, and Colorado Springs for General W. A. J. Palmer of the Denver and Rio Grande Railroad. But none of these Easterners identified the "West" with "the commonplace domesticated area within the agricultural frontier," for each man's imagination was captured by the "exhilarating region of adventure and comradeship in the open air" beyond it.[1] The sense that this region drifted and floated, limitless in scope and devoid of the confining social aspects of the East—devoid, in fact, of society in any form—gave the West its special flavor.

Even the Wild West, of course, was not without a social structure, nor was it lacking nineteenth-century social historians with their own conceptions of western "civilization." But the primary concern of eastern chroniclers of the West in the half century beginning with the 1830s was not the drama of internal social relationships in that vast continent beyond the frontier but rather the degree to which society (or the lack of it) in the wilderness represented an alternative to the social structure of the East. One can say, for example, that the Leatherstocking novels of Fenimore

1. Henry Nash Smith, *Virgin Land* (New York, 1959), pp. 4, 55.

Cooper are "social" in that they attempt to picture kinship and status groupings in Templeton, within the Hutter family, or among the Bush clan. But their drama comes not so much from the conflict between Judge Temple and Oliver Effingham or from family quarrels among the Bushes as it does from the opposition of the anarchic world of Natty Bumppo to the social order itself.

There seems to be a special relationship between Natty Bumppo's "natural" world and the wildness of his wilderness environment. Natty's disdain for the laws of Templeton in *The Pioneers* is reinforced by the abundance and order of his natural habitat. "You may make your laws, Judge," he cries, "but who will you find to watch the mountains through the long summer days, or the lakes at night? Game is game and he who finds may kill; that has been the law of these mountains for forty years to my sartain knowledge."[2] Phrases such as "game is game and he who finds may kill" suggest that Natty doubts that the laws of the social order have any relevance to the wilderness, which has its own codes of justice. As a native of the wilderness, he is outside the social order, enjoying his own rights and privileges and taking his own risks. And in each Leatherstocking novel Natty's abundant natural surroundings provide him with an escape from the oppressive aspects of social organization. The laws of Templeton, the charms of Judith Hutter, the lost love of Mabel Duncan, the rapacity of the Bush family—all these may be avoided by a passing westward into the forest or, at last, a return to an Indian village, to die seated in a chair at the foothills of the Rockies, his gaze "fastened on the clouds which hung around the western horizon."

Cooper establishes a pattern for the mid-nineteenth-century Easterner's response to the West by suggesting that the impetus of the wilderness is somehow away from, and even beyond, the social order. Part of the western drama, to be sure, is the imposing of man's institutions upon the forest—the erection of settlements, the passage of wildlife legislation, the slaughter of buffalo, and the conquest of the Indian—and Natty Bumppo, in a sense, is in the vanguard of the western movement, "the foremost in that band of pioneers who are opening the way for the march of the nation across

2. James Fenimore Cooper, *The Pioneers*, 2 (2 vols. Philadelphia, 1843), 211.

the continent."[3] But although he may hint of things to come, he remains firmly allied with a wilderness glorious in its antipathy to the established customs of eastern civilization.

This drama of society and solitude, in which the wilderness, with its vast scope, strange inhabitants, and unknown dangers, served as almost an antisocial force, lent a dual character to the westward movement in America. For the bulk of the nineteenth century, West was to remain synonymous with wilderness, and the pattern of eastern response established by Cooper was to undergo only slight changes. As the frontier receded into the middle of the continent, such literary Easterners as Washington Irving and Francis Parkman were to find that the West contained deserts and mountains as well as forests and prairies, but for all intents and purposes it remained a great empty continent outside, and perhaps beyond, the social order.

"What!" cried a London critic in 1835, upon receiving a copy of Washington Irving's *A Tour on the Prairies,* a narrative of his visit to Oklahoma territory in 1832, "Irving a buffalo-hunter on the Prairies? . . . It was but as yesterday we saw this same Washington Irving in London, a quiet, gentlemanly, douce, little, middle-aged man." It is still something of a surprise to find that the same man who delighted European salons commented critically on the "bustling" entrepreneurial society to which Rip Van Winkle awoke, and seemed to spend much of his time sitting down to a sumptuous five-course dinner, could have confessed to a "charmed interest" in the "hazardous errantry" of fur traders in the "wild parts of our vast continent," and vanished into the Indian country west of the Mississippi to partake in a "few months of rough outdoor life with frontiersmen, trappers, Indians, and border soldiers." Irving's interest in the West, nevertheless, rivaled his love of Dutch yeomanry and English gentlemen. In addition to *A Tour on the Prairies,* he wrote two other books on western subjects: *Astoria,* a history of John Jacob Astor's fur-trading enterprises in the Rocky Mountains and the Pacific slope, and *The Adventures of Captain Bonneville,* an account of a French soldier-of-fortune's trapping expeditions across the Great Plains and among the foothills of the Rockies. As

3. James Fenimore Cooper, *The Prairie* (New York, 1950), p. 429.

a consequence of these books, Irving, in the eyes of one historian of western Americana, "became an authority on the fur trade and one of the best informed persons in the United States on the western frontier."[4]

Certainly Irving was the first Easterner of established literary reputation to have had authentic contact with the "howling wilderness" West of the Mississippi. Like Cooper, many of his western experiences were vicarious; he gleaned most of the material for *Astoria* and *The Adventures of Captain Bonneville* from "the journals and letters . . . of the adventurers by sea and land employed by Mr. Astor in his comprehensive project," "collateral lights supplied by the published journals of other travellers who have visited the scenes described," and a "mass of manuscript," consisting primarily of Bonneville's traveling notes, to which Irving gave "a tone and coloring drawn from my own observation." But whereas Mark Twain was able to immortalize Cooper's lack of firsthand knowledge of the wilderness about which he wrote, Irving, according to recent scholarship, possessed a remarkable knowledge of western sites he had never seen. As Edgely Todd notes:

> The descriptions of terrain in Irving's *Astoria* and the *Adventures of Captain Bonneville* are faithful to the land. The rivers flow in the right directions, and the passes and mountains are where Irving says they are. . . . After returning from his own tour west of the Mississippi, Irving read widely in whatever he could find pertaining to the Far West and kept notes on his reading. He studied carefully before writing *Astoria,* and the preparation for that book added greatly to his knowledge. He talked to and corresponded with the participants in events narrated in both *Astoria* and the Bonneville book. He sought out such men; he read their diaries and letters; he read the newspapers closely. In a word, Irving knew his subject.[5]

So faithful, in fact, was Irving to the historical mode in his writings on the West that he refrained as much as possible from commenting upon the events which he described. His own characteriza-

4. Quoted in Edgeley W. Todd, ed., *The Adventures of Captain Bonneville* (Norman, Okla., 1961), pp. xvii, xviii; Washington Irving, *Astoria* (Geoffrey Crayon ed., New York, 1888), p. 8; Todd, *Bonneville,* p. vii.

5. Irving, *Astoria,* pp. 9, 10; Todd, *Bonneville,* pp. xlvi, liii.

tion of *A Tour on the Prairies* as "a simple narrative of every day occurrences" could also be applied to *Astoria* and *Bonneville:* they are narrative histories written by an author who remains for the most part impersonal. But the rare moments when Irving is moved to comment are of sufficient clarity and consistency to enable one to see strong parallels between his conception of the West and that of Cooper.

The western environment for Irving had more positive attributes than the mere absence of civilization. Like numerous other Easterners of the early nineteenth century, he was taken with the relationship of man to nature and tended to emphasize the "romantic" qualities of the western wilds. "It is not easy to do justice," he notes in *Bonneville,* "to the exulting feelings of the worthy captain at finding himself at the head of a stout band of hunters, trappers, and woodmen; fairly launched on the broad prairies, with his face to the boundless West. The tamest inhabitant of cities, the veriest spoiled child of civilization, feels his heart dilate and his pulse beat high on finding himself on horseback in the glorious wilderness." Nature worship is a persistent theme of *Bonneville:* Irving finds that a view from the crest of the Rocky Mountains is "astonishing" and "overwhelming in its immensity," that valleys are "deep and solemn," lakes "treasured," streams "mighty," and rapids "wild and beautiful to the eye." In particular, the wilderness of the West has an attraction for its own sake: "there was something pleasingly solemn and mysterious," he notes, "in floating down wild rivers at night."[6] Similarly, in *Astoria,* the fur traders pass by "noble" forests with "majestic" pines, "lovely" meadows, and "magnificent" mountains. The atmosphere has a "purity and elasticity," the sky "a delicious blue"; the sun "shines with a splendor unobscured by any cloud or vapor"; a starlight night on the prairies is "glorious." And Irving is careful to associate the beauties of the West with its wildness, thereby reinforcing the lure of its primitive qualities. Lakes, streams, and valleys are often "remote," mountain ranges "vast" and "unexplored," and the life of trappers and frontiersmen "savage" and "lawless."

A consideration of the components of life in the wilderness enables Irving to return to his theme of the "grand enterprise" of

6. Todd, *Bonneville*, pp. 18, 189, 190, 222, 311.

civilization's trek across the American continent. Upon investigating "the details" of such "adventurous expeditions" as those of the Astor fur traders and Captain Bonneville, Irving finds in every peak and valley of the West tensions between the charms of the wilderness and the precursors of civilization who attempted to defy its perils. Accordingly, he focuses upon the role of those "pioneers of the fur trade," the "hardy band of trappers" who "first broke their way through a wilderness where everything was calculated to deter and dismay them." Their "adventures and exploits," for Irving, "partake of the wildest spirit of romance."[7]

Yet Irving, like Cooper, is quick to impart to his characterization of the trappers, hunters, and mountain men who inhabited the western frontier the full range of his discriminating eastern social sensibilities. Although he speaks in *Astoria* of Canadian "voyageurs" as "the lords of our internal seas," the "great navigators of the wilderness," and, as such, "themes . . . for romantic associations," he also refers to them as a "motley" group of "half-savages" who are "prone to pass their time in idleness and revelry about the trading posts or settlements; squandering their hard earnings in heedless conviviality, and rivaling their neighbors, the Indians, in indolent indulgence and an imprudent regard of the morrow." And in the same breath that Irving describes the "perfect freedom of the wilderness," he notes the "licentiousness" of those "loose Western adventurers who identified themselves with the savages among whom they dwelt."[8]

The condescension with which Irving viewed the denizens of his "romantic" wilderness environment indicates that his response to the West was as characteristically eastern as Cooper's. Within the wilderness the trapper is a heroic figure—self-reliant, knowledgeable, free from the "restraints" of civilization. Apart from the western environment, such a man is a vagabond, a ne'er-do-well, a child, and a savage. In *Astoria* Irving makes clear the distinctions between a romantic wilderness life and the kinds of men who led it. "The immense wilderness of the far West," he writes, "defies cultivation, and the habitation of a civilized life"; as such it is an environment that offers "perfect freedom" to the individual. But the "rugged

7. Irving, *Astoria*, pp. 8, 145, 309; Todd, *Bonneville*, p. 6.
8. Irving, *Astoria*, pp. 37, 75, 78.

defiles and deep valleys" of Irving's West formed "sheltering places for restless and ferocious bands of savages . . . who carry into their mountain haunts the fierce passions and reckless habits of desperadoes." As Irving maintains:

> It is to be feared that a great part of [the West] will form a lawless interval between the abodes of civilized men. . . . Here may spring up new and mongrel races, like new formations in geology, the amalgamation of the "debris" and "abrasions" of former races, civilized and savage, the remains of broken and almost extinguished tribes; the descendants of wandering hunters and trappers; of fugitives from the Spanish and American frontiers; of adventurers and desperadoes of every class and country, yearly ejected from the bosom of society into the wilderness.[9]

The Adventures of Captain Bonneville concludes with similar praises of the wilderness life and expressions of anxiety about the social inadequacies of its inhabitants, but Irving's vision is tempered by his sense that "a life of savage independence" is one in which "there is nothing to tempt the cupidity of the white man." He prophesies for the West "the amalgamation of various tribes, and of white men of every nation," which "will in time produce hybrid races like the mountain Tartars of the Caucasus," and goes on to say that these mongrelized groups "may, in time, become a scourge to the civilized frontiers as they are at present a terror to the traveller and the trader." In the final sentence of *Bonneville,* he allies himself firmly with the forces of "civilization," calling for "a mounted force to protect our traders in their journeys across the great western wilds" and the pushing of "outposts into the very heart of the singular wilderness we have laid open, so as to maintain some degree of sway over the country."[10]

Irving's only firsthand experience with the uncivilized West, his hunting expedition to Oklahoma in 1832, lent, as he said, a "tone and coloring" to the rest of his western writings. *A Tour on the Prairies,* the narrative of that expedition, exhibits the same patterns of response to the wilderness and its inhabitants found in Irving's

9. Ibid., p. 303.
10. Todd, *Bonneville,* pp. 371, 372, 373.

later works. At the outset he is careful to indicate the social rank of
each of his traveling companions: Henry Ellsworth, from "the society of deacons, elders and select men on the banks of the Connecticut"; Charles Latrobe, a squired Englishman of Huguenot
extraction; and Count Albert de Pourtales, who, as befits his French
origins, is "full of talent and spirit . . . galliard to the extreme, and
prone to every kind of wild adventure." Passing on to a "personage
of inferior rank," he describes "the squire, the groom, the cook, the
tent man . . . and, I may add, the universal meddler and marplot of
our party, a little swarthy meagre French Creole named Antoine,
but familiarly dubbed Tonish." According to his own account,
notes Irving, Tonish "had a wife in every tribe; in fact, if all this
little vagabond said of himself were to be believed, he was without
morals, without caste, without creed, without country, and even
without language; for he spoke a jargon of mingled French, English and Osage." But Tonish tempered his other qualities by being
"a notorious braggart and a liar of the first water." At the bottom
of the social scale is the half-breed hunter, Pierre Beatte, whom
Irving finds "lounging about in an old hunting frock and leggings
of deer skin, soiled and greased, and almost japanned by constant
use." "I confess," writes Irving, "I did not like his looks when he
was first presented to me." He "had altogether more of the red than
the white man in his composition; and as I had been taught to
look upon all half-breeds with distrust, as an uncertain and faith-
less race, I would gladly have dispensed with the services of Pierre
Beatte."[11]

Such attitudes continued to manifest themselves throughout the
narrative of *A Tour on the Prairies*. At the last trading post prior
to departure into the wilderness, Irving comments on "the sprin-
kling of trappers, hunters, half-breeds, creoles, negroes of every
hue; and all that other rabble rout of nondescript being that keep
about the frontiers," likening them to "those equivocal birds, the
bats, which hover about the confines of light and darkness." A
short time later he denounces the "high-handed conduct" of a
"raw-boned, sinister-visaged, hard-winking frontiersman" in chas-
tising a young Indian who had returned his stray horse. "He was

11. Washington Irving, *A Tour on the Prairies* (Oklahoma City, 1955), pp. 3–4,
13–14.

for tying [him] to a tree," we learn, "and giving him a sound lash-ing," and he was "quite surprised at the burst of indignation which this novel mode of requiting a service" drew from Irving and his party. In the same vein Irving terms "the wild youngsters of the frontier" a "raw, undisciplined band," none of whom "had any idea of the restraint and decorum of a camp"; notes that Tonish and his "half-breed compeers" "bang and beat back the pack horses with volleys of mongrel oaths"; and compares the march of his party, with its ragged attendants, to a band of "bucaneers pene-trating the wilds of South America, on their plundering expeditions against the Spanish settlements."

But the class of discontents and desperadoes which Irving finds in the western wilderness remains distinct from the wilderness itself. There is a "grandeur and solemnity" in the spacious forests, and Irving "always felt disposed to linger until the last straggler dis-appeared among the trees and the distant note of the bugle died upon the ear, that I behold the wilderness relapsing into silence and solitude." He could conceive of "nothing more likely to set the blood into a flow, than a wild wood life of the kind, and range of a magnificent wilderness, abounding with game, and fruitful of ad-venture." "We send our youth abroad to grow luxurious and effemi-nate in Europe," he notes: "it appears to me that a previous tour of the prairies would be more likely to produce that . . . simplicity and self-dependence most in unison with our political institu-tions."[12]

Pierre Beatte, for example, whom Irving had found initially repulsive, acquires a certain stature as a veteran Westerner. "An Indian hunter on a prairie" he muses, "is like a cruiser on the ocean, perfectly independent of the world, and competent to self-protection and self-maintenance. He can cast himself loose from everyone, shape his own course, and take care of his own fortunes. I thought Beatte seemed to feel his independence, and to consider himself superior to us all, now that we were launching into the wilderness." Here Irving is responding to those aspects of the west-ern experience that rendered it outside eastern society and gave to its tenants an independence regardless of their social rank. "We of society," he maintains, "are slaves, not so much to others, as to ourselves; our superfluities are the chains that bind us, impeding every movement of our bodies and thwarting every impulse of our souls." Later in his narrative Irving indicates that Beatte has "risen in his estimation," and toward the end he is calling the half-breed "staunch as a veteran hound."[13]

Thus Irving, for all his abhorrence of the manners of the frontier and his characterization of the prairie as the future locus of brigandage, follows the pattern of Cooper by juxtaposing the rude march westward with the vast wilderness which serves as its track, resists it, and stands apart from it. On the one hand, he turns up his eastern nose at the lack of manners and social grace on the frontier, and on the other he describes a "wild wood life" as free from the chains that bind one, such as manners and grace.

The most celebrated pre-Civil-War response to the western experience came from the upper-class Boston historian Francis Parkman, whose nine volumes on France and England in the New World, professing to portray the "history of the American forest," have received considerable attention from students of American culture. Vernon Parrington sees Parkman's *Oregon Trail* as one of the few instances in which that stuffy group of New England Brahmins took any interest in the West at all. Bernard DeVoto chastises Parkman for his indifference to the glories of westward expansion and Manifest Destiny and "aches for the book that might have been added to our literature if God had a little thawed the Brahmin snobberies." Henry Nash Smith suggests that Parkman had a severe case of "primitivism," the "slightly decadent cult of wildness and savagery which the early nineteenth century took over from Byron." And Howard Doughty maintains that "the chief meaning of the West for Parkman was the meaning . . . of everything that the very legitimate impulse 'to get for a while out of the nineteenth century' could contribute by way of focus and perspective, to a comprehension of the nineteenth century." "Here for a young man whose birthright was the upper level of American society in its most complex and highly developed form," continues Doughty, "the Western periphery, with its aspects of strangeness and danger, with the drift of uprooted, atomized life along its trails, with its microcosm of utter social otherness in the lodges of the

13. Ibid., pp. 15–16, 20, 128, 150.

Oglala Sioux, offered the best of schools for completing his initiation into the varieties and possibilities of the human condition and orienting himself among them."[14]

Of these responses Doughty's is the most accurate, for all of Parkman's writing must be seen in a highly personal context. A product of mercantile wealth and Unitarian theology, Parkman underwent a series of violent dissociations with his Boston heritage in his early youth and from his eighth to his thirteenth year abandoned Boston to live on his grandfather's farm in Medford, where he roamed the woods and played truant from "Mr. Angier's School." When he returned to Boston to attend a day school, he was considered "docile" for a time, but his energy burst forth in a series of wilderness forays into the White Mountains and the region around Lake George while at Harvard. "The forest," he recalled, "possessed my waking and sleeping dreams."[15]

Parkman rejoiced in activities not usually related to the "mild, decorous, rational" world of his parents. Though he did not possess a strong constitution, he nevertheless craved physical exercise and wore out more than one of his fellow adventurers in his efforts to plunge deeper and deeper into the forest. Toughness, endurance, and other aspects of a cult of masculinity were his foremost concerns. As a child he had drawn pictures of soldiers in his journals, and in his writing he was to impute to his heroes such masculine qualities as awesome strength, boundless energy, and "self-abnegation," that quality of repressing one's psychic energy which he considered "the highest form of heroism."[16] Indeed, all of Parkman's heroes—James Wolfe, the backwoodsman Robert Rogers, the explorer La Salle, the Jesuits Brébeuf and Garnier, William Pitt, Generals Braddock and Amherst—are men of action, and the fact that Parkman rarely describes the family background of any of his protagonists but spends endless sentences on their exploits is indicative of the degree to which the Proper Bostonian found a man's heritage paling before his actions, particularly in the wilderness.

14. Vernon L. Parrington, *Main Currents of American Thought*, *1* (3 vols. New York, 1954), 430–31; Bernard DeVoto, *Year of Decision* (Boston, 1943), p. 115; Smith, *Virgin Land*, p. 551; Doughty, *Francis Parkman*, pp. 118–19.

15. Doughty, pp. 6, 13, 15–16, 22; Mason Wade, ed., *The Journals of Francis Parkman* (2 vols. [paged continuously] New York, 1947), p. 3.

16. Wade, *Journals of Francis Parkman*, pp. 6, 51; Francis Parkman, *The Jesuits in North America* (Boston, 1905), p. 491.

Moreover, the extent to which Parkman identifies with characters whose social backgrounds are antithetical to his own, such as the Jesuit priests and Robert Rogers, indicates that his histories should be read on several levels.

Nevertheless, Parkman, like Irving, imparts to his observations of mankind on his journey to Oregon in 1846 his Brahmin sense of mankind's inherent inequalities. In New York, making preparations, he sneers at the "little, contemptible faces—the thin weak, tottering figures—that one meets here on Broadway," and "feels savage with human nature." Passing by Harrisburg, he notices a man lounging by the river bank, and asks: "Is it not true, that the lower you descend in education and social position, the more vicious men become?"[17] While on the trail to Oregon itself, Parkman does not hesitate to comment on the rudeness and ill-breeding of certain of his associates, such as the group of uncouth figures he finds around his fire one evening, shivering in the drizzling rain. "Conspicuous among them were two or three of the half-savage men who spend their reckless lives trapping among the Rocky Mountains, or in trading for the Fur Company in the Indian villages. . . . Their hard, weather-beaten faces and bushy mustaches looked out from beneath the hoods of their white capotes with a bad and brutish expression, as if their owners might be the willing agents of any villainy. And such in fact is the character of many of these men." Like Irving, Parkman finds the West disturbing in its ethnic heterogeneity, terming a group of mountain men on the banks of the Platte River members of "a mongrel race."

Although Parkman considered the three weeks he passed in a village of the Oglala Sioux "the central experience" of his journey to Oregon, he was not overjoyed with his Indian companions. "For the most part, a civilized white man can discover very few points of sympathy between his own nature and that of an Indian. With every disposition to do justice to their good qualities, he must conclude that an impassable gulf lies between him and his red brethren. Nay, so alien to himself do they appear, that after breathing the air of the prairie for a few months or weeks, he begins to look upon them as a troublesome and dangerous species of wild beast." Upon rejoining fellow Bostonian Quincy Adams Shaw at Fort Laramie

17. Wade, *Journals of Francis Parkman,* pp. 405, 406.

near the end of his journey, Parkman confesses that "the change was a most agreeable one, from the society of savages and men little better than savages, to that of my gallant and high-minded companion."[18]

Nevertheless, the life led by certain men of a ruder stamp meets with Parkman's approval. The world of trappers he finds "of contrast and variety." Once in pursuit of game the trapper

> was involved in extreme privations and perils. Hand and foot, eye and ear, must always be alert. Frequently he must content himself with devouring his evening meal uncooked, lest the light of his fire should attract the eye of some wandering Indian; and sometimes having made his rude repast, he must leave his fire still blazing, and withdraw to a distance under cover of darkness, that his disappointed enemy, drawn thither by the light, may find his victim gone and be unable to trace his footsteps in the gloom.[19]

This is the kind of masculine doggedness with which Parkman strongly identified in his later histories; in *The Oregon Trail* he asserts that traders, hunters, and other pioneers must be alert, self-reliant, clever, and strong to survive the dangers of their solitary existence.

Parkman's wilderness takes on a quality of sternness and loneliness not so evident in Irving's majestic forests. At one spot near Laramie Creek, Parkman finds "something exciting in the wild solitude of the place"; at another he notes that "if a curse had been pronounced upon the land, it could not have worn an aspect more forlorn"; at a third he admits that "the naked landscape is, of itself, dreary and monotonous enough; and yet the wild beasts and wild men that frequent the valley of the Platte make it a scene of interest and excitement to the traveler." There is for Parkman "something impressive and awful" about the prairie, with its gloomy plain, fierce winds, and harsh temperatures. Most impressive is the sense of solitude: "I and the beasts were all that had consciousness for many a league around," he notes at one point.

Throughout *The Oregon Trail,* as in Irving's *A Tour on the*

18. Francis Parkman, *The Oregon Trail* (Garden City, N.Y., 1946), pp. 56, 61, 91, 231, 240.
19. Ibid., p. 207.

Prairies, the image of the wilderness increases in size and stature until it dwarfs the trapper and swallows up the Indian. Near the close of his narrative Parkman comes upon an ancient member of the Oglala Sioux seated, immovable as a statue, among the rocks and trees of a mountain glen. "Looking for a while at the old man," he relates, "I longed to penetrate his thoughts. . . . To an Indian all nature is instinct with mystic influence, and he watches the world around him as the astrologer watches the stars. So closely is he linked with it that his guardian spirit, no unsubstantial creation of the fancy, is usually embodied in the form of some living thing . . . and Mene-Seela, as he gazed intently on the old pine tree, might have believed it to enshrine the fancied guide and protector of his life."[20]

Upon leaving the Indian at his vigil, Parkman longs himself for some communion with the wilderness and, looking up, spies a tall peak rising among the woods:

> Something impelled me to climb; I had not felt for many a day such strength and elasticity of limb. An hour and a half of slow and intermittent labor brought me to the very summit; and emerging from the dark shadows of the rocks and pines, I stepped forth into the light. . . . Looking between the mountain peaks to the westward, the pale blue prairie was stretching to the farthest horizon, like a serene and tranquil ocean. The surrounding mountains were in themselves sufficiently striking and impressive, but this contrast gave redoubled effect to their stern features.

It is not surprising that when Parkman does praise members of the community, he relates their prowess to their interaction with the wilderness. A "French hunter from the mountains" is pictured as representative of "that race of restless and intrepid pioneers whose axes and rifles have opened a path from the Alleghenies to the western prairie"; and Henry Chatillon, the much-celebrated guide of Parkman's narrative, "from the age of fifteen years had been constantly in the neighborhood of the Rocky Mountains," "had as his school the prairies," and possessed as "no better evidence of the intrepidity of his temper" the common report that he had

20. Ibid., pp. 226–27.

killed more than thirty grizzly bears. At the close of *The Oregon Trail* Parkman returns East with the thought that his rifle, now in Henry's hands, may "perhaps at this moment be startling the echoes of the Rocky Mountains" with its sharp voice.[21]

Parkman's chief contribution to the western theme is his highly personalized characterizations of hardy trappers and mountain men opening a path through the prairies or of Indians keeping their noiseless vigils in the shadows of the mountains. By frankly identifying with those on the western scene who battled against the omnivorousness of the wilderness, he came to understand its signs. In a social setting these men were rude, uncouth, half-savage, and Parkman was glad to escape their presence; but the wilderness claimed them for its own, for the wilderness was never, in an eastern sense, social.

The eastern chroniclers of the West before the Civil War may be said to be both social historians and literary primitivists. On the one hand, they depicted social rankings in the western community with relish and acumen; on the other, they focused their imagination on the tensions between the march of civilization across the continent, and the resistance of the wilderness to that march. They created a dual role for the individual who inhabits the borderland between savagery and civilization. As a member of the social order, Natty Bumppo, Pierre Beatte, or Henry Chatillon is among the lowest class of beings on the social scale, but as a citizen of the wilderness he exemplifies heroic qualities which are associated with freedom from social restraint. His heroism, therefore, is restricted to a societyless setting, and one can identify with him only if one assumes that the course of western American civilization will be away from rather than toward the social order.

Paradoxically, each of the important western chroniclers of the early nineteenth century was closely identified with an established social order and, in the course of his literary career, wrote portraits of that order in which he eulogized individuals whose values were in apparent opposition to those of anarchic wilderness figures: "gentlemen" heroes who functioned in an environment dominated by social distinction.[22] Like Irving and Parkman, Cooper presented

21. Ibid., pp. 3, 11–12, 227, 228.
22. Cooper's *Precaution* (1820), Irving's *Bracebridge Hall* (1822), and Parkman's *Vassal Morton* (1856) contain gentlemen protagonists of this type.

a picture of the stages of society, from East to West, which clearly associates the western regions with the lowest forms of human life:

> The gradations of society, from that state which is called re-
> fined to that which approaches as near barbarity as connexion
> with an intelligent people will readily allow, are to be traced
> from the bosom of the states, where wealth, luxury and the
> arts are beginning to seat themselves, to those distant and ever-
> receding borders which mark the skirts and announce the ap-
> proach of the nation, as moving mists precede the signs of
> day.[23]

Such writers could demonstrate the moral superiority of Natty Bumppo's natural philosophies to those of the social order, suggest that a western experience be used as a training ground for the youth of America since it was more in harmony with our social and politi-cal institutions, and call the imperturbability with which a ragged Jesuit watched his flesh cut off "the highest form of heroism," but at the same time they revealed their affinity for a form of social organization which considered the Wild West furthest removed from "that state which is called refined." Like the paradoxes pro-duced in pre-Civil-War America by a stable social order which en-couraged individual initiative, the contradictory attitudes antebel-lum Easterners exhibited toward the relationship of an individual to society had not been resolved but exemplified themselves in imaginative recountings of the societyless West.

The wilderness of Cooper, Irving, and Parkman maintained much of its wildness in the decade after the Civil War, but the perspective from which Easterners viewed that wilderness was drastically changed. The result, in its broadest sense, was a shatter-ing of the delicate ambivalence which had marked previous eastern attitudes toward civilization and nature, West and East, and the emergence of a stance toward western America that retained only the condescension of a former generation. Like previous visitors to the West, most eastern tourists of the Civil War decade were suc-cessful individuals of high social status and closely identified with the social order, but the framework of that order had changed.

23. James Fenimore Cooper, *The Prairie, 1* (2 vols. Philadelphia, 1827), 88.

Progress, in eastern terms, now meant industrial progress; the march of civilization westward entailed the spread of urbanization; and man had become nature's architect instead of her worshiper.

The pattern of eastern visits to the West in the 1870s and early 1880s was dictated by the types of visitors and the tastes of the times. Certainly "the tourist was a gentleman, at least to his banker," for a coast-to-coast railroad trip cost approximately $300, not including meals. The celebrated Raymond Tours, first organized by a New England railroad magnate in 1879, advertised winter trips to California, with hotel expenses included, for $750. Small wonder that "a superior class" of Easterners traveled westward in this period: "it costs too much to get here for the scum of the earth to be among them," a Californian noted. As coast-to-coast travel increased, Pullman cars grew more lavish, with stained glass windows, carpeted floors, and frescoed ceilings. Lord Charles Russell, visiting the United States in 1883, noted that one of the strongest attractions of the Pullman was "that it enabled the rich to create the clearest possible inequality in the conditions of even ordinary travel." Some wealthy Easterners, such as Ralph Waldo Emerson, who went West in 1871, rented private cars; one family traveled in a four-car train with a maid, several cooks, nurses, and porters, and a Pinkerton detective. The exclusive tours, such as Raymond's, published previous passenger lists in their advertisements and noted that their tourists were of a "refined and cultured class."[24]

Once arrived in the West, the tourist of the seventies and eighties rarely roughed it. According to Earl Pomeroy, "The typical gentleman or gentlewoman tourist moved his bags into a hotel that offered, on a more expansive scale, comforts similar to those promised on the trip." The grand hotels that came to dot the West were products of railroad capital and sprang into being in the late seventies at stations on the transcontinental railroad lines. The Hotel de Paris in Georgetown, Colorado, was located at a spectacular stretch of mountain scenery on a narrow-gauge line winding northwest from Denver, the Windsor in Denver and the Palace in San Francisco were on the main route west, and the Del Monte in Monterey was but three hours from San Francisco by the Del Monte

24. Earl Pomeroy, *In Search of the Golden West* (New York, 1957), pp. 7–9, 10; Lord Charles Russell, *Diary of a Visit to the United States* (New York, 1910), p. 46; William Seward Webb, *California and Alaska* (New York, 1891), pp. vi–vii, 14, 204.

Limited. The hotels functioned as small cities, with shops, post offices, gardens, daily sun porches, and nightly entertainment, so that tourists could simply reproduce the comforts of the fashionable East in a more rural setting.[25]

The western resort, such as Manitou at Colorado Springs, was also a product of this period. Founded in 1871 by W. A. J. Palmer of the Denver and Rio Grande Railroad, Manitou was intended to be a "first class Colorado watering place and spa" and surpassed even General Palmer's expectations. "Fashion so embraced Manitou," notes Pomeroy, "that the social ritual developed apparently with relatively little reference to hotel facilities or to their natural environment." Women brought their most glamorous outfits, men their fox-hunting coats, and the social whirl spun on. "The ladies breakfast toilets are good enough for the dinner table, while for dinner they dress as we do for the opera," commented Daniel Pidgeon, an English visitor to Manitou. "American ladies never walk, but they go out 'buggy-riding' in dancing shoes and ball dresses, or amble about on ponies in highly ornamental riding habits. All this seems very odd among the mountains." And at the fashionable Cheyenne Mountain Country Club, in Broadmoor, three miles from Manitou, men shot clay pigeons, played polo, and rode out to hounds, substituting coyotes for foxes. In short, the "great Western hotels" of the seventies and eighties "drew many who cared little for the outdoors. The guests . . . who rode out to the hunt at the sound of a horn probably had moved West only geographically."[26]

The creation of such resorts and hotels suggests that in the urban age many traveled West for the healthful effects upon their constitutions, but few for the effects upon their souls. Replacing that immersion in the wilderness experience which Irving and Cooper recommended are attempts to channel and shape the wilderness to suit oneself. "People [go there]," wrote a visitor to one of the grand hotels, "not to worship nature, but to see and be seen by their kind. They play tennis and golf, swim in warmed tanks, drive behind fine horses, dress for dinner, and do all these things in the conventional and polite way."[27]

25. Pomeroy, *In Search of the Golden West,* pp. 16, 19–20.
26. Ibid., pp. 20–21; Daniel Pidgeon, *An Engineer's Holiday* (London, 1883), p. 140.
27. Charles S. Greene, "Where the Gray Squirrel Hides," *Overland, 30* (July 1897), 62.

To the Pullman rider and salt-bath fancier the term "wilderness" had taken on negative connotations. Disregarding Cooper's and Irving's sense of the West's majesty, visitors concentrated on its wasteland qualities. Thus J. W. Buel described Nevada in the eighties as "the very nakedness of bleak desolation [which] stretches its cursed length through a distance of 600 miles"; Ernest Ingersoll called Arizona "one of the very worst portions of the United States . . . repulsive plains of dry and thirsty sand, whose dreary waste is diversified only by jagged buttes and the splintered remains of volcanic dikes"; and J. T. Reister said of Pikes Peak in the seventies, "The dreariness of the desolate peak itself scarcely dissipates the dismal spell, for you stand in a hopeless confusion of dull stones piled upon each other in odious ugliness, without one softening influence, as if nature, irritated with her labor, had slung her confusion here in utter desperation." The absence of man and the presence of space, so momentous to the mid-century romantics, had simply become a source of irritation to the urban pioneers.[28]

Easterners were reluctant to envisage a broadly conceived western community whose members enjoyed perfect freedom from social restrictions.[29] In a world increasingly concerned with social stratification, a man was measured more and more by his relation to the social order; dissociation from this order, once heroic, came to be wholly synonymous with lawlessness. As the frontier raced westward after the Civil War, the societyless figure of Natty Bumppo evolved into the range cowboy, whose presence evoked far different responses from Easterners of the 1870s. In that decade, according to Henry Nash Smith, the term "cowboy" usually "called up the image of a semi-barbarous laborer who lived a dull, monotonous life of hard fare and poor shelter." President Arthur's first message to Congress in 1881 referred to "a disturbance of the public tranquility by a band of armed desperados known as 'Cowboys,' probably numbering from fifty to one hundred men, who had for months been committing acts of lawlessness and brutality in Arizona and Mexico," and asked for legislation empowering the Army

28. J. W. Buel, *America's Wonderlands* (Boston, 1893); Ernest Ingersoll, *Knocking Round the Rockies* (New York, 1883), pp. 163–64; J. T. Reister, *Sketches of Colorado* (Macon, Mo., 1876), pp. 51–52.

29. See A. N. Kaul, *The American Vision* (New Haven, 1963), for a perceptive discussion of the relation between society and community in mid-nineteenth-century eastern literature.

to intervene. As late as 1891 the cowboy was still attempting to correct his bad public image. Smith quotes Prentiss Ingraham's defense
of the cowboy class in *Buck Taylor, the Saddle King:* "I know well,
that a great many wicked men have crept into the ranks of our cowboy bands; but there are plenty of them who are as true as steel and
honest as they can be. . . . We live a wild life, get hard knocks, rough
usage, and our lives are in constant peril, and the settling of a difficulty is an appeal to revolver or knife; but after all, we are not as
black as we are painted."[30]

Post-Civil-War Easterners had been conditioned to see the cowboy as a desperado by a long linking of wildness and anarchy with
the western experience. They needed only to reverse their judgment on the merits of a wild life, shifting from the social revulsion
and imaginative attraction which had characterized earlier impressions of the West to attempts to transplant urban social patterns to
the most rural of settings. While retaining Cooper's, Irving's, and
Parkman's sense of the inferiority of western social groupings, the
gentlemanly tourists of the seventies and eighties had lost any conception of the West as an ultimate counterpoint to the East.

The image of the wilderness and a wild life as an alternative to the
social order retained its power, however, and as eastern society became more complex, rigid, and urbanized in the last years of the
nineteenth century, this image was to reassert itself in a cult of
westernizing which profoundly influenced the American imagination. In 1881 President Arthur was aghast at the violent deeds of
certain bands of "Cowboys," but by 1901 the occupant of the White
House, a graduate of Harvard and a member of Porcellian, was
known as the Rough Rider. In 1875 Laura Winthrop Johnson
spoke in *Lippincott's Magazine* of "rough men with shaggy hair
and wild, staring eyes, in butternut trousers stuffed into great rough
boots," but by 1902 a soft-spoken, hard-riding cowboy called the
Virginian had catapulted the novel that bore his name to the top of
the best-seller lists. And in 1895 a former Yale art student and foot-
ball player, who had failed to sell any of the sketches of western life
that he had brought with him to New York ten years before, found
himself the leading illustrator in the nation. Together Theodore
Roosevelt, Owen Wister, and Frederic Remington rode the crest of

30. Smith, *Virgin Land*, pp. 122, 124.

the western wave. All eastern men of social and financial prestige, they were heavily responsible for a sudden and dramatic restatement of the western theme and a reexamination of the American West in an industrial and urban context.

3. Remington, Roosevelt, Wister: The East and Adolescence

Just as an ocean voyage and the "grand tour" of Europe were oft-recommended antidotes for mysterious illnesses in the early nineteenth century, so the trip westward via Pullman car and grand hotel symbolized potential relief from the dyspepsia and delirium of the Gilded Age. This health-seeking ranged from the salt-bath chatter of gilded ladies at Manitou and Del Monte to Parkman's grim attempt to battle his "enemy" in the huts of the Oglala Sioux.

An aura of health-seeking surrounded Frederic Remington's journey West in 1881 and those of Theodore Roosevelt and Owen Wister in 1884 and 1885. Each man had experienced prior to his departure a sense of frustration, disappointment, or personal tragedy, and sought in the West a moratorium, a momentary stay against confusion, or a chance to begin life from a new perspective. Moreover, each traveled West when he was making the transition from adolescence to adulthood—"that period of the life cycle," according to Erik Erikson, "when each youth must forge for himself some central perspective and direction, some working unity, out of the effective remnants of his childhood" and the hopes of his anticipated life as an adult.[1] From such an "identity crisis," according to Erikson, an individual may "eventually come to contribute an original bit to an emerging style of life."[2]

The twenty-odd years during which Wister, Remington, and Roosevelt passed from childhood to the threshold of adulthood have previously been characterized as years of rapid social change. In the last of these years the three men journeyed West and deviated from past eastern conceptions of the American West to carve out an original and influential image of that wilderness beyond the Mississippi. Certain connections between the anxieties each of the

1. Erik H. Erikson, *Young Man Luther* (New York, 1958), p. 14.
2. Ibid., pp. 14–15.

three had associated with his adolescence in the East and the imaginative response which his initial western journey stimulated can be established, although a professional evaluation of possible identity crises in the adolescence of Roosevelt, Wister, and Remington is beyond the scope of this study.

According to Erikson, "at a given age, a human being, by dint of his physical, intellectual, and emotional growth, becomes ready and eager to face a new life task, that is, a set of choices and tests which are in some traditional way prescribed and prepared for him by his society's structure." Cultures achieve a degree of permanency in their social organization by correlating the various roles demanded by the social structure with the changing mental and physical capabilities of individuals, but "a new life task" in adolescence often presents "a crisis whose outcome can be . . . an impairment of the life cycle which will aggravate future crises."[3] In American culture a smooth transition from the "effective remnants" of childhood to the "hopes of anticipated adulthood" is usually dependent upon a basic agreement between the adolescent and his parents on the social role he is to perform—a role intimately related to the adolescent's prospective occupation. "The child," as Erikson writes, "can manage the fact that there is no return to the mother as a mother and no competition with the father as a father only to the degree to which a future career outside the narrower family can at least be envisaged in ideal future occupations."[4] If the adolescent is uncertain about his future occupation or in conflict with his parents over its future, he may feel unqualified or disinclined to perform the occupational role which the culture, as represented by his parents, demands, or he may envisage, in Erikson's terms, some alternative future occupation which his parents or other forces of authority decline to sanction.

My brief analyses of the adolescent years of Remington, Roosevelt, and Wister will focus upon each man's relations with his parents and each man's search for an attractive occupational role. Of particular interest is the kind of role each of the trio's parents imagined their son as performing. In an age in rapid transition, with its fluctuating economic and social trends and its changing

3. Ibid., p. 254.
4. Ibid., p. 258.

styles of life, the set of choices and tasks which the social structure
prescribed for young adults was undergoing its own severe modifi-
cations. The Roosevelt and Wister families had become accustomed
to the possession of wealth and prestige in a nonindustrial age,
while the Remington family had in part remained untouched by
post-Civil-War changes in the metropolitan East. Although the
three men grew up in an urban and industrial society, their child-
hoods were remarkable for their contact with areas and subjects
such as natural science, art, and music, which were far removed
from industrial enterprise. Nevertheless, members of the Wister
and Remington families became influenced by the values of industrialism to the extent that they questioned the relevance of their
sons' training, and a series of misfortunes in late adolescence served
to convince Roosevelt that he too was ill-prepared and unfit for life
in the East.

At the hub of the anxieties which preceded their western journeys in the 1880s was the sense on the part of each man that he was
disinclined or ill-equipped to perform the occupational role which
his parents had envisaged his performing. This sense, itself a manifestation of the rapid economic and social change which characterized late nineteenth-century eastern America, was to provide a
jumping-off point for the large attraction Remington, Roosevelt,
and Wister were to feel for the West, and their subsequent articula-
tion of this attraction in original and imaginative terms.

The development of the heavily populated and highly industrialized metropolitan complexes which dotted the northeastern seaboard in the latter portions of the nineteenth century was marked
by profound social and economic fluctuations, which had far-
reaching effects on all of eastern America, but countless individuals
in the post-Civil-War East lived out their lives in environments
widely different from that of the urban seaboard. Such an environment was that of Frederic Remington's youth: the small town of
Canton, New York, located in St. Lawrence County in the extreme
northern portion of the state, some 130 miles north and slightly east
of Syracuse. In 1861, the year Remington was born, Canton had no
public school, no circulating library, no town hall, and a fire department with only a rotary hand pump. Its population of 3,000
was ethnically homogeneous, with a smattering of German and

Irish Catholics, no immigrants from southeastern Europe, no individuals of Jewish descent, and no Negroes. Saw and grist mills represented the town's major industries, with lumbering increasing in importance in the 1880s. Canton could in fact be termed, in contrast to the eastern seaboard cities of the seventies and eighties, pre-industrial. As late as 1890 no major railroad connected it with New York City; as late as 1909, the year of Remington's death, no effective telephone system had been established; and its population remained at about 3,000 through 1900.[5] A less likely setting for rapid changes in the distribution of wealth and resultant status anxieties and power struggles can hardly be imagined.

The Remington family could nevertheless be considered, by Canton standards, an exceptional and prominent one. Frederic's grandfather, minister of the powerful Universalist Church, had raised funds to build St. Lawrence University, whose charter the New York state legislature had granted in 1856. That same year the St. Lawrence *Plaindealer* had been formed as a Republican campaign paper, under the editorship of Seth Remington, Frederic's father.[6] By the close of the Civil War, Seth Remington had become heavily involved in military and political affairs, having formed early attachments to a victorious Union army and a triumphant Republican party, and was by all accounts a man of influence in the circumscribed circles of northern New York.[7]

Seth Remington spent a remarkable length of time away from his home during the first years of his son's life. The fact that Frederic never saw his father until he was six years old, the colonel having left with his regiment in June of 1861, two months before the birth of his son, and having remained absent for six additional years, may be related to his celebrated fear of women. One of Remington's biographers, for example, claims that as a child he felt "awkward, tongue-tied, and oversized" in the presence of women; another discusses his reluctance to paint them; a third com-

5. Foote's Followers Yorker Club, *Canton—The Town Friendliness Built* (Canton, N.Y., 1955), pp. 7, 9, 14–20.

6. Ibid., p. 17.

7. On Seth Remington's career see Harold McCracken, *Frederic Remington: Artist of the Old West* (Philadelphia, 1947), pp. 24–27, 29; Robin McKown, *Painter of the Wild West: Frederic Remington* (New York, 1959), pp. 12–16, 18–19, 21–23, 27, 31, 32; and Atwood Manley, *Some of Frederic Remington's North Country Associations* (Canton, N.Y. 1961), pp. 10–12.

mentator points to a time when the mature Remington was un-
nerved by the presence of a lady passenger on a European train.[8]
Moreover, from the time of his marriage to Eva ("Missie") Caten
in 1884 until only a few years before his death in 1909, Remington
apparently felt a compulsive desire to make long trips to distant
environments unaccompanied by his wife. These excursions were
primarily to regions with a sparse female population, and Remington's occasional letters to his wife, whom he called "kid," while not
without animation, are generally without warmth and almost exclusively without acknowledged affection.

It is tempting to examine Remington's extraordinary affinity for
exclusively masculine endeavors, a point which will be in turn developed in reference to his western writings, in terms of his father-
less first six years. Unfortunately, ample evidence for such a study,
even by professionally trained hands, does not exist. But the little
information available concerning the personality of Clara Bascomb
Sackrider Remington, Remington's mother, is suggestive.

A photograph of Clara Remington with her husband, taken in
1868, reveals a stolid, impassive woman with a blunt jaw, wide
frame, full face, and protruding eyes. Though her gaze is wistful
and she wears a bow in her hair, she has allowed herself to be photo-
graphed with her hair rumpled and her dress stretched tightly
across her shoulders. The portrait is that of a woman with little
imagination and a low tolerance of what she might consider irre-
sponsibility. By contrast, Seth Remington, with his bushy eyebrows,
tangled hair, drooping mustache, string tie, velvet collar, and ex-
traordinarily bright, piercing eyes, appears as a picturesque combination of hayseed and gambler.[9]

Throughout young Remington's adolescence the differing per-
sonalities of his parents manifested themselves in conflict over
Frederic's occupational training. When Seth Remington returned
to Canton in 1867, he found an adulatory son, who supposedly
claimed, "When I grow up, I'm going to be a soldier like father."
The colonel encouraged this interest in the armed services, send-

---

8. McKown, *Painter of the Wild West*, p. 18; McCracken, *Frederic Remington*,
pp. 80–82; Poultney Bigelow, *Seventy Summers*, *1* (2 vols. New York, 1925), 312–14.

9. The photographs of Seth and Clara Remington are in Robin McKown's collection of Canton memorabilia; see also illustrations in Manley, *Some of Frederic
Remington's North Country Associations*.

ing his son at fifteen to the Highland Military Academy in Worcester, Massachusetts, but thoughts of a service career for Frederic fizzled; Remington confessed in a letter to a chum "I don't amount to anything in particular."[10] At the same time, however, the colonel was encouraging Frederic's other major childhood interest: according to one account, when he discovered his son, in his eighth year, drawing crude sketches of a neighbor's horse, he prophesied that Frederic "was going to be a great artist." He saw that his son's talents were indulged at Highland and arranged for him to go to art school at Yale in his seventeenth year.

The curious blend of the aesthete and the roughneck in Remington had coupled with his inordinate aversion to the opposite sex to produce a distinctive stance toward life. In a letter to a contemporary, Scott Turner, Remington waxed indignant over Turner's sketches of "women and dudes," asked to see a drawing of a battle between "Russians and Turks or Indians," and accompanied a photograph of himself with the caption: "You can burn it but don't throw it into the back yard or it may scare some wandering hen to death." One biography of Remington has him confiding to Turner that "he had never drawn a woman—except once and then had washed her out."[11] And at this point in Remington's adolescence the only woman with whom he had had a lasting acquaintance, his mother, chose to make the first of a chain of comments on the relevancy and worth of her son's adolescent education.

Frederic's mother reportedly balked at the notion of his attending Yale Art School. She felt that he "would never make a living by painting pictures" and that he "should take some business courses." When Colonel Remington died in February 1880, his mother's bias against art studies no doubt influenced his decision to abandon Yale. Her influence is also evident in Remington's occupational efforts for the remaining period he spent in the East before his first journey to Montana in August 1881: a grocery job

10. McKown, *Painter of the Wild West*, pp. 12, 14; Manley, *Remington's North Country Associations*, p. 18; Frederic Remington, *Men with the Bark On* (New York, 1900), p. 171; on Remington's Highland Park career, see Orin Edson Crooker, "A Page from the Boyhood of Frederic Remington," *Collier's, 14* (September 1910), 28. Remington attended the Burlington Episcopal School in Burlington, Vermont, for a year before matriculating at Highland Park; see Manley p. 17.

11. Quoted in McKown, *Painter of the Wild West*, p. 21.

in Ogdensburg, a clerkship in the governor's office in Albany, and five or six other positions in the Albany statehouse. Of the clerkship she was apparently most proud, referring to her son as being in "politics," which "to her meant a brilliant future."[12]

The relative values Clara Remington placed on art and business strikingly exhibit themselves in an extraordinary journey she made to visit her son in Kansas City in 1884, when Frederic was polishing a portfolio of sketches he had assembled from a brief tour of the Southwest he had made earlier that year. According to Mrs. Nellie Hough, who was a friend of the younger Remington and had witnessed the scene, Clara pleaded with her son "to give up his foolishness and take a 'real man's job.' " She did not "have one word of encouragement for [Remington's] art studies," and left after it had become apparent that he had "turned a deaf ear to her pleading."[13] Clara realized her own entrepreneurial ambitions by marrying an Ogdensburg hotel manager in 1890 and entering with him into joint ownership of a hotel in Carthage, New York. According to one account, Remington told his mother that she had "no right to even consider such a thing," to which she rejoined, "You've never paid any attention to what I told you to do. Now I'm going to do what I want."[14]

The deep antipathy Remington came to feel for industrial enterprise, coupled with his great attraction for masculine environments, particularly those of a military sort, may well have been spawned in the seven years he spent confronted with the images of an absent, idealized father, off somewhere "in the war," and a strong-willed, stubborn mother, who had come to symbolize unchallenged and perhaps detested authority.

Some accounts of Remington's career have correlated his initial journey West with a spell of ill-health brought on by the failure of his suit for Missie Caten in the summer of 1880, but it is of interest that Remington waited almost a year after Missie's father had refused him before leaving for Montana and, upon his return from that excursion, waited almost a year and a half before setting out

---

12. Ibid., pp. 21, 31, 32–34.

13. On the encounters between the Remingtons in Kansas City in 1884, see Mrs. Nellie Hough, "Remington at Twenty-Three," *International Studio*, 76 (February 1923), 413–15.

14. Quoted in McKown, *Painter of the Wild West*, p. 102.

for Kansas on a "permanent" basis in 1883. In the interval between these journeys Remington, though in the Ogdensburg area, made no effort to see Missie and reportedly resolved that "he would be better off if he cut women out of his life altogether."[15]

A more probable explanation is that his father's death in 1880 deprived Remington not only of the foremost of his childhood heroes but of the major financial and ideological force behind his intended career as an artist. From the time he returned to Ogdensburg in February 1880, there is no record of his attempting sketching or painting; instead, he turned to business and politics, occupations to which his mother gave a high priority. During the summer his romance with Eva Caten, whom he had known for over a year, took on a particular intensity; no doubt living with his mother had an effect upon the timing of his proposal, since Remington was only nineteen, an unusually young age to marry in the 1880s, when he asked for Eva's hand.

Thus the crucial factor in Remington's oft-mentioned "ill-health" of the eighteen months ending with the trip to Montana in August 1881 may well have been his constant occupational frustration. Work would have been a natural outlet to relieve tensions caused by his father's death, his mother's omnipresence, and his sweetheart's inaccessibility, but the fact that he held seven or eight different jobs in eighteen months indicates that, if anything, it brought on greater tensions. It is significant that when Remington left New York, he chose to move to a nonindustrial environment; according to one biographer he desired to go to "any place that's not cluttered up with office buildings."[16] At twenty he had begun what was to be a lifelong description of industrial civilization as a cramped and crowded existence which impinged upon a man's freedom.

In simplest terms, Frederic Remington was encouraged by his father to prepare for one role and then told by his mother to perform another, and the inadequacy he must have felt as a clerk was surely coupled with his resentment at the lack of viable alternative occupational possibilities. As he departed for Peabody, Kansas, in March 1883, to begin a career as a sheep rancher, he had not yet

15. McKown, *Painter of the Wild West*, p. 45; the lost love and ill-health theories appear in McKown, p. 35; McCracken, *Frederic Remington*, p. 32; and Manley, *Remington's North Country Associations*, p. 22.

16. McKown, *Painter of the Wild West*, p. 35.

resolved his doubts and uncertainties, but had merely transferred them to what he felt would be a more pleasant setting.

Theodore Roosevelt moved at the center of the social and occupational circles from which sprang the Eastern Establishment, and the main themes of his adolescence are intimately related to the fluctuations in wealth, power, and status that served as the setting for the formation of Establishment institutions.

It was characteristic of the Roosevelts that they "closed ranks" in times of crisis. Twice in Theodore's youth they joined to pay tribute to one of their own: once upon the occasion of Theodore Roosevelt, Sr.'s death in 1878; once at the double funeral of Roosevelt's first wife, Alice Lee, and his mother, Martha Bulloch Roosevelt, in 1884. Such occasions served as reminders of the force of their heritage. Theodore's letter to his younger sister in 1878 was representative: "What an inestimable blessing to have such a home as I have."[17]

Roosevelt's succession to the presidency, clouded as it was by the tragedy of McKinley's death, was an equally momentous and emotion-filled occasion; significantly, his first meal at the White House was a private family dinner with his two married sisters and their husbands. His sister Corinne remembered that the awesome solemnity of the moment did not preclude the ritual of passing boutonnieres to the gentlemen with their coffee, and "on that night the flower offered Theodore was a saffron yellow rose." As the new President placed it in his buttonhole, he "was heard to murmur, 'Isn't it strange. This is the rose we always connect with my father.' "[18] The enactment of a formalistic ritual in a closed social situation, the extraordinary circumstances surrounding that situation, and the omnipresent memory of Theodore Roosevelt, Sr., served to make that dinner a logical extension of the new President's adolescent experience.

In an age in which economic and social upheavals were manifesting themselves in struggles for financial power and familial prestige, the Roosevelts exhibited a remarkable strength of forces. The mar-

17. Theodore Roosevelt to Corinne Roosevelt, in Elting E. Morison et al., eds., *The Letters of Theodore Roosevelt, 1* (8 vols. Cambridge, Mass., 1951), 32.
18. Corinne Roosevelt Robinson, *My Brother, Theodore Roosevelt* (New York, 1921), p. 207.

riage of Theodore Roosevelt and Martha Bulloch had blended "six generations of solid, reputable citizens" from New York, the last five of which "had carried public responsibilities of various kinds," with four generations of Georgia forebears, each of whom "was reputable in private life and made some contribution to his community and country."[19] And the economic standing of the Roosevelts was as impressive as their social position, for it had managed to effectively change its focus to meet the needs of the expanding American economy. Founded in the early nineteenth century, it had originally been concerned with hardware, had expanded to building supplies, then, under Theodore, Sr., to the "importation and distribution of plate glass," and finally to banking. By the time of his marriage in 1853, Theodore, Sr. was already a partner, and at his death in 1878 his net estate was valued at approximately $750,000, an extraordinary sum for times which had not yet become acquainted with the million-dollar trust.[20]

As might be expected under such circumstances, Theodore, Jr.'s, youthful experiences were more broad-ranging and exceptional than most. In 1869 he embarked with his family for a year's tour of western Europe, three years later he spent another twelve months in Germany and the Near East, by 1873 he had begun intensive tutoring for the entrance examinations at Harvard, and in 1876 he matriculated at that university. The advantage of his family situation had enabled him, in the meantime, to supplement his intellectual endeavors with adventures of a physical orientation: between 1870 and 1872 he spent summers in the Adirondacks and northern Maine, making notes on the fauna and quoting Browning by the shores of lakes.[21]

The pattern of exercise in the outdoors had a particular significance for the Roosevelt family, and especially for young Theodore, for it marked an attempt to cope with his celebrated childhood illnesses. One of Roosevelt's earliest recollections of his childhood was his father's carrying him in arms as they walked up and down the nursery, while "Teedie" tried to draw a breath. Another is "sitting

19. Carleton Putnam, *Theodore Roosevelt: The Formative Years* (New York, 1958), pp. 5, 8, 9.

20. Putnam, *Theodore Roosevelt*, pp. 5, 337n.

21. On Roosevelt's European and Near Eastern journeys and his excursions to the Adirondacks and Maine, see Putnam, *Theodore Roosevelt*, pp. 51–116.

up in bed gasping, with my father and mother trying to help me."
In the summer of 1870, Roosevelt's twelfth year, he "was sent from
place to place for a change of air"—from the family's summer home
in Spuyten Duyvil, New York, to Philadelphia, to Saratoga Springs,
to Richfield, New York, to Oyster Bay—until by autumn, according
to one account, "the whole family, including Theodore himself,
apparently felt that they had had enough." Theodore, Sr., sum-
moned his son, and the famous conversation ensued at which the
father challenged his namesake to "make your body," and the son,
throwing back his head and flashing his teeth, determined that he
would.[22]

The most oppressive of Roosevelt's childhood illnesses was
asthma, and the psychological effects of shortness of breath may
have resulted in his identification of wilderness environments such
as northern Maine as places of refuge. But he clearly also responded
to them because they were physically taxing. Throughout his adolescence he turned to physical exercise as a means for gaining health
and relieving anxiety, and the method proved remarkably successful: by his freshman year at Harvard he was allotting two-and-a-half
hours to daily exercise and feeling "bully," his asthma having sub-
sided to an occasional attack.[23]

The uniqueness of his family's social position and the well-
developed childhood pattern of response to adversity came together,
for young Roosevelt, in the person of his father, who had petitioned
him to "live like a brave Christian gentleman," and advised him
upon entering Harvard to "take care of your morals first," while at
the same time remaining the chief inspiration for his son's dogged
attempts to improve his health. Thus Roosevelt at Harvard was
"inordinately conscious of his position as a 'gentleman,' " "cautious
and discriminating" in his choice of friends, and quick to identify
himself with socially prominent campus institutions, while retaining and reinforcing his commitment to health through exercise
with trips to Maine in September of his sophomore year and March
of his junior year. In June 1878, some five months after his father's

22. Theodore Roosevelt, *An Autobiography*, Vol. 22 of the *Complete Works of
Theodore Roosevelt* (Memorial Edition, 22 vols. New York, 1925), p. 17. Hereafter
cited as Roosevelt, *Works*, with volume and page numbers; unless otherwise indicated, the Memorial Edition is used.
23. Putnam, *Theodore Roosevelt*, pp. 26, 138.

death, he summed up the themes of family solidarity, ill-health, and paternal guidance that had characterized his life up to that point: "I owe everything I have or am to Father. He did everything for me, and I nothing for him. . . . I realize more and more each day that I am as much inferior to Father morally and mentally as physically."[24]

Roosevelt had nevertheless resolved "to lead such a life as Father would have wished me to," to "do something to keep up his name,"[25] and from 1878 increasingly turned his attention to the kind of life he intended to pursue after Harvard. Though his occupational alternatives were not as painfully disjointed as those of Remington, they nevertheless served to highlight some of the major themes and tensions of his youth.

The relatively sheltered nature of Roosevelt's childhood, not in terms of range of experience but in terms of human contacts, was consistent with a somewhat bookish life. At the time he entered Harvard he had never been outside of his family circle for any length of time, and his health could be best described as uncertain. During the semi-invalidism of his early years he read voraciously on a host of subjects, but his chief interest was in natural science. While at Harvard he had seriously discussed the prospect of natural science with his father, who had tempered his encouragement with a warning that the academic life did not lead to financial triumphs. Nevertheless, there is little doubt that when he resolved in the winter of 1878 to "think what I shall do when I leave college,"[26] natural science loomed largest in his mind.

During Roosevelt's junior and senior years a series of factors combined to pose alternatives to a career as a naturalist. As Carleton Putnam points out, he found "a new pulsing interest in people," no doubt the product of his wide-ranging social affairs at Harvard and his improved health, and it is quite conceivable that "the

24. Theodore Roosevelt, letter to Martha Bulloch Roosevelt, March 24, 1878, in E. Morison, *Letters, 1,* 33; Theodore Roosevelt to Corinne Roosevelt, November 26, 1876, in Theodore Roosevelt Collection, Harvard College Library; Putnam, *Theodore Roosevelt,* pp. 115, 136, 150–51.

25. Putnam, *Theodore Roosevelt,* pp. 151–52.

26. Quoted ibid., p. 177; Roosevelt, *Works, 22,* 30–31. In his autobiography Roosevelt claimed that his father advised him that "if I went into a scientific career, I must definitely abandon all thought of the enjoyment that could accompany a money-making career, and must find my pleasures elsewhere."

prospect of the relatively narrow discipline of natural science, even of the faunal naturalist, was raising doubts in his mind as to its range of satisfactions." Moreover, he became more conscious of his family heritage with his father's death and his forthcoming marriage to Alice Lee, of Chestnut Hill, Massachusetts, in the fall following his senior year. Alice was very much a Victorian maiden, and Theodore felt keenly his masculine role as provider and protector: in March 1880 he wrote a friend, upon announcing his engagement, that he had "made everything subordinate" to winning Alice, "so you can perhaps understand a change in my ideas as regards science." By March 25 he had decided to abandon natural science as a profession: "I shall study law next year," he wrote, "and must do my best, and work hard for my little wife."[27]

This decision indicates how closely Roosevelt, in making decisions that he considered of prime importance, identified with his family and, in a broader sense, his "class." Not only had the "total environment on Chestnut Hill, the traditions and outlook of the older generation of Saltonstalls and Lees," associated with his future wife, "almost certainly discouraged any thought of natural history as a career," but the specter of his father as businessman, philanthropist, and government official loomed large in his mind. The crisis regarding an occupational decision came not during the period of choice itself but after his role had apparently been established.

In the years between 1880 and 1884 Roosevelt pursued the path he had laid out for himself. In 1880 he entered Columbia Law School and joined the Twenty-First District Republican Association in Manhattan. In 1881 he was elected Republican candidate to the New York State Assembly from the Twenty-First District, and in 1883 he was reelected to the same post. At Albany he overcame initial reservations on the part of his fellow delegates to gain their respect as an uncompromising foe of machine government, and the fact that he "dressed and played the gentleman, outwardly as well as inwardly," did not hurt his popularity in the fashionable District,

27. Putnam, *Theodore Roosevelt*, pp. 177, 179; Roosevelt to Henry Minot, in E. Morison, *Letters*, *1*, 43. On Alice, Roosevelt wrote in his diary on March 26, 1889, two months after he had become engaged: "It is perfectly impossible to tell how much I love her. . . . She is sweet and tender and loving, and so absolutely pure and innocent."

although it provoked a certain amount of sarcasm in the New York press. By 1884 Roosevelt felt so secure in his position in the state assembly that he made a bold campaign for Speaker of the House and almost captured the post, being thwarted at the last minute by a secret deal characteristic of the party jealousies and controversies which racked the Garfield-Arthur years. Rebounding vigorously from his close defeat, he spent the remainder of 1884 attempting to pass legislation to reorganize the structure of municipal government in New York, balance the city's chaotic budget, and establish high fees for liquor licenses in the state, thereby "striking at the close alliance between the machine politicians and the liquor interests."[28] Within three years he had become an entrenched favorite in his district and a rising star in the assembly.

Nor did Roosevelt neglect his role as family man and preserver of his heritage in his first years of married life. The young couple entertained with a flourish at Albany and New York, and in 1883 Roosevelt not only acquired a cattle ranch in Dakota as a supplementary business and a base for hunting trips but watched construction begin on a permanent home for his family at Oyster Bay. In February of 1884, as the Roosevelts prepared for the birth of their first child, all signs pointed to a successful and prominent life in the best tradition of his family.[29]

When, on Tuesday, February 12, 1884, Roosevelt received a telegram announcing the birth of his first child, he was, according to a contemporary, "full of life and happiness," but the next morning he received a second telegram informing him that his wife and mother were seriously ill. He hastily departed for New York and arrived in time to witness his mother's death from typhoid and, the next day, his wife's from Bright's disease. Dazed and stunned by this double tragedy ("he does not know what he does or says," a friend said at the time), Roosevelt wrote in his diary that "the light has gone out of my life," and "for joy or for sorrow my life has now been lived out."[30]

28. A full account of Roosevelt's years at Columbia and the New York State Assembly may be found in Putnam, *Theodore Roosevelt*, pp. 238–312.

29. See Hermann Hagedorn, *The Roosevelt Family of Sagamore Hill* (New York, 1954), esp. pp. 1–10, for the construction of the Oyster Bay House; see Putnam, *Theodore Roosevelt*, pp. 313–46, for Roosevelt's acquisition of his Dakota ranches.

30. Arthur Cutler, letter to William W. Sewall, quoted in William W. Sewall, *Bill Sewall's Story of T.R.* (New York, 1919), p. 11; Putnam, *Theodore Roosevelt*, p. 389.

Frantically throwing himself into his work ("I think I should go mad if I were not employed," he wrote a sympathizer two days after the double funeral), Roosevelt turned with fury to politics, only to see his promising career receive a devastating setback. He led the New York reform delegates in their support of George F. Edmunds of Vermont for the 1884 Republican presidential nomination, but the Edmunds forces were balked in their effort and James G. Blaine, whom Roosevelt had often castigated as an enemy of reform, was nominated. Reporters at the convention in Chicago found Roosevelt in a fighting mood, and certain hasty comments of his, such as "Mr. Blaine's nomination I regard as the result of mistaken public enthusiasm," were reprinted in the eastern press. To make matters worse, on June 9, a day after the convention, the St. Paul *Pioneer Press* printed an interview with Roosevelt in which he reportedly said: "I shall bolt the nomination of the convention by no means. I have no personal objections to Blaine . . . I believe Blaine will be elected. . . . I have been called a reformer but I am a Republican."[31]

Roosevelt's attacks on the Republican nominee, coupled with his supposed disavowal of reform for party loyalty, served to alienate both party regulars and "independents," the latter a group upon which he had based much of his political support in the New York Assembly. On July 19, 1884, when Roosevelt made public his support of the Republican ticket, "immediately all the newspapers which had repudiated Blaine repudiated Roosevelt." Old Harvard classmates cut him in the streets, and he received "shoals of letters, pathetic and abusive," from friends who seemed "surprised that I have not developed hoofs and horns." By the end of July, Roosevelt was "disinclined to talk about the political situation," and in August he suddenly left New York for a prolonged hunting trip through the Dakota Badlands. Returning to campaign half-heartedly for the national Republican ticket in October, he turned down one nomination for the state assembly and one for Congress. At this same time he wrote that he "would make ranching my regular business," and, according to Putnam, "renounced all thought of politics and centered his life around Dakota."[32]

31. Quoted in E. Morison, *Letters, 1,* 66, and in Putnam, *Theodore Roosevelt,* p. 390; New York *Tribune,* June 7, 1884; St. Paul *Pioneer Press,* June 9, 1884.

32. New York *Tribune,* October 14, 1884; E. Morison, *Letters, 1,* 73; Putnam, *Theodore Roosevelt,* p. 507.

In many ways Roosevelt's adolescence had been a preparation for long-term success in the East. That had been virtually assured, but tragedy had caused him to pull up his stakes and head westward. With his wife's and mother's deaths, the continuity and kinship of the Roosevelts had become fragmented, and Theodore obviously wished a respite from those symbols of his heritage which now mocked him: Oyster Bay, the assembly, even his sisters and his baby girl.[33] He had long thought of a spartan life in the outdoors as a means of alleviating physical and mental duress; and the "grimness" he was to find in the Badlands particularly suited his mood in the fall of 1884. Plunging, in a physical sense, into a new task had been a characteristic method of coping with adversity in his youth, and his purchase of the Dakota ranch now guaranteed that the task would be associated with the kind of environment which particularly suited his needs.

The anxiety which in a large part motivated Roosevelt's decision to turn West likely manifested itself in profound doubts about his own identity. The very fact that he seriously considered becoming a cattle rancher indicates the degree to which he felt thwarted, occupationally as well as personally, by developments in his late adolescent years in the East. In this sense the psychological pattern which preceded Roosevelt's first major journey West was not unlike that of Remington as he departed for Kansas in 1883.

Owen Wister's eastern boyhood presents an equally striking example of restlessness and anxiety brought about by a crisis in choice of vocation. As a youth, Wister was plainly creative and socially inclined, and his family every bit as intellectually curious and perhaps even more socially self-conscious than the Roosevelts. At six Owen was left in a Swiss boarding school for three months while his parents toured Europe; at ten he enrolled in another school in Hofwyl, Switzerland; at eleven he lived in England with his aunt and uncle for a year, attending a day school. Like Roosevelt, he had spent a full two years of his life outside the United States before he was fifteen and was brought up in a household "intensely intellectual" and upper class—"a part of the upper circle of Philadelphia." Sarah Butler Wister, Owen's mother, was "the great lady of her

33. See Sewall, *Bill Sewall's Story,* esp. pp. 40–49, for an indication of the frustration and melancholia which accompanied Roosevelt to Dakota.

neighborhood," who "swept into the opera and symphony concerts in black velvet and white lace," and carved at the table while wearing white kid gloves, and whose friends and correspondents included Henry James, Mendelssohn, Thackeray, and Browning.[34] His grandmother, the Shakespearean actress and playwright Frances Anne (Fanny) Kemble, was as noted for her distinctive views on social life as for her theatrical talent: she left fashionable New York aghast in the early seventies by remarking that that city had never heard of a finger bowl.[35] In 1875 she settled down at "York Farm," across the road from Butler Place, the "gracious country estate" six miles north of the Philadelphia City Hall where the Wisters resided until 1925.

Fanny Kemble's memoirs are full of life at York Farm and Butler Place in the period of Owen's youth, and if one takes her literally, her daughter Sarah Wister had a remarkable incapacity to maintain tolerable relations with individuals "beneath her station," particularly servants. Though the bulk of her references to her daughter concern themselves with domestic problems, there is an occasional pointed insight into Sarah's character. On November 29, 1874, Miss Kemble noted: "S - - was as fond of her baby as I think she could be of any creature too nearly resembling a mere animal to excite her intellectual interest, which is pretty much the only interest in infants or adults that she seems to me to have." Indeed, when Sarah was not frantic about servants, she was concerned with the theatre, her father's Georgia plantation, the writing of an occasional unsigned article for the *Atlantic Monthly*, or the low state of American political affairs in the 1870s. In the whole of Fanny Kemble's memoirs, which cover the years at York Farm (1874 to 1883), there is never a mention of any special tenderness between Sarah and her husband, Dr. Owen Jones Wister, or between Sarah and her son.

One "regular visitor to Butler Place" is alleged to have spoken of a "temperamental clash between Dr. and Mrs. Wister,"[36] and indeed Owen's father was of a considerably different disposition from

34. Frances Kemble Wister Stokes, ed., *Owen Wister Out West* (Chicago, 1958), pp. 4, 6; interview with Owen J. Wister, November 21, 1965.

35. Van Rensselaer, *The Social Ladder*, p. 127.

36. Frances Anne Kemble, *Further Records* (New York, 1891), p. 52; Stokes, *Owen Wister*, p. 5.

his wife. According to his daughter, he was "not intensely social, as his wife was, and did not enjoy dining out and entertaining as she did." A "humorous, methodical" descendant of a series of prosperous Philadelphia merchants, he may be said to have been as relaxed as his wife was intense and as pedestrian as she was imaginative. Two aspects of Dr. Wister's relations with his son emerge from anecdotes of the years at Butler Place: a certain hearty companionship lacking in Owen's relationship with his mother, and a seeming indisposition on Dr. Wister's part toward his son's creative impulses, which tended to mitigate against this companionship.

When Owen showed promise as a pianist and composer at St. Paul's, where he had been sent in 1873, and decided to continue his music studies upon his entering Harvard, there is no record that Dr. Wister lost his sense of humor. But a talent indulged was one thing, and a musical career quite another. In June of 1882 Owen graduated from Harvard with highest honors in music. He then resolved to "become a composer of operas and symphonic poems"; "this had been the only thing I wanted to do since I discovered, as a boy at St. Paul's school, that I could make tunes and devise harmonies." Dr. Wister, however, was skeptical: in later life Wister noted that his choice of career "did not at all appeal to my father, who insisted upon an authoritative European judgment before he would give his consent."

Thus young Wister journeyed abroad and, before enrolling at the Conservatoire in Paris, visited Franz Liszt with a letter of introduction from his grandmother. "Grandfather Liszt," as Wister called him, was impressed with his old friend's grandson, writing to Miss Kemble that Owen had "un talent prononcé" for music.[37] Ernest Guiraud of the Conservatoire was equally pleased with his pupil, and Wister spent a profitable winter in Paris. But Dr. Wister was not happy that his son, upon whom he "doted," was in the wrong atmosphere pursuing the wrong goals. When Major Henry Higginson of the Boston brokerage firm of Lee, Higginson and Co. (which Morison sees as closely connected with the inner circle of Harvard's clubdom) mentioned to Dr. Wister that he "would like to

37. Interview with Mrs. Frances K. W. Stokes, November 21, 1965; Owen Wister, *Roosevelt, the Story of a Friendship* (New York, 1930), p. 22; Stokes, *Owen Wister*, pp. 8–10.

have [Owen] start in [his] office," the good doctor was only too happy to have the opportunity to summon the prodigal.

In the spring of 1883 Owen "was brought back to State Street," but a shortage of positions at Lee Higginson forced him "below stairs into the Union Safe Deposit Vaults," where he "sat on a high hard stool computing interest at 2½ per cent on the daily balances of our depositors." Finally, after a year, when "still there was no place for me at Lee Higginson . . . and . . . no prospect of the Vaults ending," Wister wrote a letter to his father. "I would go," he said, "to the Harvard Law School, since American respectability accepted lawyers, no matter how bad, which I was likely to be, and rejected composers, even if they were good, which I might possibly be."[38]

Dr. Wister accepted the proposal, and Owen returned to Philadelphia in the spring of 1885, where he "sat nibbling at Blackstone in the law office of Francis Rawle until the Law School should begin a new year in the Autumn." Then came one of those turning points which supposedly change the lives of men: Wister's health "very opportunely broke down," and his cousin, Dr. S. Weir Mitchell, recommended a trip to a ranch in Wyoming as a cure. Early in July 1885 Wister boarded a train from Philadelphia for the West, and "this accidental sight of the cattle-country settled my career":

> Never before had I been able to sustain a diary, no matter how thrilling my experiences. . . . But upon every Western expedition I kept a full, faithful, realistic diary: details about pack horses, camps in the mountains, camps in the sagebrush, nights in town, cards with cavalry officers, meals with cowpunchers, roundups, scenery, the Yellowstone Park, trout fishing, hunting with Indians, shooting antelope, white tail deer, black tail deer, elk, bear, mountain sheep. . . . I don't know why I wrote it all down so carefully. I had no purpose in doing so, or any suspicion that it was driving Wyoming into my blood and marrow, and fixing it there.[39]

Although Wister was to continue in law school and join the Philadelphia bar in 1888, pursue his law practice until his father's death

38. Wister, *Roosevelt*, pp. 22, 27.
39. Ibid., pp. 28, 29.

in 1896, and keep his office at Francis Rawle for twenty years after that, his first journey West in 1885, like Remington's four years earlier, settled his career.

One critic has suggested that Wister suffered a nervous breakdown in the spring of 1885, and though the evidence is too scanty for such a conclusion,[40] it is safe to assume that certain anxieties related to uncertainty over his future occupation and the larger question of his identity as a citizen of post-Civil-War Philadelphia had accompanied him West, as they accompanied Remington and Roosevelt. It is important to emphasize that none of these larger questions had been fully answered by the time that Remington, Roosevelt, and Wister returned to the East in 1885, 1886, and 1892, respectively; in this sense, their adolescence continued throughout their prolonged stays beyond the Mississippi. Hence each of the trio was no doubt conscious during his years in the West of the possibility that within its boundaries might lie a potential career, a new way of life, or a greater understanding of oneself and one's eastern heritage.

The adolescent consciousness of alternative possibilities lent to the response of Wister, Roosevelt, and Remington an intensity and expansiveness that were eventually to enhance an eastern understanding of the wild region past the Ohio Valley. The deep appreciation they felt for the unique "westernness" of those regions was to prove remarkably harmonious with the style of life emerging in the postbellum industrial East, which had in fact provided the impetus for their western explorations.

The anxiety surrounding occupational choices in the trio's adolescence stemmed in large part from the effect an industrialized society had upon their youthful patterns of preparedness. "The proliferation of knowledge and the great strides made in science and technology" in late nineteenth-century America, writes William O'Neill, "created new occupations . . . which grew partly by meeting the needs of an enormous, industrialized population, and partly by absorbing some of the functions previously monopolized

40. George Thomas Watkins, "Owen Wister and the American West: A Biographical and Critical Study," unpublished doctoral dissertation (University of Illinois, 1959), pp. 48–50. Watkins' dissertation, which is of uneven quality, is the only full-length study of Wister's life and work presently available.

by the traditional all-purpose professions."[41] Such all-purpose professions as those of Theodore Roosevelt, Sr., Dr. Owen Jones
Wister, and, on a smaller scale, Colonel Seth Remington, were out-
growths of a civilization in which the possession of wealth, power,
and status was relatively diffused and stabilized. Men whose families
had long enjoyed positions of prominence in their communities and
had accumulated a certain degree of wealth had grown to cultivate
an ideal of gentlemanly well-roundedness and diversity of interests.

The value placed upon diversification in the age of the all-purpose profession is best illustrated in the kind of education which
Wister, Roosevelt, and Remington received. Their schooling consistently encouraged the pursuit of interests (music, natural science,
and art) that were conceived of as avocational rather than vocational. Since only the elder Roosevelt seriously envisaged his son's
continuing his boyhood interest on a professional basis, and that
with reservations, it may be assumed that the parents of Remington,
Roosevelt, and Wister saw no striking disparity between the major
adolescent interests and the future adult roles of their progeny. But
the balanced ideal of such education was disturbed when men like
Remington and Wister exhibited a reluctance to pursue account-
ing and brokerage at the expense of art and music.

In choosing an occupation, Remington and Wister expressed a
distaste for certain aspects of industrial enterprise, a dissatisfaction
with parental guidance, and a discomfort with their future roles in
the East at a time when the impetus of industrialism was already
changing the occupational shape of that region. In an age whose
focus now lay in specialization and technological innovation,
scholarly and cultural pursuits were rapidly becoming fringe interests. "Our class at Harvard," Wister later wrote of his educational
experiences, "like all classes then, had been forced to learn stuff that
was utterly worthless in Wall Street and little good for turning a
dishonest penny anywhere. . . . Higher education was satisfied to
turn out, year after year, an absurd product known as the college-
bred man; a youth whom it had brought face to face with subjects
utterly behind the times."[42] Certainly Roosevelt, with his political
career in ruins, must have been painfully aware in 1884 of how

41. William C. O'Neill, *Divorce in the Progressive Era* (New Haven, 1967), p. 195.
42. Wister, *Roosevelt*, p. 21.

the very educational institutions which had come to be viewed as training grounds for future leaders of the East had remained blissfully unaware of the kind of focus needed in an age of industrial specialization.

As each man realized how ill-prepared or unwilling he was to cope with the style of life evolving in post-Civil-War eastern America, his bitterness or disillusionment with his heritage was soon coupled with desire to escape to a noneastern environment. The great exuberance with which Remington, Roosevelt, and Wister responded to the American West of the 1880s and 90s, exemplified in their compulsion to put the West down on paper, reflects the spirit of freedom and relief they felt the wild environment instilling in themselves. Like children suddenly freed from but ever mindful of authority, they delighted in reminding themselves how the new environment had added a dimension to their lives which their friends back home could barely comprehend.

However, the late nineteenth-century readers of Remington, Roosevelt, and Wister in fact made every effort to comprehend the noneastern aspects of the West. For life in the post-Civil-War East had come to be what one historian has aptly termed an experience of "fundamental ambiguity."[43] Three manifestations of this ambiguity have been considered in the first portion of this study: the clash between the presence of a preindustrial, eighteenth-century status system and nineteenth-century developments in industrial enterprise; the complication of the mid-century balance between nature and civilization through a disproportionate urbanization of the "civilized" East; and the subsequent development, in a broad sense, of a gap between the adolescent experience of individuals born around the decade of the 1860s and that of their parents.

When Remington, Wister, and Roosevelt went West for the first time in the 1880s, they went in at least three capacities: as participants in a reorganization in status, with particular overtones for families of established wealth but with ramifications for all of eastern America; as late nineteenth-century descendants of a line of creative-minded Easterners who had turned their attention to the wilderness of the West; and as members of three eastern families attempting to cope with the personal effects of cultural change. The

43. William Goetzmann, *Exploration and Empire* (New York, 1966), p. 305.

tensions each man associated with his adolescence in the East suggest that the industrialist ethos which had emerged with the Civil War decades had failed to resolve the ambiguities in its cultural patterns; instead, it had merely focused them around a variety of responses to the presence of an urban civilization.

Part II: The West

"Contrary to Turner's hypothesis," writes William Goetzmann, "the Western experience in the main appears not to have brought distinctiveness as such to bear on the country, but instead has offered a theater in which American patterns of culture could be endlessly mirrored." Goetzmann's view of the relation between the West and American culture appears essentially accurate for the half-century ending about 1885, when eastern conceptions of the West essentially mirrored culture patterns in the East, but certain developments toward the opening of the twentieth century seem to suggest that the West had by that time established an identity of its own. The Populist movement of the late eighties and nineties, symbolized for many Americans in Bryan's capture of the Democratic presidential nomination in 1896, lent to the West a political distinctiveness. Dime novels of the same decades attempted to describe a particular set of values which characterized life in the "wide open spaces," while more sophisticated writers, the local colorists, produced volumes filled with the dialects and customs of the Great Plains, the Rocky Mountains, and the Southwest. And a young historian from Wisconsin, recalling the successive generations of settlers that had swarmed through the South Pass of the Rockies on their way to the Pacific, saw with the closing of the frontier in 1890 the closing of an experience at once uniquely western and intrinsically American.[1]

Frederic Remington, Theodore Roosevelt, and Owen Wister were not only fortunate enough to witness the changes which transformed the West from wilderness to region and "securely wedded [its future] to the fortunes of the nation" but to play important parts in that transformation, at least to the extent that their accounts of their western experiences contributed to a changing conception of the West among the literate eastern public. While they were certainly not directly responsible for any changes that occurred in the West during the twenty-odd years after 1885, when they gave it their close attention, the interaction between these changes and the sets of attitudes each man brought to bear upon them helped to determine the kind of West Easterners would read about.

1. Goetzmann, *Exploration and Empire*, pp. xiii, 599; George F. Whicher, ed., *Bryan and the Campaign of 1896* (Boston, 1953), passim; Smith, *Virgin Land*, pp. 99–135; Claude M. Simpson, ed., *The Local Colorists* (New York, 1960), Introduction.

Since the response of each man to his eastern heritage was, despite certain broad similarities, idiosyncratic, each developed a different view of the West conditioned by the legacy of his eastern youth. The individualistic quality of each man's response was reinforced by his distinct experiences in the West. Among the mountains of Wyoming, Wister looked back at Proper Philadelphia with renewed interest and mixed emotions; in the Badlands of Dakota, Roosevelt once more battled adversity; on the plains of Kansas and Arizona, Remington attempted to shed every portion of his "civilized" skin.

The three men had shared a common experience, having grown up in the postbellum industrial East; and their separate Wests also had an overriding similarity. The concept of the West as one of the stages of civilization—as Cooper expressed it in 1823, of the "gradations of society" which could be traced from "that state which is called refined" to "that which approaches . . . barbarity"—reappeared in their writings, but in a fundamentally different sense. Cooper was attempting to fit the West into a preconceived conception of the nature of man, which related the degree of one's "savagery" or "refinement" to the contact one had with an established social order, as symbolized by "the bosom of the states," while Wister, Remington, and Roosevelt saw the West as a stage in the history of American civilization. It was "an iron age that the old civilized world had long passed by," a "land about to vanish forever," an "extraordinary phase of social progress," or even "the true America."[2] Aware of the extraordinary changes taking place in eastern America, they saw the West in a state of rapid transition as well and tried, as historians, to capture part of it before it passed on.

2. Cooper, *The Prairie, 1* (1827 ed.), 88; Roosevelt, *Works, 4,* 454; Frederic Remington, "A Few Words from Mr. Remington," *Collier's* (March 18, 1905), quoted in McCracken, *Frederic Remington,* p. 36; Owen Wister, journals for 1885 and 1891, reprinted in Stokes, *Owen Wister Out West,* pp. 33, 112.

4. Roosevelt's West: The Beat of Hardy Life

Theodore Roosevelt threw himself into his new career as a Dakota cattle rancher with customary energy, but not without a touch of sadness. He had initially conceived his stay in the Badlands, which began in earnest in August 1884, as a two- or three-year interlude of ranching, hunting, and writing: a refuge from the "very harassing" winter and spring of that year, which had left him "both tired and restless." But the loneliness and desolation of the plains must have seemed peculiarly suited to his feelings, for it appeared that his life in the East was "behind him, and nothing but Dakota remained." Carleton Putnam is convinced that Roosevelt meant to be a rancher on a permanent basis: "No man invests a fifth of his fortune in two ranches and writes of ranching, 'I shall make it my regular business,' if he is only seeking a stopgap. Roosevelt . . . loved the West for the outdoor life it brought him and ranching because it gave that outdoor life a *raison d'être*. In the West he could experiment with a literary career as well as business, the West itself providing a subject for his pen." Nevertheless, one senses that Roosevelt took the West in desperation, as his comment to Henry Cabot Lodge in August 1884 implies: "The Statesman (?) of the past has been merged, I fear for good, into the cowboy of the present." The grim memories of the past year still haunted him: he confided to William Sewall in the fall of 1884 that "he would never become reconciled to his loss [of his wife] nor expect to find happiness again" and that his baby girl would be just as well off without him.[1]

It was this gloom in Roosevelt's heart, mingled with the bleakness of his new surroundings, which conditioned his first extensive literary response to the West. "Nowhere," he wrote in 1884, "does a

1. Putnam, *Theodore Roosevelt*, p. 507; Roosevelt, letter to Henry Cabot Lodge, in Henry Cabot Lodge, ed., *Selections from the Correspondence of Theodore Roosevelt and Henry Cabot Lodge, 1884–1918*, 2 vols. (New York, 1935), 1, 7; Sewall, *Bill Sewall's Story*, p. 47.

man feel more lonely than when riding over the far-reaching, seemingly never-ending plains; and after a man has lived a little while
on or near them, their very vastness and loneliness and their
melancholy monotony have a strong fascination for him . . . nowhere else does one seem so far off from all mankind."[2] He found
the isolated life of a ranchman in harmony with his wistful and reflective thoughts, and his first impressions of the West in 1884 concern themselves with the composites of loneliness on the vast and
monotonous plains, which "stretch out in deathlike and measure-
less expanse, and . . . will for many miles be lacking in all signs of
life."

Loneliness is also associated with the forbidding qualities of
nature on the Great Plains. In summer, "when the grassy prairies
are left and the traveler enters a region of alkali desert and sage-
brush, the look of the country becomes even more grim and forbidding. In places the alkali forms a white frost on the ground that
glances in the sunlight like the surface of a frozen lake; the dusty
little sage-brush, stunted and dried up, sprawls over the parched
ground, from which it can hardly extract the small amount of
nourishment necessary for even its wizened life"; at the hottest
times "all objects that are not nearby seem to sway and waver."
There are few sounds to break the stillness save the "soft, melancholy cooing of the mourning-dove, whose voice always seems far
away and expresses more than any other sound in nature the sadness of gentle, hopeless, never ending grief." Other birds are still,
but "now and then the black shadow of a wheeling vulture falls on
the sun-scorched ground."[3]

In winter, loneliness in the Badlands takes on a rigorous quality
not associated with silent thoughts in the shade of a veranda.
"When the days have dwindled to their shortest, and the nights
seem never-ending, then all the great northern plains are changed
into an abode of iron desolation. Sometimes furious gales blow out
of the north, driving before them the clouds of blinding snow-dust,
wrapping the mantle of death round every being that faces their
unshackled anger." Or, "not a breath of wind may stir; and then

2. Roosevelt, *Works*, *1*, 183–84; Anna Roosevelt Cowles, *Letters from Theodore
Roosevelt to Anna Roosevelt Cowles* (New York, 1924), p. 59.

3. Roosevelt, *Works*, *1*, 184; *4*, 408.

the still, merciless, terrible cold that broods over the earth like the shadow of silent death seems even more dreadful in its gloomy rigor than is the lawless madness of the storms." Then "all the land is like granite; the great rivers stand still in their beds, as if turned to frosted steel. In the long nights there is no sound to break the lifeless silence."[4]

It is in the winter passages particularly that Roosevelt associates the grim loneliness of the plains environment with the lives of men who inhabit the Badlands: the cattlemen, ranchers, and hunters who battle with the elements:

> For ranchmen, winter is . . . often an irksome period of enforced rest and gloomy foreboding . . . there is much less work than at any other season, but what there is involves great hardship and exposure . . . the men in the line camps lead a hard life, for they have to be out in every kind of weather, and should be especially active and watchful during the storms. . . . Even for those who do not have to look up stray horses, and who are not forced to ride the line day in and day out, there is apt to be some hardship and danger in being abroad during the bitter weather. A man must be careful lest he lose his way, for the discomfort of a night in the open during such weather is very great indeed. . . . I have known of several cases of men freezing to death when caught in shelterless places by a blizzard, a strange fact being that in about half of them the doomed man had evidently gone mad before dying, and stripped himself of most of his clothes, the body when found being nearly naked.[5]

Thus the initial reflective serenity (masking his inner tensions) with which Roosevelt first viewed the lonely Badlands environment gives way to a fascination for the savage "iron desolation" of a winter on the Great Plains, an awed reverence for the power of a blizzard that can freeze a man to death and drive him mad in the process, as Roosevelt's old love of the arduous and the terrible in nature begins to supersede his initial attraction to loneliness for loneliness' sake. Responding to the violent natural environment, the chief adversary of a ranchman with his characteristic vigor, by

4. Ibid., *4*, 446.
5. Ibid., pp. 447, 449, 450, 451.

December he speaks of "returning by moonlight from a successful hunt after mountain sheep" in conditions where the thermometer was twenty-six below zero and he had had no food for twelve hours. "I became numbed," he notes, and "before I was aware of it had frozen my face, one foot, both knees, and one hand."[6] Once again Roosevelt was meeting a challenge.

Roosevelt's accounts of the men who inhabit the western land-scape find in them qualities associated with survival in the most severe and forbidding of environments. "We still live in an iron age that the old civilized world has long passed by," he wrote in 1885. "The men of the border reckon upon stern and unending struggles with their iron-bound surroundings; against the grim harshness of their existence they set the strength and the abounding vitality that come with it." There are the hunters, who "led hard lives, and the unending strain of their toilsome and dangerous existence shattered even such iron frames as theirs." There are the trappers, whose perilous existence had fascinated Parkman forty years earlier; Roosevelt recounts the story of one, possessed of a "certain uneasy, half-furtive look about the eyes," who had battled for his life against famine and the ravenous madness of his travel-ing companion one recent Dakota winter. And finally, there are the cowboys, whose life "forces them to be both daring and adven-turous, and the passing over their heads of a few years leaves printed on their faces certain lines which tell of dangers quietly fronted and hardships uncomplainingly endured."[7]

For these men severe experience had been a most demanding teacher, but for the most part they had stoically learned its grim lesson; in praising them, Roosevelt resorted to epithets many of his contemporaries had come to associate with success in the masculine world of industrial enterprise. Hunters are "frank, bold, and self-reliant," fearing "neither man, brute, nor element"; a representa-tive specimen of them is "an image of bronzed and rugged strength." Cowboys are "as hardy and self-reliant as any men who ever breathed—with bronzed, set faces, and keen eyes that look all the world straight in the face without flinching." Peril and hardship may "draw haggard lines across their eager faces," but it cannot dim

6. Ibid., p. 451.
7. Ibid., *1*, 8; *4*, 454, 457, 461.

the cowboys' eyes nor "break their bearing of self-confidence."[8] In short, the inhabitants of the Badlands are overwhelmingly masculine, and their masculinity is both a product of their environment and a prerequisite for success in coping with it.

Roosevelt's notes on the scenery and citizenry of the Badlands were part of his own vigorous effort to become a Westerner. "I have been fulfilling a boyish ambition of mine," he wrote his elder sister in June of 1884, "playing at frontier hunter in good earnest," and the transition was not an easy one, even for such an accomplished and inveterate actor. A reporter from the Pittsburgh *Dispatch*, encountering Roosevelt on his way West in April 1885, described him as a "pale, slim young man with a thin piping voice and a general look of dyspepsia about him . . . boyish looking . . . with a slight lisp, a short red mustache and eye glasses, [who] looks the typical New York dude." His first appearances in cattle country had created a similar impression. Hermann Hagedorn, in his study of Roosevelt's years in the Badlands, states that "Roosevelt was in those first days considered somewhat of a joke. Beside Gregor Lang, forty miles to the south, he was the only man in the Badlands who wore glasses. Lang's glasses, moreover, were small and oval; Roosevelt's were large and round: making him, in the opinion of the cowpunchers, look very much like a curiously nervous and emphatic owl. They called him 'Four Eyes' and spoke without too much respect of 'Roosenfelder.' " Adding to this general conception were the incidents of Roosevelt's encouraging one of his men to round up a stray cow with a piping "Hasten forward quickly there," and a local railroad man's description of Roosevelt as "a slim, anemic-looking young fellow dressed in the exaggerated style which newcomers on the frontier affected, and which was considered indisputable evidence of the rank tenderfoot."[9]

Indeed, Roosevelt was guilty of the most blatant attempts to affect a cowboy style of dress. Soon after his arrival in Dakota he confessed to his frontier companion Lincoln Lang that he was "most anxious to get a buckskin suit." Buckskin to Roosevelt was

---

8. Ibid., *4*, 371, 457, 459.

9. Letter to Anna Roosevelt Cowles, June 23, 1884, in Cowles, *Letters*, p. 59; Pittsburgh *Dispatch*, April 15, 1885; Hermann Hagedorn, *Roosevelt in the Bad Lands* (Boston, 1921), pp. 101–02.

"the most picturesque and distinctively national dress ever worn in America. It was the dress in which Daniel Boone was clad when he first passed through the trackless forests of the Alleghenies and penetrated into the heart of Kentucky . . . the dress worn by grim old Davy Crockett when he fell at the Alamo." The tenderfoot prevailed upon a Mrs. Maddox of Sand Creek, Dakota, to make him a buckskin shirt, and he no doubt felt a greater sense of belonging to "the old race of Rocky Mountain hunters and trappers, of reckless, dauntless Indian fighters . . . [who] have been the forerunners of the white advance throughout all of our Western land." When Roosevelt returned to New York for the Christmas season of 1885, he brought with him the trophies of his recent bighorn sheep hunt in eastern Montana and that same shirt. As Hagedorn tells it:

> he solemnly dressed himself up in the buckskin shirt and the rest of [his] elaborate costume . . . and had himself photographed. There is something hilariously funny in the visible records of that performance. The imitation grass not quite concealing the rug beneath, the painted background, the theatrical (slightly patched) rocks against which [Roosevelt] leans gazing dreamily across an imaginary prairie . . . with rifle ready and finger on the trigger, grimly facing dangerous game which is not there.[10]

Certain brushes with the wilder elements of the West, however, served to initiate Roosevelt into the cowboy community where the buckskin shirt had failed. The first of these was his "scrape" with the "Mingusville bully," as recounted in his *Autobiography*. In April 1885, according to one source,[11] Roosevelt reached the little settlement of Mingusville, thirty-five miles west of Medora, after dark. The only hotel in Mingusville was "Nolan's," which had both a dining room and a bar in its lobby. As he approached Nolan's, he

10. Hagedorn, *Bad Lands*, pp. 95, 235, 256; Roosevelt, *Works, 4,* 455.

11. Putnam, in his *Roosevelt,* places the Mingusville episode "in the latter part of April 1885"; Hagedorn in his *Bad Lands* has it in June 1884. Putnam, through "as close a day-by-day source study of Roosevelt's whereabouts in 1884 and 1885 as the available sources permit," sees little likelihood of Roosevelt's undertaking a horse-hunting trip to Mingusville in June 1884. Of the two sources Putnam is more generally reliable, being less inclined to rely on the recollections of aged Dakotans. Moreover, it is hard to imagine the same Roosevelt who dressed himself up in a hunting shirt in December 1884 and who was still a "dude" for the Pittsburgh reporter in April 1885 reacting to the bully in such a "western" fashion by June 1884.

heard shots in the lobby and "was reluctant to enter, but it was a cold night and there was no place else to go." Entering "as unobtrusively as possible," Roosevelt noticed that "inside . . . were several men, who, including the bartender, were wearing the kind of smile worn by men who are making believe to like what they don't like." "A shabby individual was walking up and down the floor talking with strident profanity. As soon as he saw me he hailed me as 'Four-eyes,' in reference to my spectacles and said: 'Four-eyes is going to treat.' I joined in the laugh and got behind the stove and sat down, thinking to escape notice. He followed me, however, and though I tried to pass it off as a jest this merely made him more offensive, and he stood leaning over me, a gun in each hand, using very foul language." As Roosevelt notes:

> He was foolish to stand so near, and, moreover, his heels were close together, so that his position was unstable. Accordingly, in response to his reiterated command that I should set up the drinks, I said: "Well, if I've got to, I've got to," and rose, looking past him. As I rose, I struck quick and hard with my right just to one side of the point of his jaw, hitting with my left as I straightened out, and then again with my right. He fired the guns, but I do not know whether this was merely a convulsive action of his hands or whether he was trying to shoot at me. When he went down he struck the corner of the bar with his head. It was not a case in which one could afford to take chances, and if he had moved I was about to drop on his ribs with my knees; but he was senseless. I took away his guns, and the other people in the room, who were now loud in their denunciation of him, hustled him out and put him in a shed. I got dinner as soon as possible, sitting in a corner of the dining-room away from the windows, and then went upstairs to bed where it was dark so that there would be no chance of any one shooting at me from the outside. However, nothing happened. When my assailant came to, he went down to the station and left on a freight.[12]

The news of Roosevelt's encounter in Mingusville "spread as only news can spread in a country of few happenings and much conversation." It was, according to Hagedorn, "the kind of story that

12. Roosevelt, *Works*, 22, 146–47.

the Bad Lands liked to hear. . . . 'Four-eyes' became, overnight, "Old Four Eyes," which was another matter."

A large share of hard work at the spring round-up served to confirm the Dakota cowboys' new opinion of Roosevelt, and the "dude" evolved into the "boss."[13] But other men of the plains and mountains were not so easily convinced: upon arriving at Thompson Falls, Montana, preparatory to a hunting expedition through the Rocky Mountains, Roosevelt made a poor impression on the man he had asked to guide him on the trip. Jack Willis noticed two men climbing down from the Pullman at the Thompson Falls station. "One of them," he tells us, "had on the corduroy knickers and a coat of a tenderfoot. I knew he was Roosevelt, and he looked too much like a dude to make any hit with me. He had red cheeks, like those of a brewer's son I knew, and that didn't help any. The only thing about him that appealed to me at all were his eyes. They were keen and bright and dancing with animation. . . . But in spite of that I didn't like his looks."[14] Roosevelt, however, eventually convinced Willis that he was "a Westerner at heart and had the makings of a real man," and the two set out on a hunt for mountain goats, accompanied by William Merrifield, Roosevelt's foreman on his Maltese Cross ranch. "It was hard going," Willis notes, "for the goats are at home only in rough country. Being accustomed to it, I walked so fast that Roosevelt was forced into a jog trot most of the time to keep up with me. But he never complained, nor did he ever ask me to slacken my speed. . . . That satisfied me as to his gameness, for which I came to have the highest admiration as we got to know each other better." By the end of the trip Willis was satisfied that Roosevelt "could keep up with me on almost any trail, no matter how hard the going."[15]

There were other aspects of hunting life that Roosevelt could not instantly master, no matter how desperately he wanted to. Early in the trip Willis told him that the proper way to shoot pheasant was in the head, for "a big rifle bullet in the body would tear one of the birds to pieces." Shortly after that admonition Roosevelt creased a pheasant, knocking it senseless. "As he stopped to pick it

    13. Putnam, *Roosevelt*, pp. 522–27.
    14. Jack Willis, with Horace Smith, *Roosevelt in the Rough* (New York, 1931), p. 9.
    15. Ibid., pp. 11–13.

up," Willis states, "he put his foot on its head and seized it by the legs, with the intention of pulling its head off and making it appear that it had been shot off. I suspected what had happened and what he was up to and caught him right in the act. . . . It was some time before I stopped twitting him about that incident. He took it good-naturedly, but I noticed that his answering smile was largely restricted to one side of his face."

Though Roosevelt exhibited an anxiety to convince Westerners of his merit before he himself was convinced, even to the point of a slight fabrication to help ride him over the first uneasy moments, he nevertheless learned fast. After missing a mountain goat in the afternoon of his first day out with Willis, Roosevelt "occupied himself entirely that evening with lamentations over his poor marksmanship, but the next day he drew a bead on the same goat and brought him down from a distance of a quarter of a mile, with a twenty-mile-an-hour wind blowing. "It was a lucky shot," writes Willis, "but that didn't alter the fact that he got what he shot at, and I took off my hat to him." Roosevelt was ecstatic. The "yell of delight he let loose could have been heard for two miles in any country," and since "nothing would do but he must have a picture of the goat," Willis walked six miles back to camp after the camera and Merrifield, whose sore feet had incapacitated him that day. When the three returned to camp, Roosevelt insisted on developing the picture immediately and eventually had it reproduced "for private distribution among his friends,"[16] an indication of the delight he felt in finally succeeding in the role of a huntsman.

The hunting trip with Willis and Merrifield gave Roosevelt confidence in his outdoorsmanship and an education in the perils of wilderness living. At one juncture he slipped on a narrow ledge of slaty rock and fell off the edge of a sixty-foot precipice, but he landed in the top of a tall pine tree, which broke his fall, and eventually came to rest "on a bunch of moss that was as thick as a feather bed and much more comfortable." He was unhurt and even recovered his glasses and his rifle, which had made the trip with him. Another time Roosevelt had himself lowered by a rope into a gulch to snap pictures of a waterfall and found that Willis and Merrifield were unable to pull him back up. Eventually Willis

16. Ibid., pp. 14–17.

secured another rope and lowered Roosevelt to a spot some thirty-five feet above the water, which boiled with whirlpools at the foot of the waterfall. Swimming out to the spot above which Roosevelt was suspended, Willis caught Roosevelt's camera and brought it safely ashore. He then built a raft from logs along the shore and pushed it back out to the area underneath Roosevelt. Merrifield cut the rope and Roosevelt dropped into the water, disappearing under the surface close to the raft. He came up "sputtering weakly," but in less than a minute Willis "had him stretched out on the raft and away from all danger."[17]

Even Willis, to whom such adventures were routine happenings, was impressed by his first experiences with "what afterward came to be known as 'Roosevelt luck.'" "But I never have accepted that explanation of the good fortune which attended him," the mountaineer was later to say. "To my way of thinking it was simply the natural reward of a dauntless courage."[18]

Roosevelt's most significant brush[19] with the Wild West in his Badlands years was the capture of Mike Finnigan, which serves as the basis for Chapter 8 of his *Ranch Life and the Hunting Trail*. In the midst of a March thaw in Roosevelt's third year in Dakota, Mike Finnigan, "rather a hard case" who had been "chief actor in a number of shooting scrapes," and two companions stole a boat Roosevelt used for daily trips across the Little Missouri River, which cut through his Elkhorn ranch. In their effort, Finnigan and his comrades reckoned without Roosevelt's vaunted energy and righteous wrath. He wrote:

> Our loss was very annoying . . . but the determining motive in
> our minds was neither chagrin nor anxiety to recover our prop-
> erty. In any wild country where the power of the law is little
> felt or heeded, and where every one has to rely upon himself
> for protection, men soon get to feel that it is in the highest de-
> gree unwise to submit to any wrong without making an imme-
> diate and resolute effort to avenge it upon the wrong-doers, at

17. Ibid., pp. 18–22.
18. Ibid., p. 18.
19. Chronologically, the Finnigan episode occurred before the excursion with Willis, the capture of Finnigan taking place in March and April 1886 and the Willis hunting trip in August and September of that year.

no matter what cost of risk or trouble. To submit tamely and meekly to theft or to any other injury, is to invite almost certain repetition of the offense, in a place where self-reliant hardihood and the ability to hold one's own under all circumstances rank as the first of virtues.

Determined to prove once again that he could hold his own, that he would not "submit tamely and meekly" to anything, Roosevelt had his men build a flat-bottomed boat, and set off down the river after the thieves.

After an arduous three days Roosevelt came upon Finnigan's camp and "felt a thrill of keen excitement . . . for it seemed likely that there would be a brush." No confrontation was forthcoming, however, for the only thief in camp was an old German, "whose viciousness was of the weak and shiftless type." Finnigan and his partner were absent on a hunting foray, and Roosevelt and his companions were able to surprise them on their return. "When they were within twenty yards," Roosevelt "shouted to them to hold up their hands—an order that in such a case, in the West, a man is not apt to disregard if he thinks the giver is in earnest." Finnigan "hesitated for a second,, his eyes fairly wolfish"; then, as Roosevelt approached with his rifle, "he saw that he had no show, and with an oath . . . held his hands up beside his head."

Later, Roosevelt was to note that that tinge of excitement he felt when he anticipated a "brush" was "almost the only moment of much interest," for "the capture itself was as tame as possible." But if corraling the fugitives had been easy, bringing them to justice was certainly not. Roosevelt was forced to spend another eight days conducting his companions to the nearest sheriff's office, and upon his arrival there he appeared to an onlooker as "the most bedraggled figure I'd ever seen . . . all teeth and eyes . . . clothes in rags . . . scratched, bruised, and hungry, but gritty and determined as a bull dog." That same man noted that "the average westerner would have hanged the thieves out of hand. But that evidently did not occur to Roosevelt."[20] Hanging was probably the last course Roosevelt would have resorted to; indeed, he conceived of the Finnigan episode as a

---

20. Roosevelt, *Works, 4,* 497, 498, 499, 502–04, 507, 511–13; unidentified, undated newspaper article in Hermann Hagedorn's collection of notes for his *Bad Lands,* quoted in Putnam, *Roosevelt,* pp. 568–69.

matter of enforcing the law and maintaining his good name. While a concern for justice and honor had been intrinsic to his eastern heritage, a concern for his reputation in the eyes of other potential thieves was both a matter of practical necessity and a personal vendetta.

The Finnigan episode occurred less than two years after Roosevelt's unfortunate arrival at Medora and marked, in a sense, the culmination of his westernizing experiences. That previous summer the same correspondent for the Pittsburgh *Dispatch* had chanced to run into the pale, slim, piping-voiced dude he had described only four months before. "What a change!" exclaimed the reporter. "He is now brown as a berry and has increased 30 pounds in weight. The voice which failed to make an echo in [Albany] when he climbed upon his desk and shook his little pocket handkerchief and piped, 'Mistah Speakah,' is now hearty and strong enough to drive oxen." At that time Roosevelt had won his physical battle with the Badlands; with the capture of Finnigan he won his mental battle. "Think we have all got our names pretty well up by this scrape," one of Roosevelt's companions wrote after the thieves had been captured. "Don't think we will have anything more stolen from *us*."[21] He could have made, in Roosevelt's eyes, no greater tribute to his chief's effort to pass from being an admirer of cowboys and hunters to being one of them. By 1886 that effort had succeeded.

Another challenge met, Roosevelt's uncommonly restless spirit could look elsewhere, and in the years after 1886 his chief interest in his ranches was as a base for autumn hunting trips, which "he made in each year through 1896, with the exception of 1895. Thereafter the pressures of his career and his interest in hunting in other parts of the country ended his Dakota expeditions. Save for a hurried political trip along the line of the Northern Pacific as Governor of New York and candidate for the Vice-Presidency in 1900 and another even more hurried transit as President in 1903, he did not see the Bad Lands again."[22] The great winter of 1886, when Roosevelt lost most of his cattle, no doubt helped prompt his decision to

21. Pittsburgh *Dispatch*, August 23, 1885; Putnam, *Roosevelt*, p. 569.
22. Putnam, *Roosevelt*, p. 595.

face East again, as did his forthcoming marriage to Edith Carow and pressures from his silk-stocking friends to run for mayor of New York. Ultimately, Roosevelt's Badlands excursion, which he had conceived as an interlude and then considered as a way of life, became, of necessity, an interlude again, for its challenge had been mastered; but he continued to treasure throughout his life the image of the West which had emerged from his Dakota experiences. "In that land," he wrote in his *Autobiography,* "we led a free and hardy life. . . . We knew toil and hardship and hunger and thirst; and we saw men die violent deaths as they worked among the horses and cattle, or fought in evil feuds with one another; but we felt the beat of hardy life in our veins, and ours was the glory of work and joy of living."[23] This "beat of hardy life," for Roosevelt, was associated with all the toughening and trying experiences of an environment supremely masculine.

In Roosevelt's writings about the West after 1885 his epithets for masculinity—strength, self-reliance, determination—recur again and again. Hunting in the western wilderness symbolizes "the free, self-reliant, adventurous life"; "the chase" cultivates "that vigorous manliness for the lack of which in a nation, as in an individual, the possession of no other qualities can possibly atone." The wilderness hunter "must not only show skill in the use of the rifle and address in finding and approaching game, but he must also show the qualities of hardihood, self-reliance, and resolution needed for effectively grappling with his wild surroundings." On a more general level, "the men among us who have stood foremost in political leadership . . . have been of stalwart frame and sound bodily health. When they sprang from the frontier folk, as did Lincoln and Andrew Jackson, they usually hunted much in their youth, if only as an incident in the prolonged warfare waged by themselves and their kinsmen against the wild forces of nature." That "greatest of Americans, Washington, was very fond of hunting . . . both with rifle and fowling-piece, and especially with horse, horn and hound. . . . Essentially the representative of all that is best in our national life, standing high as a general, high as a statesman, and highest of all as a man, he could never have been what he was had he not taken delight in feats of hardihood, of daring and bodily prow-

23. Roosevelt, *Works,* 22, 112–13.

ess."[24] These passages give an indication of the degree to which Roosevelt's westernizing experiences influenced his ideological beliefs and his reading of history. He finds a strong frame and an iron will prerequisites for success in any environment: "the men among us who have stood foremost in political leadership . . . have been of stalwart frame and sound bodily health."

These same assumptions reappear in Roosevelt's historical writings about the West. He expected those men who waged warfare against "the wild forces of nature" to be men among men, and he honored them for it. Thomas Hart Benton, in Roosevelt's biography, is characterized as a man of "abounding vitality, rugged intellect, and indomitable will . . . deeply imbued with the masterful, overbearing spirit of the West . . . the possession of which is certainly a most healthy sign of the virile strength of a young community." This spirit became the theme for Roosevelt's history of the settlements of the Ohio territory and Kentucky, *The Winning of the West*. "The West," he writes, "was neither discovered, won, nor settled by any single man . . . it was the work of a whole people, of whom each man was impelled mainly by sheer love of adventure; it was the outcome of the ceaseless strivings of all the dauntless, restless backwoods folk . . . to each penetrate deeper than his neighbors into the remote forest hunting grounds where the perilous pleasures of the chase and of war could best be enjoyed."

Because "the life of the backwoodsmen was one of long struggle," frontiersmen whom Roosevelt singled out in his history of the westward movement naturally possessed all the qualities he associated with manliness. Daniel Boone is "dauntless and self-reliant"; James Robertson, who helped settle eastern Tennessee, is "robust" and "masterful," with "a look of self-contained strength"; John Sevier, another Tennessee woodsman, although "a gentleman by birth and breeding," has "skill and dashing prowess" as an Indian fighter and "dauntless, invincible courage"; and George Rogers Clark's "executive ability" stems from his "far-sighted daring and indomitable energy." When he could, Roosevelt took pains to imply that the majority of the western settlers were not unlike those he singled out: at one point in *The Winning of the West* he describes two Kentuckians as "tall, spare, and athletic . . . like so many other

24. Ibid., 3, xxi, 19, 418–19, 421.

backwoodsmen." "There were perhaps some three hundred men in Kentucky," he continues, "a hardy, resolute, strenuous band."[25]

In passage after passage of *The Winning of the West* Roosevelt attributes to western settlers "the fundamental virtues of hardihood and manliness"; this is another indication of the extent to which masculinity and the ways in which it was exhibited had become inextricably bound up with his image of the West by the time of his abandonment of Dakota in 1886. The love of the outdoors which had been a kind of balance to his social and intellectual pursuits at Harvard and a welcome diversion from personal pressures in New York had evolved into a cult of manliness with all its trimmings—aggressiveness, belligerency, belief in "hardihood" as a "fundamental virtue"—that seemed to be enjoyed largely for its own sake. In the "free and hardy life" of the West he found an outlet for his creative energies; there he buried his sorrows; there he found health and confidence of a lasting nature.

25. Ibid., *8*, 18, 27; *10*, 101, 102, 113, 133, 136, 163, 166, 169, 261, 262, 357, 374.

5. Remington's West: Men with the Bark On

Although both Theodore Roosevelt and Frederic Remington launched western ranching careers in 1883, the extent of each man's undertaking was determined by the context in which it was launched. Roosevelt considered his Dakota enterprise as another investment in a life of large financial ventures, and after consulting his banker uncles, established his Badlands cattle ranch with a capital output of $40,000. Remington, on the other hand, chose to raise sheep, which was considerably less expensive, and purchased two quarter-sections (320 acres) of land in central Kansas for a little over $4,600.[1] The $40,000 Dakota investment represented less than a fourth of Roosevelt's potential income, whereas Remington had gambled nearly all his patrimony on his Kansas ranch.[2] Moreover, Roosevelt's previous trips to Dakota had given him some understanding of the ranch business, while Remington had never been to Kansas before 1883 and bought his ranch sight unseen. If Roosevelt's enthusiasm for ranching had grown in direct proportion to his difficulties in the East, he had at least maintained a financial perspective on the situation; Remington's sheep venture can be best described as an impulsive attempt to associate himself with the West in some capacity, even if such an association threatened him with bankruptcy.

Roosevelt never forgot his eastern ties while in the Badlands. Self-consciousness best describes his state of mind throughout his years in Dakota—whether in the form of indulgent melancholy, frontier role-playing, or the maintenance of a certain distance from his cowboy associates. Toward the close of his Dakota interlude a reporter from the Bismarck *Tribune*, while noting that Roosevelt's

---

1. Putnam, *Theodore Roosevelt*, pp. 343–44; Robert Taft, *Artists and Illustrators of the Old West* (New York, 1953), p. 361.

2. Putnam, *Roosevelt*, p. 337; on Remington's patrimony see Taft, *Artists and Illustrators*, p. 361, and Manley, *Some of Frederic Remington's North Country Associations*, pp. 20–21.

interests in the Badlands "were such that he did not believe he could ever leave the territory permanently," nevertheless identified him as "the famous young New York reformer . . . the New York boomer . . . the reform politician, orator, and literateur," as well as "the millionaire Dakota ranchman." By contrast, Remington's three turbulent years in Kansas and the Southwest were sufficient, in the words of two magazine editors who saw him upon his return to New York in 1886, to transform him into "an unspoiled native genius dealing with Mexican ponies . . . cactus, lariats, and sombreros" who "looked like a cowboy just off a ranch."[3] Remington's transformation was the result of an indiscriminate examination of particle after particle of the dust-life of the central plains and Southwest.

Remington's first impressions of the West stemmed from the years he was based in Kansas, from March 1883 until the late summer of 1885. These years are less remarkable for their creative output (the bulk of Remington's writing and painting was done after his return East) than for the zeal with which he responded to his new environment. In the face of the surroundings into which Remington entered, this was no mean feat. The sheep ranch which he had purchased was located in northwest Butler county, a "rolling upland that lies on the extreme western edge of the Flint Hills, a high escarpment running north and south which roughly divides the eastern third of Kansas from the remainder of the state." Although it was far from urbanized, Remington's immediate neighborhood, according to Robert Taft, "could by no means be regarded as frontier." Ten years before his arrival "there had been frontier difficulties with horse thieves and vigilantes," but these difficulties had passed by 1883. "Life on a Kansas sheep ranch," Taft maintains, "was a far more prosaic affair than life in the West was so luridly built up to be by the newspapers of the period."[4]

Sheep ranching was not unpleasant in the warmer months, especially "when boys of the neighborhood could be hired to herd the flock," but during the winter "it was a herculean task to protect the bleating animals from the sudden northern blasts." Dipping the

---

3. Bismarck *Daily Tribune*, July 9, 1886; J. Henry Harper, *The House of Harper*, quoted in McCracken, *Frederic Remington*, p. 48; Bigelow, *Seventy Summers*, *1*, 304.
    4. Taft, *Artists and Illustrators*, pp. 199, 200, 201.

sheep and lambing were time-consuming operations, and the problems of transporting and selling wool were considerable, particularly after 1884, when market prices dipped sharply. Remington,
according to his neighbor rancher, Robert Camp, "didn't take a
great deal of interest in the actual work of the sheep ranch," pre-
ferring to chase jack rabbits or race horses across the plains, box and
"swap yarns" with his neighbors, or make side trips into Indian territory, only a few miles south of Butler county.[5]

From his initial shock at arriving in such a bleak and monotonous environment, which manifested itself in extreme fluctuations
of disposition (one of his contemporaries characterized him as
"moody beyond anything I had ever seen in man" and noted that
"in moments of despair he was not only morose but recluse; he hid
from the majority of all his fellows"), Remington swiftly moved to
a cheerful acceptance of his role, if not as a working ranchman, at
least as a citizen of Butler county. "In the development of his new
life," Taft notes, "Remington soon became more jovial and was
well known and popular over the countryside."[6] At times this
joviality spilled over into sheer boisterousness: during a Christmas
Eve party in 1883 Remington and his ranching colleagues attacked
"a prominent member of the community who had incurred their
dislike." As soon as they caught sight of "the bald head belonging
to the object of their dislike, the target was irresistible"; paper
wads and balls of mud "began to fly toward the gleaming bald
dome." Such conduct was immediately reprimanded, and Remington and his friends were ushered out of the schoolhouse. Once outside, one of them "spied a pile of straw," which was "hastily piled
outside the window and set blazing with a cry of 'Fire! Fire!',", resulting in a "near panic" among the occupants of the schoolhouse.

The incident culminated in a suit, with Remington paying the
damages. The "wild and wooly" boys of "the northwest," as the
Walnut Valley Times termed them, had the honor of having one
of their number referred to as "Billy the Kid" by a prosecuting
attorney.[7] Strange as it may seem, the lawyer had associated that
famous desperado with a pudgy blond cherubic-faced fugitive from
the East, and if Remington had not been incensed by the fine, he

5. Ibid., pp. 210–11.
6. Ibid., p. 204.
7. Ibid., pp. 209–10.

might have warmed to the appellation. By the close of the trial most of Butler county knew him as "one of the boys."

Chasing jack rabbits, discussing the merits of horses with his ranching cronies, and occasional mischievous whims such as the schoolhouse prank helped sustain Remington's boyish enthusiasm during his months as a rancher, but they could not obviate his growing impatience with the drudgery of his chores. When wool prices plummeted in the spring of 1884, Remington attempted to sell his ranch, and by May 31 he had left his erstwhile career behind and set out in search of other adventures.[8]

From Peabody he wandered briefly to Kansas City, then southwest through Indian territory to Arizona, and finally to Mexico for a hunting expedition, returning to Kansas City in the late summer of 1884. This excursion was "the first on which Remington devoted any really serious effort to making sketches in the field"; he apparently had a portfolio of drawings which he tried to peddle upon his return to Kansas City. Meeting with only moderate success, he attempted to further his fortunes by becoming a silent partner in a saloon, only to discover that his business accomplices had unscrupulously deprived him of his holdings. According to one account, "with his six-gun in hand and blood in his eyes," Remington searched for his partners "to even up the score," and "only the intervention of a friend persuaded him that gunplay was not a satisfactory way to settle the matter."[9] The western laws of vengeance and violence had by this time made their mark upon him.

Remington returned East in the fall of 1884 and bid once more for the hand of Eva Caten, this time successfully. Apparently little reference was made to the fact that four years ago, upon his initial rejection, Remington "had been a young man with an inheritance," while at this point he was penniless.[10] The Remingtons established themselves in Kansas City in the fall of 1884, but within less than a year Eva had returned to Gloversville and Remington had set out again for the Southwest. Their marriage had been a love match, but hardly a financial success: the $250 Remington had received from the sale of one of his paintings had "dwindled with appalling rapidity," and by the summer of 1885 expenses had so far exceeded in-

8. Ibid., p. 211.
9. McCracken, *Frederic Remington*, pp. 37, 38, 40.
10. McKown, *Painter of the Wild West*, p. 69; McCracken, p. 40.

come that Remington urged his wife to return to Gloversville for a visit to her family, while he remained West to try to "pick things up."[11]

In the summer of 1885 Remington set out on a prospecting expedition to the south side of the Pinal Range in Arizona Territory. Although he allegedly had been attracted by the lure of "a fabulously rich mine" supposedly discovered "by a Negro named Seminole Bill, who had subsequently disappeared," it is more likely that he had once again succumbed to his wanderlust and his desire to gather more material for sketchbooks. In this case his material was well at hand: on May 17, 1885, a Chiricahua Apache named Geronimo had led 42 warriors and 92 women and children in an escape from the San Carlos Reservation in southeast Arizona across the Mexican border to the Sierra Madre mountains of Sonora and Chihuahua, and at the time Remington was pushing southward in search of gold, Geronimo was eluding the pursuit of General George Crook and the Third United States Cavalry.[12] Though he was undistinguished except for his "thoroughly vicious, intractable, and treacherous" character, Geronimo has received an inordinate amount of attention over the years, primarily on account of his remarkable ability to evade the United States Army. The deep affection of Americans for the renegade who successfully defies authority made him into a kind of villainous superman, although his flight into the Sierra Madres represented simply another episode in the frustrating and often ill-conceived attempts by the Army to administer the Southwest. Eastern newspapers were filled in 1885 and 1886 with accounts of the treachery and violence of Indians of the Southwest, much to the disgust of those Apaches who were attempting to come to terms with the white man's culure. Remington was to profit by this large interest in the Geronimo affair, although his experiences among Apaches were confined to a sketching session on the San Carlos Reservation and a mysterious visit three hungry renegades paid to his campfire one night. He never saw Geronimo at large, nor was, in fact, within 200 miles of him,[13] but he had seen

11. McKown, pp. 70–71.

12. Ibid., p. 73; Robert M. Utley, in Britton Davis, *The Truth about Geronimo* (New Haven, 1963), pp. viii, x, xi.

13. Davis, *Geronimo*, pp. xiii, xvii; McCracken, *Frederic Remington*, p. 43; Frederic Remington, "On the Indian Reservation," *Century*, 38 (July 1889), 394–405.

and drawn countless Apaches, soldiers, and cowboys of Kansas and the Southwest. As he headed for New York in the fall of 1885, the would-be prospector's portfolio was to prove to be filled with gold.

Remington had kept no journal of his western experiences, had made no notes on cowboy dress, and had written no letters home about the picturesque qualities of his new companions. Individual events, such as a horse race on the Kansas plains, a meeting with Apaches, or a disagreement with his business partners had passed into his consciousness, but he had apparently made no attempt to identify them as intrinsically "western." His vision in the two years after 1883 was at times that of the artist, occasionally that of the expectant entrepreneur, often that of the impulsive adolescent, but rarely that of the Easterner. His western economic ventures had proved no more profitable, if a little less burdensome, than those in the East, and he had returned to sketching with a consuming interest. When he wanted to determine once and for all whether he could make a living by his pencil and paintbrush, he assembled a portfolio of sketches and set forth to peddle them in the nation's largest and most prestigious art market. Though his years in the West had not decreased his dislike for the routine of industrial enterprise, upon his return to New York he secured a job keeping books for American Express to better the reunited Remington household's woeful financial position. He quit after a week, however, borrowed money from his uncle to attend classes at the Art Students League, and descended upon the art editors of New York magazines with his sketches of the West.[14]

The timing of Remington's entrance into the New York art world with his western scrapbooks was felicitous. He had acted, as in the past, on impulse, but the Geronimo affair had already focused the attention of the eastern public upon the conflict between soldier and Indian in the Southwest. Ten of Remington's first eleven illustrations in *Harper's Magazine,* beginning in January 1886, were of soldiers and Apaches in Arizona. Furthermore, an old Yale friend of Remington's, Poultney Bigelow, was by chance the art editor of *Outing* magazine, which was about to publish a series of articles on the Geronimo campaign, and Remington's experience in the Southwest made him a natural for the task of illustrating them.

14. McKown, *Painter of the Wild West,* pp. 83–84.

Bigelow was later to describe his memorable encounter with Remington which resulted in the partnership:

> One day at the *Outing* office I was hard at work making up a forthcoming number. I was interrupted by a vast portfolio in the hands of some intruding one. . . . Feeling cross and weary, I did not even look up at the huge visitor, but held out a hand for the drawings. He pushed one at me, and it was as though he had given me an electric shock. Here was the real thing, the unspoiled native genius dealing with Mexican ponies, cowboys, cactus, lariats and sombreros. No stage heroes these; no carefully pomaded hair and neatly tied cravats; these were men of the real rodeo, parched in alkali dusk, blinking out from barely opened eyes under the furious rays of the Arizona sun. . . . I looked at the signature—Remington. "It's an odd coincidence, I had a classmate at Yale . . ." I said to him. But before I could let another word out, he roared: "Hell! Big—is that you?" And so it was—after a ten-year interval! He had turned himself into a cowboy and I had become a slave at my desk. . . . I pulled forth from pigeon-holes every manuscript likely to interest such a pencil. Anything that might serve as an excuse for introducing horses, cowboys, army types and frontier background was eagerly sought. . . . Genius was in those rough drawings, and I loved them for their very roughness. Of course I bought out all he had in the portfolio, and I loaded him with orders likely to keep him in every number of the magazine for two or three years.[15]

Not only had the "unspoiled native genius" aroused Bigelow's desire for "frontier background" and "roughness," but Remington's very crudeness in technique identified him all the more with the region that he was portraying. In his artistic amateurishness the slaves to eastern desks found a fascination.

Harold McCracken suggests that Remington's rise to a position of artistic prominence in the years after 1886 may be traced to the "verve and realism of his work," the "depth and accuracy of his knowledge" of the West, and his "unbiased understanding of Indian nature," which combined to mark him as "an authority on a

15. Bigelow, *Seventy Summers, 1,* 303–04.

subject little known and just then very much in the minds of thoughtful people."[16] The depth of Remington's understanding of the West and the degree to which his impressions of it approximated reality are certainly debatable issues; as will be seen, Remington's image of the West had both its complex and superficial, its "realistic" and "romantic" aspects, and his understanding of Indian nature exhibited for the most part a considerable bias. But there is little doubt that from 1886 on, Remington's eastern contemporaries looked to him and other articulate exponents of western life to dramatize the meaning of a region remarkably unlike their own and yet very much in their minds.

The Bigelow interview marked a turning point in Remington's career: in the decade beginning with 1886 he developed and capitalized on his image as an "expert" on the West. In 1887 *Harper's Weekly* published 12 of his illustrations and *Outing* 71, the bulk of which were sketches made on his trips into Arizona and Mexico in 1884 and 1885 and an additional expedition in June 1886, in which Remington joined forces with General Nelson Miles and his cavalry units on their relentless pursuit of Geronimo. When the celebrated renegade finally surrendered, Remington was back in New York, complying with *Harper's* art editor Henry Mills Alden's request "to see everything he drew about the Southwest and the Apaches." Those drawings which Alden rejected, Bigelow accepted, it seemed, and as Remington's illustrations in *Harper's Weekly* and *Outing* began to attract attention, other members of the New York art world sought him out: in 1887 the American Water Color Society and the National Academy of Design each accepted one of his Arizona paintings for hanging in their exhibitions.[17]

In 1888 Remington struck a bonanza. Three paintings of his were hung in the National Academy, one of which, "Return of a Blackfoot War Party," won the Hallgarten and the Clarke prizes. The American Water Color Society exhibited him again, and the magazine world flocked to his door. *Harper's Weekly* ran 54 of his illustrations; *Outing*, 32; *Youth's Companion*, 27; and that august

---

16. McCracken, *Frederic Remington*, p. 53.

17. McCracken, *Frederic Remington*, pp. 52–53; McKown, *Painter of the Wild West*, p. 85.

symbol of eastern gentility, the *Century*, included 64 Remington sketches in its pages and commissioned the erstwhile saloon keeper to write and illustrate a series of articles on the Southwest to be published in 1889. The last enterprise was the product of an interview between Remington and Richard Watson Gilder, editor of the *Century*, in which that refined advocate of the genteel tradition reportedly passed Remington a box of cigars and said, "Tell me about the West."[18]

The *Century* commission (inspired by none other than Theodore Roosevelt, who had been taken with Remington's 1887 sketches in *Outing* and recommended him to Gilder as an illustrator for *Ranch Life and the Hunting Trail*, which appeared in article form in the *Century* in 1888) marked the beginning of Remington's career as a writer. He had written a brief article on his jack-rabbit hunting experience in Kansas for *Outing* in 1887 but had reportedly confessed to Gilder that "the best writing I've ever done was to sign my name on the back of a railroad pass."[19] Within the next eight years, however, Remington was to publish 4 illustrated articles on the West in *Century*, 7 in *Harper's Monthly*, and 19 in *Harper's Weekly*.

Gilder's decision to send Remington West as a correspondent wrought significant changes in the former sheep rancher's career. From 1887 until 1891 Remington spent his summers in the West, material-hunting, and his winters in New York, writing and painting. In 1888 he joined the Tenth Cavalry in Arizona and revisited the San Carlos Reservation, returning with the material for his 1889 articles in *Century;* in 1889 he journeyed to Mexico to make sketches for a serial which appeared in *Harper's Weekly;* and in the fall of 1890, after spending a summer working on the plates and text drawings for Longfellow's *Hiawatha*, which permanently established his reputation as an illustrator, Remington joined one of General Miles' scouting parties in Dakota, where the Sioux were in rebellion. The result of this foray was a series of illustrated articles on the Sioux uprising in *Harper's Weekly* for 1891. As in the Geronimo campaign, Remington was slightly on the fringe of the action: the famous Wounded Knee Massacre of December 29, 1890, took place on the same day that Remington left an encampment

18. McCracken, p. 53; McKown, p. 96.
19. McCracken, p. 53; McKown, p. 96.

near Wounded Knee Creek on his way to the Pine Ridge government agency to prepare to return to New York. He managed to see the victorious troops pass in review after Wounded Knee, but to his regret missed the battle entirely.[20]

On first glance, Remington's trips west from 1886 through 1890 may seem distinctly similar to those he made before 1885. But although the experiences—trailing after cavalry campaigns, sketching Indians on reservations, chasing game in the mountains of northern Mexico—were often the same, the manner with which Remington responded to them was of necessity different. He now viewed the troopers and vaqueros and Indian renegades through the eyes of an eastern magazine correspondent, an "expert" who was searching for the unique and picturesque in behavior which might have once seemed ordinary. Since eastern readers accepted his views as authentic, he was forced to stand back and examine his West, to discuss it in terms they could understand. This necessitated a reevaluation of his own role in terms of East and West— that is, of New York and Kansas, illustrating and ranching, social recognition and the delights of solitude. The result was the merging of the bits and pieces of life in Arizona, Mexico, and the Dakotas that provided Remington material with his sense that he was identified with and yet apart from that material.

This merging of artist and subject matter was to result in the crystallization within Remington of a distinct conception of western life, an approach sufficiently different from his view of the West in later life to be considered as marking a phase in his creative development. The phase is best illustrated in *Pony Tracks*, a mélange of nine articles reprinted from issues of *Harper's Weekly* between 1890 and 1895 and six articles from *Harper's Monthly* which had appeared over a two-year period beginning in 1893. Eleven of the articles were directly related to Remington's western journeys in the four years after 1889: four grew out of Mexican trips in 1889 and 1893, four were products of his expedition across Dakota in 1890, and the remaining three stemmed from fishing and hunting excursions through Canada and the Northwest in 1890 and 1893.

20. McKown, p. 97; McCracken, pp. 60, 61; Frederic Remington, "Lieutenant Casey's Last Scout" and "The Sioux Outbreak in South Dakota," in his *Pony Tracks* (Norman, 1961), pp. 17–40, esp. p. 31.

The *Pony Tracks* articles are for the most part isolated descriptions of events. Remington makes little attempt to see each event beyond its immediate context or to make connections between the various experiences he describes. Yet it is possible to see emerging from the collection as a whole a sense on Remington's part that the climatological and topographical diversity of his West did not preclude its having an environmental sameness. The characters and settings vary, but for Remington the process through which an individual confronts the world about him has a fundamental similarity. It is this process of confrontation, the result of an interaction between a certain kind of environment and, for all his sizes and shapes, a certain kind of individual, which Remington came to see as uniquely western.

Nature as an oppressive force was a persistent theme of *Pony Tracks*. Upon arriving in Dakota, Remington, like Roosevelt, was struck by the "tangled masses of the famous Badlands," which he saw as "a place for stratagem and murder, with nothing to witness its mysteries but the cold blue winter sky." "No words of mine," he wrote, "can describe these Badlands. They are somewhat as Doré pictured hell." In the Southwest he found "tortuous rivers thick with scorching sand" and "never-ending burnt plains," over which wound an occasional dusty trail. Yellowstone Park, in the northwest corner of Wyoming, was in turn filled with "treacherous mazes" of "spongy mountain meadows," "nasty" chasms, "dirty slough-holes," and above all, the "thin and hazardous" geyser formations, over which Remington rode gingerly, for "to break through is to be boiled." At one point "two jets of boiling water shot a hundred feet in the air, and came down in rain on the other side." The roar of the geysers was to Remington "like the exhaust of a thousand locomotives"; he wrote that one of his companions "nudged me and remarked, 'Hell's right under here.'" "Nature has made her wildest patterns here," Remington said of Yellowstone, "let us respect her moods."[21] The western experience implied to him the presence of man in potentially hostile natural surroundings.

Whether the constant trials of oppressive nature had their effects upon individual western psyches, or the stern settings of the West

21. Remington, *Pony Tracks*, pp. 20, 23, 41, 110, 112, 118, 120.

attracted men of a coarse fibre, the inhabitants of *Pony Tracks* are as fearsome and hostile as their surroundings. A Brûlé Sioux in Dakota is "a perfect animal" with a face "replete with human depravity—stolid, ferocious, arrogant, and all the rest—ghost shirt, war-paint, feathers, and arms. As a picture, perfect; as a reality, horrible." Indians of this stamp, to Remington, precipitated feelings such as those expressed by a veteran of the 1890 Sioux uprising, who noted that when he got out of the hospital he was going to reenlist, "and I hope I get back . . . before this trouble is over. I want to get square with these Injuns." "You see," notes Remington, "there was considerable human nature in this man's composition."[22]

Brutality and repulsiveness are by no means restricted to the Sioux and the Apache. In the Southwest Remington noticed "a certain individual who, as he engulfed his food, presented a grimy waste of visage only broken by the rolling of his eyes and the snapping of his teeth," and an old fiddler who "looked as though he had had his share of a very rough life; he was never handsome as a boy . . . but the weather and starvation and time had blown him and crumbled him into a ruin which resembled the pre-existing ape from which the races sprang. If he had never committed a murder, it was for lack of opportunity."[23]

The combination of brutish men in a grim setting occasionally led Remington to a conception of the West as a land of random yet constant danger. "At times," he notes, "instant and awful death overtakes the puncher—a horse in a gopher hole, a mad steer, a chill with a knife, a blue hole where the .45 went in, a quicksand closing overhead, and a cross on the hillside are all." Every stranger, in such a land, becomes a potential enemy, every notch and crevice an invitation to suicide. The following passage, written about the Southwest, Remington felt could serve for all "that country which . . . lies beyond the high plains":

> There is the serious side of the life. The Apache is an evil which Mexicans have come to regard as they do the meteoric hail, the lightning, the drought, and other horror not to be averted. They quarrel with themselves over land and stock, and there are a great many men out in the mountains who are

22. Ibid., pp. 28–29, 39.
23. Ibid., pp. 49, 58.

proscribed by the government. Indeed, while we journeyed on the road and were stopping one night in a little mud town, we were startled by a fusillade of shots, and in the morning were informed that two men had been killed the night before, and various others wounded.[24]

The logic of the serious side of western life, fraught with actual and potential perils, seemed to dictate that its inhabitants be of a special ilk and adopt a specific stance toward their environment. Like Roosevelt, Remington sees western men as overwhelmingly masculine. "Anglo-American foremen" in the Southwest exhibit the same qualities Roosevelt noticed in the inhabitants of Dakota: they "have all the rude virtues," such as "perfect courage," strength, "moral fibre," and, of course, self-reliance. "If a man," notes Remington, "is to hold down a big ranch in Northern Mexico, he has to be 'all man,' because it is 'a man's job.' " Soldiers in Dakota impressed Remington with their jokes about death in the midst of battle: "Nothing," he wrote, "can be taken seriously by men used to danger." An American ranchman in Mexico likewise "faces the Apache, the marauder, and the financial risks" with "his strong spirit, the embodiment of generations of pioneers."[25]

The "spirit" with which the strong men of the West confront their world is for Remington a descriptive term for the manner with which one comes to terms with the western experience. In some cases, primarily those of the Anglo-Americans, the process of confrontation produces the same grim determination Roosevelt saw as essential to success in Dakota and eventually in all of America. In others, particularly those of the vaqueros of the Southwest, the natural result of constant confrontations with an oppressive environment is a philosophic fatalism. "Such is the life of the vaquero," writes Remington, "a brave fellow, a fatalist, with less wants than the pony he rides," whose pleasures consist of "the *baile*, the song, the man with guitar"—and who "under all this" has "little hates and bickerings, as thin as cigarette smoke and as enduring as time." The Mexican cowboys "are grave," Remington notes, "and grave even when gay; they eat little, they think less, they meet death calmly."[26]

24. Ibid., pp. 48, 50, 100.
25. Ibid., pp. 32, 51, 62.
26. Ibid., p. 61.

Whether an individual's search for meaning in the western experience resulted in a determination to rely on his strength of body and mind or on a tossing of his destiny to the chinook and the prairie storm was of less consequence to Remington than his conviction that to live in the West was to confront life at its "most real," devoid of the "luxuries" of eastern civilization. On Indian fighting, Remington mocks the "sentimentalist" who from his "place of security" pleads to "try to avoid bloodshed." "Who is to weep for the men who hold up a row of brass buttons for any hater of the United States to fire a gun at?" he asks. "Are the squaws of another race to do the mourning for American soldiers?" On the amusements of cowpunchers, he distinguishes between their songs, which are "largely about love and women and doves and flowers," and their "real life," in which they take "only a perfunctory interest" in such "nonsense." On the manners of ranch hands, he points out that "the fact that a man bolts his food or uses his table-knife as though it were a deadly weapon counts very little in the game they play in their lonely ranch life," for these men are "untainted by the enfeebling influences of luxury and modern life." "I believe," Remington said of his experiences in the Sierra Madres, "that a man should for one month of the year live on the roots of the grass, in order to understand for the eleven following that so-called necessities are in reality luxuries."[27]

At the same time that Remington was applauding the fact that his natural men of the West possessed minds "which, though lacking all embellishments, are chaste and simple, and utterly devoid of a certain flippancy which passes for smartness in situations where life is not so real," he was rapidly moving up the eastern social ladder. His address changed from Brooklyn to Central Park at 58th Street in 1888 and to a "more spacious home" on fashionable Mott Avenue and 138th Street the following year. In 1890 the Remingtons bought a large house overlooking Long Island Sound in New Rochelle, where the erstwhile prospector erected a studio which was twenty feet high, forty feet long, and twenty feet wide, with double doors "wide and high enough so that a mounted horseman could ride in and out."[28] By 1891, riding on the success of the

---

27. Ibid., pp. 34, 50, 62, 73, 82.

28. Ibid., p. 61; McCracken, *Frederic Remington*, p. 58; McKown, *Painter of the Wild West*, p. 103.

Hiawatha plates, Remington had begun to make his mark in New York literary circles. The Players Club, which featured Charles Dana Gibson, Childe Hassam, architect Stanford White, and popular dramatist Augustus Thomas, offered him membership, and his house in New Rochelle became a weekend watering place for successful New York artists.

Remington was a generous host, challenging friends to match him in food and liquor consumption, but his conviviality did not extend to a genuine fondness for the luxuries of civilization. In the midst of plush settings he would hearken back to his days on the prairie: one account of his years in New York in the nineties has him dressed in a "tall silk hat, fashionable dark blue coat, tan kid gloves, patent-leather shoes, and staunch walking stick with a buckhorn handle," addressing his Players Club friends in "terse epigrams and cursewords derived from army friends, cowboy comrades, and Spanish vaqueros." On a trip to Europe in 1892 he claimed that the "collars, cuffs, foreign languages, and cut and dried stuff" of the Old World were "sure poison for me; it's time I got back to the Sierra Madre and the Big Horn and the Grand Canyon where I belong."[29]

In the ten years after 1886 Remington's close attachments to a formalized social order may have paradoxically reinforced his deep antisocial tendencies. It was in the midst of his entrance into the New York art elite, according to Augustus Thomas, that he came to cultivate the "cowboy habit and point of view, and finally the cowboy standard and philosophy." Thomas was suggesting that Remington in his initial creative phase did more than dramatize the hardships of western environment and the celebrated manner in which its inhabitants responded to those hardships; he adopted the attitudes of "army friends, cowboy comrades, and Spanish vaqueros" as his own. "The cow-men are good friends and virulent haters, and if justified in their own minds, would shoot a man instantly, and regret the necessity, but not the shooting, afterwards," Remington wrote in *Pony Tracks*. "Sensitive as an Indian, he liked instinctively and enduringly, hated intuitively and long," Thomas wrote of Remington in the New Rochelle years.[30]

29. McKown, pp. 110–11, 130.
30. Remington, *Pony Tracks*, p. 62; Augustus Thomas, "Recollections of Frederic Remington," *Century, 86* (July 1913), 354.

A letter to Poultney Bigelow in 1893 demonstrated the extent to which Remington had come to view American civilization in terms of the "cowboy philosophy" he had set down in *Pony Tracks:*

> Jews, Injuns, Chinamen, Italians, Huns—the rubbish of the Earth I hate—I've got some Winchesters and when the massacring begins, I can get my share of 'em, and what's more, I will. . . . Our race is full of sentiment. We invite the rinsins, the scourins, and the Devil's lavings to come to us and be *men*—something they haven't been, most of them, these hundreds of years. I don't care a d - - n how a man gets to Heaven— how he takes care of his soul—whether he has one or not. It's all nothing to me. But I do care how he votes and lives and fights."[31]

In this remarkable outburst a provincial suspicion of strangers appears as racism, an affinity for things masculine as a frantic assertion of masculinity, a sense of violence as belligerency, and a smattering of fatalism as a blunt unconcern for "how a man takes care of his soul." Remington's attempt to extend a stance toward life which he saw evolving from the western experience to the crowded ethnic shores of urban America is expressed with blatant lack of control. One imagines him picking up his Winchester and asserting his independent-violent-masculine self at the expense of the first immigrant to cross his path.

This lack of control may have been a product of Remington's awareness that the very individuals whose philosophy he had adopted were disappearing from the American scene. The battle of Wounded Knee was to be the last great struggle between the soldier and the Indian; the census of 1890 had shown only pockets of frontier on a closed continent; and Remington had perhaps come to the realization that "the cowboy—the real thing, mark you, not the tame hired man who herds cattle for the mere wage of it, and who lives for weeks at a time in convention store clothes"—was vanishing "with the advent of the wire fence."[32]

31. Quoted in Poultney Bigelow, "Frederic Remington; with Extracts from Unpublished Letters," *New York State Historical Association Quarterly Journal, 10* (1929), 46–48.

32. Remington to Perriton Maxwell, in Perriton Maxwell, "Frederic Remington, Most Typical of American Artists," *Pearson's, 18* (October 1907), 407.

Despite having resolved to go back to the Sierra Madres and the Little Big Horn "where I belong," Remington made no major excursions West after 1895. He spent the next eight years busily recreating western scenes, the belligerent aspects of his cowboy philosophy were tested in a campaign against the Spaniard in Cuba, and the coming together of eastern industrial civilization and the Wild West received his anxious attention. While his response to western America was, if anything, more intensive in the 1896–1902 period, it incorporated a physical and psychological distance between the artist and his patented subject matter.

A substantial change in his conception of the West marked the initiation of Remington's second creative phase, which may be dated from the appearance in 1896 of the first of a collection of nine articles from *Harper's Monthly* and one from *Harper's Round Table*, which were published together in 1898 under the title *Crooked Trails*. The starkness of his earlier western portraits was tempered with the softer elements of legend and romance. Royal Cortissoz highlights the change that took place in his paintings:

> Remington . . . left far behind him the brittleness of the pen drawings which he had once scattered so profusely through magazines and books. His reds and yellows, which had blared so mercilessly from his canvases, began to shed the quality of scene painting and took on more of the aspect of nature. Incidentally the mark of the illustrator disappeared and that of the painter took his place.[33]

In Remington's writings after 1896 the merciless reality of the cowboy existence becomes a jumping-off point for investigations into the history of western pioneers, the strange spirit-world of the Indian, and the tragic aspects of the western experience.

Sustained creative outbursts were not unusual for Remington, as the vast number of paintings and illustrations he produced between 1888 and 1890 testify, but the 1896–1902 period is of special interest on account of the number of occasions on which his creative impulses were expressed in writing, a form with which he was less comfortable. Even while he continued to satisfy the public's

33. Royal Cortissoz, "Frederic Remington, A Painter of American Life," *Scribner's*, 47 (February 1910), 187.

demand for his western sketches and paintings, and turned with considerable success to sculpture, four collections of his short stories and a full-length novel were published in *Harper's*. Though this period is by no means as awesome as Faulkner's "white heat" period of the late 1920s or Melville's moments of "creative equilibrium" in the early 1850s, it is nevertheless remarkable for its harmony of subject and theme.

Recognizing that the Old West was no more, Americans were seeking in the 1890s to capture its essence while at the same time demonstrating its place in the history of American civilization, and Remington was able to infuse his West with the sense of its historical and romantic possibilities. This expansion of his vision from empirical to imaginative, "realistic" to "romantic," was abetted by his growing association with the East. The discrepancy between the urban and industrial culture New York symbolized and the nomadic world of Kansas and Arizona served to put the West in perspective for Remington and further dramatized for his readers their sense that American civilization could incorporate contrasting, even clashing images which were somehow not mutually exclusive.

Crooked Trails marks Remington's first attempt to see the West in a historical context. He employs such devices as repeating stories he has heard from western characters and reproducing an older manuscript in its entirety to enhance the presence of the past. At the end of "How the Law Got Into the Chaparral," a tale of Texas in 1851 told by Colonel Rip Ford, "of the old-time Texas Rangers," Remington dramatizes the relation between past and present: "Texas is to-day the only State in the Union where pistol-carrying is attended with great chances of arrest and fine. The law is supreme even in the lonely *jacails* out in the rolling waste of chaparral, and it was made so by the tireless riding, the deadly shooting, and the indomitable courage of the Texas Rangers."[34]

This historical consciousness pervades *Crooked Trails*. Regarding an extract from the memoirs of a seventeenth-century Indian fur trader, Remington asks those who "in these days will analyze . . . and scoff" to "go to your microbes, your statistics, your volts, and your bicycles, and leave me the truth of other days." Of a letter about one of Rogers' Rangers in the French and Indian War he

---

34. Frederic Remington, *Crooked Trails* (New York, 1899 ed.), pp. 1–2, 20.

maintains that "it is history, and descends to the list of those humble beings who built so well for us the institutions which we now enjoy in this country." Other stories contain historical allusions: in "A Sergeant of the Orphan Troop" Remington speaks of the "wild days . . . in the seventies" when "if a sergeant bade a soldier go or do, he instantly went or did—otherwise the sergeant belted him over the head with his six-shooter, and had him taken off in a cart"; and in "The Essentials at Fort Adobe" he notes that "the Indian suns himself before the door of his tepee, dreaming of the past. . . . I looked at him and wondered at the new things. The buffalo, the warpath all are gone. What of the cavalrymen over at Adobe—his Nemesis in the stirring days—are they, too, lounging in barracks, since his lordship no longer leads trooping over the burning flats by day and through the ragged hills by night?"[35]

The answer to this question for Remington, writing in New York of the mid-nineties, was that "the blistered faces of men, the gaunt horses dragging stiffly along to the cruel spurring, the dirty lacklustre of campaigning . . . [are] no more." In *Crooked Trails* Remington appears compelled to contrast the West he knew with the still wilder days that preceded it and the "enfeebled" present that will soon forget it—to gather it up in a bundle before it vanishes forever. Such a compulsion led him into strange quarters to find romance, such as his flirtation in 1897 and 1898 with a French-Canadian half-breed named Sundown Leflare, who "never got mentally in sympathy with either strain of his progenitors" and consequently "knew about half as much concerning Indians as they did themselves . . . and white men in the same proportion."[36]

The four stories about Sundown that appeared in *Harper's Monthly*, beginning in September of 1897, and were published in book form in 1899 indicate the degree to which a character originally intended to play a subordinate role can capture his author's imagination and eventually shape the narrative around himself. Sundown is first introduced as an interpreter in one of Remington's characteristic tales told to him by a representative of the Old West, in this case an ancient Absaroke warrior named Paint, but as the story, "The Great Medicine-Horse," unfolds, the author has great

35. Remington, *Crooked Trails*, pp. 34, 52, 63, 92.
36. Ibid., p. 63; Remington, *Sundown Leflare* (New York, 1899), p. 3.

difficulty in getting "Paint's mysterious musings transferred to my head without an undue proportion of dregs filtered in from Sundown's lack of appreciation." Ultimately Remington must admit that "there is quite as much Sundown in this as Paint"—and with no distress, for he has become taken with this "strange man, with his curious English and his weird past":

> He is a tall person of great physical power and must in his youth have been a handsome vagabond. Born and raised with the buffalo Indians, still there was white man enough about him for a point of view which I could understand. . . . His character was so fine a balance between the two, when one considered his environment, that I never was at a loss to place the inflections. . . . And yet Sundown was an exotic, and could never bore a man who had read a little history.[37]

Remington follows Sundown as he braves a blizzard to deliver an order for General Miles and the Seventh Cavalry ("How Order Number Six Went Through"), absconds with Snow-Owl's squaw ("Sundown's Warm Spot"), gets temporarily rich at a poker game ("Sundown's Money"), and explains his religious beliefs ("Sundown's Higher Self"). Initially he has difficulty in reconciling Sundown's attractive picturesqueness with his apparent thoughtlessness: upon hearing that Sundown had sold Snow-Owl's squaw for a hundred dollars after risking death to run off with her, he wonders, "How can I reconcile this romance to its positively fatal termination?" But upon learning that Sundown has an infant child at the nearest Indian agency who is being taken care of by a white woman for three dollars a week (Sundown refuses to "put dat baby een a dam Enjun tepee"), and further hearing that the mother of the child, also white, "was run off on de dam railroad when de leetle baby was born," Remington can only conclude that "most of [Sundown's] real trouble had come of railway trains." He weeps for this creature from the older, wilder West, as he bemoans the passing of the environment that spawned him.

Sundown Leflare is a living indictment of the failure of white industrial civilization to assimilate those western descendants of a previous era. On Christianity versus "medicine," Sundown says:

37. Remington, *Sundown Leflare*, pp. 4, 21, 51.

"White man he don' know so much he think he know. Guess de speeret don't come een de board house, but she howl ron' de tepee een de wintair night. Enjun see de speerets dance un talk plenty een de lodge fire; white man he see not'ing but de coffee boil." On technological progress, Sundown notes: "White man mak de wagon un de seelver dollar, un de dam railroad, un he tink dat ees all dair ees een de country." And on changes that have taken place in his West, Sundown is explicit: "Back yondair, een what year you call '80—all same time de white man was hang de oddar white man so fas'—she geet be bad. De buffalo man she was come plenty wid de beeg wagon, was all shoot up de buffalo, was tak all de robe. Den de man come up wid de cow, un de solder he was stop chasse de Enjun. De Enjun she was set roun' de log pos', un was not wan' be chasse some more—eet was do no good. Den come de railroad; after dat bad, all bad." By the last Sundown story Remington tells us that "my romance had arrived," but it is a romance of a tragic sort, and as Remington "sat in the growing dusk of my room at the agency, before a fire," he was "somewhat lonesome," for "my stay was about concluded, and I dreaded the long ride home on the rail-road—an institution which I wish from the bottom of my heart had never been invented."[38]

Finding the grim antics of the cowboy, the symbol-ridden world of the Indian, and the stirring days of the cavalry vanishing in the wind, Remington tried to recapture them in a collection of cow-boy yarns, Indian legends, and war articles entitled *Men with the Bark On,* which viewed the inhabitants of wilder days from a modern perspective; in his only novel, *John Ermine of the Yellow-stone,* which fused the harsh reality of the plains experience with the elements of historical romance; and as a war correspondent in Cuba, where he sought an international extension of his cowboy philosophy: the chance to destroy white America's enemies in a noble war.

The Cuban campaign in 1898 was a most disillusioning experi-ence for Remington. In the nineties he had written Bigelow of his great desire to be involved in a European war, and when the bomb-ing of the *Maine* occurred in February 1898, Remington reportedly confessed to his wife that "this is what I've been waiting for all my

38. Ibid., pp. 67, 69, 70, 75, 92, 95, 103, 104.

life." He secured credentials from *Harper's* and the New York *Journal* as an artist-correspondent, had his old friend General Miles clear passage with the State Department, and headed for Tampa, Florida, to embark for Cuba. In *Men with the Bark On* he wrote that the Cuban campaign "satisfied a life longing to see men do the greatest thing which men are called on to do . . . he who has not seen war only half comprehends the possibilities of his race."

But the anticipation and the reality were miles apart. Remington was assigned to the battleship *Iowa,* which steamed up and down the Cuban coast for seven days and saw no action; he noted that "the appalling sameness of this pacing works on the nerves of everyone," and longed for his old days with the cavalry in Arizona. "I want to hear a shave-tail bawl," he cried, "I want to get some dust in my throat; I want to kick the dewy grass, to see a sentry pace in the moonlight, and to talk the language of my tribe. I resist it; I suppress myself; but my homely old first love comes to haunt me, waking and sleeping—yes even when I look at this mountain of war material, this epitome of modern science."[39]

The technological aspects of modern war were most distressing to Remington. "Grave, serious persons of superhuman intelligence" stood about the battleship—"men who have succumbed to modern science, which is modern life. Daisies and trees and the play of sunlight mean nothing to these. I believe they fairly worship this throbbing mass of mysterious iron; I believe they love this bewildering power which they control. Its problems entrance them; but it simply stuns me. . . . Don't waste your sympathy on these men below decks—they will not thank you; they will not even understand you. . . . They love their iron baby, so leave them alone with their joy." The spontaneity and glory of an Indian fight had been replaced by a mass of technological equipment which seemed to dwarf men's deeds and depersonalize their reactions.

Modern bullets and the injuries and suffering they inflicted compounded Remington's horror. On the Cuban mainland he saw "one beautiful boy brought in by two tough, stringy, hairy old soldiers, his head hanging down behind. His shirt was off, and a big red spot shone brilliantly against his marble-like skin. . . . The doctor laid his arms across his breast, and shaking his head, turned

39. McKown, *Painter of the Wild West,* p. 162; Remington, *Men with the Bark On,* pp. 14, 15, 171–72.

to a man who held a wounded foot up to him, dumbly imploring aid, as a dog might. It made my nerves jump, looking at that grewsome hospital, sand-covered, with bleeding men. . . . The thought came to me, what if I am hit out here in the bush while all alone? I shall never be found."[40]

Of his experience with the Fifth Corps near San Juan Hill, Remington wrote, "There were no bullets and shells cracking about my ears, but I found my nerves very unsettled. . . . Art and literature under Mauser fire is a jerky business; it cannot be properly systematized. I declared that I would in the future 'set pieces for dining-rooms.'" Racked with fever, haunted by the spectre of "white bodies which lay in the moonlight with dark spots on them," his taste for glory turned to ashes in his mouth, he gave in to his sickness and "concluded that I had finished." With the rest of the sick and wounded he returned to America and "never again wrote to Bigelow about how he hoped for a real war so he could join it."[41]

The disillusionment of the Cuban campaign echoes through *Men with the Bark On,* published in 1900. Seen through the smoke and dust of Cuba, the West was as grim and unrelenting as ever, but it had taken on a new meaning. The braves and scouts and soldiers of the Old West are now victims of a world of technology and "civilization." Essentially wild, they cannot cope with modern war, which dehumanizes them, or modern institutions, which dwarf them, or "progress," which passes them by: they "die like the wild animals, unnaturally—unmourned, and even unthought of mostly." Remington sees helplessness and tragedy where once he had seen glory and heroism. Ah-we-ah, the Ojibway brave, loses his wife and baby from starvation in a dry fall and cold winter, because the elements have driven away potential game. MacNeil, a "pure old warrior" from the older days, speaks with amusement of an occasion when he and a band of Crow warriors were trapped in a blizzard and barely survived. While Remington had once landed such stoic acceptance of an oppressive environment, by 1900 he had come to feel that men should be "reflective," should allow themselves to be taken "out of the present"—a "refinement" that "never came to MacNeil, and he needed it in the worst way."[42] In the face of the

40. Remington, *Men with the Bark On,* pp. 16, 17, 198.
41. Ibid., pp. 206, 207, 209; McKown, *Painter of the Wild West,* p. 169.
42. Remington, *Men with the Bark On,* dedication, p. 42.

threatening qualities of modern civilization, the threat nature had for such men as MacNeil was no laughing matter.

Nor is there any glory in sheer devotion to institutions. Sundown Leflare's battle with the snow and cold to deliver Order Number Six was treated with warmth and humor, but the attempt of Sergeant William Burling of *Men with the Bark On* to deliver a similar order ends in tragedy: he first has the order stolen from him; then, after regaining it, he is ambushed and killed by a band of Sioux. When, after noticing that his order has been stolen, Burling holds up a whole room of buffalo hunters with the threat: "Unless that paper is returned to me, I will turn both these guns loose on the crowd. I know you will kill me, but unless I get that paper I want to be killed," the routine memoranda of the army have taken precedence over his existence. When the hunters at length discover Burling's body next to the ashes of the order that he has burned, one of their party wonders, in telling the story to Remington, whether Burling's "medicine" had not "gone back on him." "No," Remington explains, "it wasn't his medicine, but the great medicine of the white man, which bothered the soldier so." "Hump! The great Washington medicine maybe so. It make dam fool of soldiers lots of time I know 'bout," is the Indian's reply.[43]

In *John Ermine of the Yellowstone* Remington attempted to unify his responses to the passing of his West and the march of industrial civilization from the East, to fuse all the elements of the plains experience in the creation and destruction of a hero of the Old West. John Ermine's experience has been an especially full and symbolic one. A white child raised by Indians, Ermine stands for all that is wild and primitive in man down through the ages. Although he has "evolved from a race which . . . got its yellow hair, fair skin, and blue eyes amid the fjords, forests, rocks and ice-floes of the north of Europe," he is linked in Remington's eyes with a still ruder heritage. As Ermine leaves an Indian village to join the army with his half-breed companion Wolf-Voice, Remington notes that "these two figures . . . were grotesque but harmonious. America will never produce their like again. Her wheels will turn and her chimneys smoke, and the things she makes will be carried around the world in ships, but she never can make two figures which will bear even a resemblance to Wolf-Voice and John Er-

43. Ibid., pp. 111, 117.

mine. The wheels and chimneys have crowded them off the earth."[44]

After demonstrating Ermine's identification with a wilder, older West in the first half of the novel, Remington devotes the remainder to his hero's confrontation with the "senseless mass of white humanity" invading from the East. In describing Ermine's eventual rejection by the "yellow-eyes" who initially welcomed him, Remington gives as searing an indictment of the hypocrisy and pettiness of white civilization as any civil rights novelist of the twentieth century. In view of Remington's acknowledged racist attitudes, his use of Ermine to expose some of the misconceptions in his own thinking indicates the depths of his disillusionment with modern, urban America, which had come to appear to him as a cancerous growth spreading across the continent, dwarfing, depersonalizing, and, worst of all, emasculating the men who had become exposed to it.

Ermine is an excellent scout and impresses the soldiers with "his low-voiced simplicity and acute knowledge concerning the matters about them." In turn, he forms "attachments for his comrades— that enthusiastic affection which men bring from the camp and battle-field, signed by suffering and sealed with blood." But this camaraderie soon disintegrates under pressure from that inevitably destructive force—a pretty woman. Ermine falls in love with Katherine, the daughter of Major Searles of the cavalry, and for the first time is awakened to the subtle social distinctions of white civilization. "Now vaguely," Remington notes, Ermine "began to feel a lack of something, an effort which he had not made—a something he had left undone; a difference and a distinction between himself and the officers." He senses that a scout cannot be a suitor of a young lady from an eastern finishing school, but his heart overrules his head. After a fortunate forest accident enables him to be Katherine's savior and nearly her lover, Ermine proposes to her at his first opportunity. Katherine responds, "I can't do that; why, my mother would never consent to it. . . . No, no, I cannot marry you. Why, what should we do if I did? We should have to live in a mule corral," and later confesses to her mother that "that horrible scout wanted to marry me. Did you ever hear of anything so ridiculous?", to which Mrs. Searles replies: "The social savagery of this place is

44. Frederic Remington, *John Ermine of the Yellowstone* (New York, 1902), pp. 22, 52, 82, 88, 90, 107.

depressing. To think of my daughter living in a log-cabin cooking bear meat for a long-haired wild man. . . . I suppose next an out-and-out Indian will want to be my son-in-law."

For Ermine the situation is both mysterious and intolerable: he cannot understand how Katherine can kiss him in the woods and scorn him in the parlor. His only conclusion is that white men "have two hearts: one is red and the other is blue; and you feel with the one that best suits you at the time. . . . You did not think I was a dog when I kept you all from freezing to death last winter; but here among the huts and the women I am a dog." Major Searles attempts to explain to Ermine that Katherine is engaged to a Lieutenant Butler, whose "people were of consequence," but this only serves to enrage Ermine, and he subsequently shoots Butler in the arm and vanishes. Immediately the soldiers set out after him: "The brotherhood of the white kind, which had promised him so much, had ended by stealing the heart and mind of the poor mountain boy, and now it wanted his body to work its cold will on."[45] Ermine escapes and holes up in the mountains for a time, but he is finally driven to return to the camp and seek vengeance on Butler and is killed in the process.

The destruction of John Ermine, in Remington's mind, symbolized the destruction of a way of life which emphasized the enthusiastic affection of the camp and battlefield and deemphasized social distinctions. Thrown up against that life was the inexorable march of eastern civilization, which constantly subordinated an individual's will to technological progress or social conventions. At one point Katherine Searles confides to her mother: "If Mr. Ermine is not sophisticated, he seems to have the primitive instincts of a gentleman." "Mr. Ermine, forsooth!" is the reply. "Is he presumptuous enough to present you with compliments? You had better maintain your distance." "He is a perfectly delightful man," Katherine returns, "so thoughtful and so handsome." "Tut, tut, Katherine; he is only an ordinary scout—a wild man."[46] That, of course, is precisely what Ermine is—a man among men of the Wild West; that is why Katherine is attracted to him, and that is why she eventually rejects him. In so doing, she demonstrates that civiliza-

45. Ibid., pp. 115, 136, 167, 211, 223, 230, 231, 236, 243.
46. Ibid., p. 196.

tion has made her as "inhuman," in Remington's terms, as the sailors on the Battleship *Iowa,* who pay homage to their iron baby at the expense of their free will. The fact that Mrs. Searles' condescension toward the "wild men" who "belong on the corral fence" is not far removed from his own condemnation of "Jews, Injuns, Chinamen, Italians, and Huns" as "the rubbish of the earth" is of no concern to Remington: Mrs. Searles speaks for a civilization that has robbed the West of its wildness and would rob a man of his free will, the essence of his masculinity. By 1902 such a civilization for Remington was anathema.

In 1898 Remington purchased an island in Chippewa Bay on the St. Lawrence River, in the same region where he was born, and after 1902 he resided there every year from March until October, when he would return to New Rochelle. His western travels altogether ceased: he said in 1907 that he had "no interest whatever in the industrial West of to-day—no more interest than I have in the agriculture of East Prussia or the coal mines of Wales." That same year he burned 75 of his old canvases, retaining only the landscape studies. As civilization continued its advance upon him, even memories became painful: in 1908 he tried to escape to a fifty-acre farm in Ridgefield, Connecticut, and burned 27 more of his best-known western paintings. Reality became a blur before his eyes: of the new impressionist school of painters he had once said "I've got two maiden aunts upstate who can knit better paintings than these," but in the last year of his life he adopted impressionist techniques.[47]

In 1905, from seclusion at New Rochelle, Remington attempted to sum up his response to the West:

> Evening overtook me one night in Montana, and I by good luck made the campfire of an old wagon freighter who shared his bacon and coffee with me. I was nineteen years of age and he was a very old man. Over the pipes it developed that he was born in western New York and had gone West at an early age. His West was Iowa. Thence during his long life he had followed the receding frontiers, always farther and farther West.

47. McKown, *Painter of the Wild West,* pp. 175, 178; Maxwell, *Pearson's, 18,* 407; McCracken, *Frederic Remington,* pp. 106, 118–19.

"And now," said he, "there is no more West. In a few years the railroad will come along the Yellowstone and a poor man can not make a living at all." The old man had closed my very entrancing book almost at the first chapter. I knew the railroad was coming. I saw men already swarming into the land. I knew the derby hat, the smoking chimneys, the cord-binder, and the thirty-day note were upon us in a restless surge. I knew the wild riders and vacant land were about to vanish forever, and the more I considered the subject, the bigger the forever loomed.[48]

In fact, Remington knew nothing of the kind. He stumbled into the Wild West, learned its codes, battled its perils, and documented its ruthless reality. He was able to put it into perspective only when the fame he found there led him back East. Although this perspective may have enabled him to see the West's glory, romance, and final tragedy, it did not soften the blow of its passing. If after 1896 he no longer insisted on a strictly "realistic" approach to his subject, he at least insisted on the relevance of a "bark on" way of life. When that, too, seemed doomed before the advance of the twentieth century, Remington came to "assert with . . . earnestness the nonexistence of the very things which he . . . taught us to accept as literal translations of real life." "Cowboys!" he would cry. "There are no cowboys anymore!"[49] Indeed, for Remington there were not, so completely had his West moved to the level of the symbolic. And that, in the end, was Remington's contribution: the raising of his "bark on" world, with its wild and virile inhabitants, to the level of history and romance.

48. "A Few Words from Mr. Remington," *Collier's Weekly* (March 18, 1905), quoted in McCracken, *Frederic Remington,* pp. 34–36.
49. Maxwell, *Pearson's, 18,* 394.

6. Wister's West: The Cowboy as Cultural Hero

On July 3, 1885, a tall, pale, dark-eyed young man and two middle-aged women stepped off the Pullman car of a Northern Pacific Railway train into the sun and dust of Omaha, Nebraska. The three were easily recognizable as Easterners: Owen Wister by his loose English flannel shirt, soft cloth hat, tailored coat, and close-fitting trousers; the Misses Maisie and Sophy Irwin by their white gloves, lace, and parasols. They were met at the train by Richard Trimble, another Easterner, who had come to accompany them to Cheyenne, Wyoming. Trimble, who had left a position in a New York dry goods company to enter the cattle business, had been in Wyoming for three years. The middle of 1885 found him co-manager of the Teschemacher and deBillier Cattle Company, which had been founded in 1879 by two Harvard classmates of Wister, Hubert Teschemacher and Frederic deBillier. Since Trimble had likewise gone to Harvard, it no doubt pleased him to see yet another schoolmate headed West.

July 3 ended with the ladies safely ensconced in a hotel in Cheyenne and with Wister and Trimble partaking of the abundant liquor supply offered by the Cheyenne Club. Founded in 1880 by "a small group of wealthy young cattlemen" who had based themselves in Wyoming, the Cheyenne Club, according to one account, "was known the world over as a sumptuous and elaborate meeting place for . . . cattle barons." If Wister had looked forward to soaking in some of its atmosphere, he was not disappointed: "No wonder they like the club at Cheyenne," he wrote in his journal. "It's the pearl of the prairies."[1]

Wister's first day and night in the West served to dramatize the two-pronged character of his eastern heritage, which was to loom large in his subsequent response to the sights and sounds of western

---

1. Owen Wister, Journal, July 3, 1885 (Western History Research Center, University of Wyoming, Laramie, Wyo.) Stokes, *Owen Wister Out West*, p. 61.

America. The Misses Irwin suggested in their presence the tea-cupped, parasoled, drawing-room portions of the world of Philadelphia, with which, through the person of his mother, Wister was to remain in painfully close contact throughout the whole of his western travels. The Cheyenne Club symbolized the other side of that world—what one historian has called the "stocks-and-bonds, havana-cigar, mahogany-and-leather side" of the East that had emerged in Wyoming in the person of the Wyoming Stock Growers Association, a group of powerful cattle companies heavily financed by eastern capital and in some cases, such as that of Teschemacher and deBillier, owned and operated by upper-class Easterners.[2] Wister's eastern background had identified him with both the Misses Irwin and the Cheyenne Club; and the implications of this dual identification were to condition his response to the West.

Wister's first recorded impressions of western life centered around the contrast he saw between the freedom of its nomadic cast and the regimentation of his Philadelphia existence. "This life has a psychological effect on you," he wrote his mother from Wyoming in 1885. "To ride 20 miles and see no chance of seeing human traces; to get up on a mountain and overlook any number of square miles . . . and never a column of smoke or a sound except the immediate grasshoppers—and then never to go upstairs. You begin to wonder if there is such a place as Philadelphia anywhere." Wister seemed particularly relieved that his western travels took him away from two major facets of his life in Philadelphia: his law practice and his close relations with Sarah Butler Wister. "Looking back at [Wister's Western] journals and letters," his daughter notes, "we see that Owen Wister freed himself from what to him was a deadly life . . . his regimented childhood and detested law practice." In 1894, when Wister had made eight trips westward and had virtually abandoned the law for a writing career, he noted that his journeys up to that point had been "holidays from . . . my perfunctory days at the office—the forgetting for a moment a detested occupation," and that "the homecoming and prospect of the office and driveling legalities was a gloomy thing."[3]

On his thoughts about being separated from his mother, Wister

2. Gene M. Gressley, *Bankers and Cattlemen* (New York, 1966), and "Teschemacher and deBillier Cattle Company," *Business History Review, 33* (Summer 1959), 121–37.
3. Wister, in Stokes, *Owen Wister Out West*, pp. 130, 201, 252.

was more subtle. In 1887, after describing some picturesque scenes on an Oregon ferryboat, he wrote her: "I keep thinking how you would hate nearly all of it. The only way you could ever come West and enjoy yourself would be inside a large party of friends who would form a hollow square whenever a public place was to be entered." Time and again his letters and journals demonstrated the incompatibility of Sarah Wister's way of life and the customs of the West. "When I've been most enjoying myself," the devoted son wrote to his mother in 1885, "I've laughed and likewise shuddered to think how you would have probably hated every minute. Everything that you most particularly abhor in practice, no matter how much you think it theoretically and democratically beautiful, has happened at least twice." Occasionally he, like his grandmother Fanny Kemble, would allude in his western journals to the coldness and rigidity of his mother's temperament. "My other news from home was not so good," he wrote from San Francisco in 1894. "Butler Place seemed on the verge of domestic troubles below stairs, which means, I know very well, that the ill-starred mistress of the house had been home long enough to harass the servants to the striking point."[4]

The freedom Wister found in the West thus had a deep personal meaning. "I don't wonder a man never comes back [East] after he has once been here for a few years," he wrote in 1885, and added: "This existence is heavenly in its monotony and sweetness. Wish I were going to do it every summer. I'm beginning to be able to feel I'm something of an animal and not a stinking brain alone." In 1889 Wister put his sentiments into verse:

> Would I might prison in my words
> And so hold by me all the year
> Some portion of the Wilderness
> Of freedom that I walk in here.

The last references to feeling "something of an animal" and finding freedom in the wilderness, when contrasted with Wister's image of his mother regarding the West inside a "hollow square" of her friends, suggest masculine rebellion against a mother's zealous overprotectiveness.

4. Owen Wister letter to Mrs. Owen Jones (Sarah Butler) Wister, July 4, 1885, Owen Wister Papers, family correspondence (Library of Congress); Stokes, *Owen Wister Out West*, pp. 47, 100, 116, 222.

Sarah kept close tabs on her only son. In 1888 Wister wrote home only once in a three-month period while in Wyoming, and his parents "worried desperately and spoke of their alarm to their relations." When Wister "realized the anxiety of his parents," his daughter maintains, "he made up his mind never to let so much time go by again without more letters." In 1902, when Wister was forty-two, the father of three, and America's best-selling novelist, he still corresponded frequently with the omnipresent Sarah.[5]

The specter of his family ties appears to have had a peculiar effect upon Wister's response to the expansiveness of his new environment. At times his western journals reflect a peevish denunciation of Proper Philadelphia, as in 1891, when he wrote from Yellowstone Park that he looked forward to a winter in the East "with unmixed dislike . . . there are a few people I care to see and who care to see me, but Philadelphia is not the place I should choose either for my friends or myself if I could help it." But more characteristic was his sense that his eastern heritage rendered him somewhat apart from the life and men he saw about him. No frantic attempts to acclimate himself to western manners and mores are apparent in his journals: far from being eager to obtain a buckskin shirt, as Roosevelt was, Wister, after nine years in the West, had to be persuaded by a cowboy friend to accept a pair of chaps as a gift, because he had "always been shy of wearing or owning these garments, as being not enough of a frontiersman to be entitled to them."

In virtually all of Wister's western fiction, which began after his fifth journey to Wyoming in 1891, a tenderfoot narrator serves as both a recounter of various anecdotes and an interpreter of them from a somewhat alien perspective. The use of this persona, who is as much a butt of his own jokes as a chorus to the action, gave Wister a mode of narration with which he felt comfortable, just as he took delight in his acknowledged success at being a "brilliant listener" who could remain "passive in the clutches" of his colorful native confidants.[6] What authenticity exists in Wister's writings on the West is derived from his ability to observe and reproduce its sights and sounds, not from an immersion in the life itself, as in the case of Remington and, to a lesser degree, of Roosevelt.

5. Stokes, *Owen Wister Out West*, pp. 30, 32, 64, 92.
6. Ibid., pp. 247, 255.

Wister's ever-present sense of his heritage did not prevent him from making the same eager exploration of the asocial and uncivilized aspects of the western experience that has been attributed to Roosevelt and Remington. In fact, it may be said to have hastened such an exploration, as an anecdote from one of Wister's railroad journeys to Wyoming will serve to illustrate. On a Northern Pacific Pullman out of Minneapolis in 1892, Wister marked the "talk between ladies and the porter about alkali water which they tell him they have been warned against"—a conversation which must have reminded him both of the heavily feminist overtones of his Philadelphia existence and certain of the gaps between East and West. "I am sure," he noted, "that the colonist sleepers ahead are more interesting than this Pullman, and thither I shall go." A day later Wister wrote that his "journey to the ordinary cars in front was a success," for he had met a cowboy who "had worked 3 years on the 7-bar-outfit," and whose "astonishing lively eyes" made him "handsome as a hawk." Early in their conversation, Wister reported, the cowboy had mentioned "that he'd made $50 a month on one job." Wister then replied, "And did you save it or blow it in?" The Westerner "burst into a most joyful explosion of laughter and cried, 'Blowed it in.' " "This mutual understanding," Wister concluded, "completely broke the ice and after a while I had the history of his life so far."[7] Similar memories of the "hollow square" within which his mother lived no doubt had a hand in stimulating Wister to make further searches that resulted in his encountering some of the wilder and more picturesque elements of the western scene.

The blending of East and West in the persons of Wister's Porcellian clubmate Richard Trimble and his partners Teschemacher and deBillier, lending their education and social prestige to the range cattle industry, was an equally memorable aspect of Wister's life in Wyoming. Their early experience on the range seemed another testimony to the gilt-edged image of the cattle industry that had filtered back to the East in the 1880s. "The number of Harvard graduates alone that appeared on the cattle frontier," writes a leading student of eastern capitalist ventures in the West, "is ample testimony to the fact that long hours were spent in the Hasty Pud-

7. Wister, Journal, July 7 and 9, 1892.

ding Club by scions of wealthy families romanticizing the West as a place for adventure." Among the Harvard men who bought stock in Teschemacher and deBillier were Theodore Roosevelt, who purchased a $10,000 certificate in October 1882, the cash being supplied by the ubiquitous Roosevelt and Son, and Robert Bacon, a close friend of Roosevelt.

One of the most successful members of the Wyoming Stock Growers Association has pictured the kind of life these Easterners lived in Wyoming of the eighties and nineties. In the spring, according to John Clay, they partook of the

> wild, free life of the cowboy, the morning cup of coffee, the long rides as they circled the cattle, the frantic scenes at the roundup, the calf-branding in the afternoon, the foundation of a cattle owner's wealth, and at night sweet sleep under clear skies, breathing refreshing air. When the spring work was over they came back to town. They had a bachelor's house where an old servant gave them coffee and rolls in the morning. During the afternoon they made a pretense at business and at lunch time they turned up at the Club. There they talked cattle and politics and afterwards played tennis. Lastly came dinner and generally a lively evening after it.

On the frequency of his appearances at the Cheyenne Club, Richard Trimble wrote his parents: "I am sorry thee has so little confidence in my ability to judge whether it is for my advantage to stay on the ranch or in Cheyenne. There are two sides to the cattle business, the theory and the practice, one is learned better in Cheyenne where cattle men congregate and the other on a ranch."[8]

Wister also came into contact in the eighties with a breed of men who took cattle ranching more seriously and who had seen the wisdom of combining forces to protect their interests. The Wyoming Stock Growers Association had been formed by Major Frank Wolcott, of Wolcott and Company, at whose ranch Wister based himself during his Wyoming travels; Francis E. Warren, of the Warren Land and Livestock Company, later U.S. Senator from Wyoming; Thomas Sturgis, founder and first secretary of the Asso-

---

8. Gressley, *Business History Review, 33,* 122–23, 130; Gressley, *Bankers and Cattlemen,* p. 275; John Clay, *My Life on the Range* (Norman, 1962), p. 76.

ciation, president of the Stock Growers National Bank, and partner of Sturgis, Lane, and Goodell, which evolved into the powerful Union Cattle Company in 1883; and John Clay, the shrewd Scottish broker who made a lifework of protecting British interests in the West and attempting to influence Wyoming politics through the stock growers lobby. For such men cattle ranching was a full-time profession, and they were willing to hire a corps of detectives to discourage rustling, become heavily involved in the political affairs of Wyoming ("the Union Pacific Railroad and the range cattle industry, the two partially mature economic agents," writes a historian of Wyoming politics, "directed the political life of the territory"),[9] and even resort to violence to insure that that profession was a profitable one.

The most celebrated case of the WSGA's use of violence to protect its interests was the April 1892 invasion of Johnson County, Wyoming, by a band of cattlemen and Texas mercenaries, "with the avowed purpose of exterminating the Rustlers in Johnson County." After killing two suspected rustlers, the vigilantes were outnumbered by the aroused residents of Johnson County and would no doubt have been slaughtered had not a troop of United States cavalry, dispatched by President Harrison, arrived in Johnson County and taken the cattlemen into custody. On April 18 the prisoners were sent to Cheyenne, where they awaited trial. Wister's friends among them included Wolcott, Teschemacher, deBillier (who was soon to suffer a nervous collapse), William C. Irvine, another member of the WSGA, and Frank Canton, a detective hired by the Association, whom Wister had met in Yellowstone Park in 1891. Also arrested in connection with the invasion, but subsequently released, was Dr. Charles B. Penrose, a Philadelphian who had accompanied the expedition in the role of surgeon. Penrose, a close friend of Wister, had written him a letter from Wyoming on May 11, 1892, in which he strongly backed the stockmen's cause.[10]

9. Gressley, *Bankers and Cattlemen*, p. 223. On the interactions between Senator Warren, Clay, Sturgis, the WSGA, and Wyoming territorial politics, see Lewis L. Gould, "Willis Van DeVanter in Wyoming Politics, 1884–1897," unpublished doctoral dissertation (Yale University, 1965).

10. Gould, "Willis Van DeVanter," p. 103; Charles B. Penrose, letter to Owen Wister, May 11, 1892, in Lois Van Valkenburgh, ed., "The Johnson County War, The Papers of Charles Bingham Penrose," unpublished master's thesis (University of Wyoming, 1939), App. A, following p. 108.

With passions aroused, his friends in jail, and deBillier's health failing, Wister's heart was no doubt in Wyoming in the spring and summer of 1892, although his person, with the exception of one mysterious week, remained in Philadelphia. Between July 6 and 14 he made a curious journey to Cinnibar, Montana, some five miles north of the extreme northwest corner of Wyoming, "just to tell George West [his guide] that he could not hunt with him that summer." Wister kept a journal of the trip, but the journal was not included in the edition of his letters and journals (*Owen Wister Out West*) released by his daughter in 1958. George T. Watkins has speculated as to why Wister undertook "the exhausting rail-road journey . . . only to discharge his guide . . . and get right back on the train for Philadelphia." "Was he afraid of the retribution upon the cattlemen and their friends that occurred almost daily that summer of 1892? Or did he undertake to deliver his message to West personally as an act of bravado, to prove to himself that he was not afraid to show himself in the West?"[11] Wister could have wired money to Omaha or corresponded with Trimble as to the status of his friends, and he certainly could have written or wired West to say that he was not coming. It is conceivable that West's whereabouts were uncertain, but a message could have been left at the telegraph station in Cinnibar.

The journal of 1892 itself fails to clarify the situation entirely. At one point Wister writes that "the only thing I don't like is that a man like Keller [a Philadelphia acquaintance] is likely to think that the reason for my giving this summer up is personal fear for my carcase," which suggests that Watkins' "act of bravado" theory is somewhat far-fetched, but in the same breath Wister points out that Dick Penrose (the son of Charles B. Penrose) "appreciated the reason" for his going to Montana. On the meeting with West himself Wister was equally elusive. His journal for July 11, 1892, written between Billings and Custer, Montana, notes that he reached Cinnibar at 12:30 P.M. on Sunday, July 10. He "found the faithful West on the platform," who did not know that Wister would not be hunting with him and "was so glad to see me and kept repeating his satisfaction with so much zest that I rather shirked telling him there was to be no trip this time." At 6:15 P.M., after an afternoon

11. Watkins, "Owen Wister Out West," p. 312.

of talking and drinking beer with West and other assorted citizens of the Yellowstone area, Wister headed again for Philadelphia, arriving there on July 14. "Of the whole 9 days journey of 4570 miles," his last journal entry reads, "it may be that I looked forward to it with unalloyed dismay, and that I look back on it with almost unalloyed pleasure and content."[12] Whether his gloom had turned to pleasure on account of a brief respite from the East is uncertain, but there is no indication that any specific act was the central focus of his seemingly purposeless journey of 1892.

One certainty about Wister's 1892 trip to Cinnibar was that it marked the end of his impressionistic wanderings through Wyoming and the beginning of his "material-hunting" through Texas, New Mexico, and Arizona. Between 1891 and 1893, the year of his first southwestern trip, Wister had established himself as a western writer, having published "Hank's Woman" in the August 1892 issue of *Harper's Weekly* and "How Lin McLean Went East," "The Winning of the Biscuit Shooter," and "Emily" in *Harper's Magazine* for that year and the following one. In June of 1893 he came to an agreement with Henry Millys Alden of *Harper's* to write a series of articles on his western experiences—"the whole adventure of the West in sketches or fiction," as Wister put it—and set out on the first of his three excursions to the Southwest in search of material. By 1894 he was noting that he had "fallen into favor with an ease that suggests how easily I might fall out and be forgotten," and nostalgically recalling his days in Wyoming, which "had an enchantment that no doubt can never be wrought again." Conceived as holidays from the law office and the rest of Proper Philadelphia, the Wyoming journeys for Wister had been delightful interludes, fraught as they were with the omnipresent reminders of his heritage. He was not again to find in the West the frolicsome adventure he had found in Wyoming. Heading home from one of his forays through the Southwest in 1895, he wrote: "As I finish this volume of notes, we are drawing near Cheyenne—and how I wish the next weeks could be on Wind River! . . . No one will ever know how unreasonably much it is to me, and how I long for it through the year. . . . Damn material-hunting! I'm filled and sick with it!"[13]

12. Wister, Journal, July 11 and 14, 1892.
13. Stokes, *Owen Wister Out West*, pp. 167, 201, 250

Wister's disaffection for certain aspects of his eastern background, symbolized to some extent in his mother's presence, had led him to seek out the wildest and most uncivilized denizens of the West for his acquaintances, such as the Wyoming stage driver who "entirely sympathized with the horse thieves and rustlers over in Johnson County and told me there were four men who ought to be killed—Wolcott, Canton, Irvine, and the other I forget."[14] To these friendships he had added his connection with their opposite numbers, the men of wealth, power, and prominence who ran the cattle industry and felt the political pulse of the territory. The Johnson County War had pitted each of these elements against the other, but, more importantly, it had signaled the end of the "wild days" in Wyoming, when barbed wire and court trials were seen as unnecessary embellishments. In vindicating themselves upon the rustlers, the cattlemen dramatized their financial plight, which was to be solved not by violence but by the adoption of efficient managerial techniques which smacked of the industrial East. Although one supporter of the invaders felt that after the war Wyoming was "a better state to live in, so far as property rights are concerned,"[15] the effect of the invasion was to place a greater emphasis on the legal safeguarding of persons and institutions, and consequently an extension of the forces of social organization in Wyoming. As Wyoming approached the twentieth century, the unfettered frontiersman disappeared from view as surely as did the part-time cattle baron.

The two-pronged nature of Wister's Wyoming experience manifested itself in his use of two radically different fictional modes, the "picaresque" and the "heroic." Concomitant with the emphasis in his early writings on the picaresque qualities of his fictional protagonists is a fascination with the violent and rustic aspects of the West and a sneering at the false trappings of eastern civilization. In his work in the later 1890s and 1900s, by contrast, Wister tended to view the West not as anticivilized but as precivilized, and to portray his protagonists as precursors to more cultured times, even possessing some smatterings of culture themselves. This distinction

14. Ibid., pp. 117, 174.
15. Clay, *My Life on the Range*, p. 277.

is not absolute, nor is there a clear break between the two phases, but an indication of the direction in which Wister moved can be gathered from contrasting his statement to William Dean Howells in 1893 that "he wanted to do a 'picaresque' novel of the West, as the life there was 'nomadic' and suited to the picaresque style," with his contention in the preface to the first edition of *The Virginian*, which appeared in 1902 and contained his most heroic western protagonist, that "What has become of the horseman, the cowpuncher, the last romantic figure upon our soil. . . . He will never come again. He rides in his historic yesterday."[16]

Wister's journals of Wyoming provide examples of both these conceptions of the West. In 1885 he called the cowboys a "queer episode in the history of the country," "purely nomadic," and "without any moral sense whatever," and in 1891 he described with fascination "the mostly blackguards" he had met, calling one "a brilliant talker in his vagabond line"; but in 1885 he demonstrated an awareness of the historic qualities of the West by prophesying that "Western life will slowly make room for Cheyennes, Chicagos, and ultimately inland New Yorks—everything reduced to the same flat prairie-like level of utilitarian civilization, and the ticket will replace the rifle." In 1891, on this same theme, he "petitioned" to be "the hand that once and for all chronicled and laid bare the virtues . . . of this extraordinary phase of social progress."[17]

The fiction of Wister's early years in the West revolves around a combination of the landscape's "wildness" and the lives of a company of men "without any moral sense." Later his feeling that the older West had now become a phase in the history of American civilization was coupled with a rediscovery of some of the attractive features of his life in the East. The result was a curious return to the days of the Cheyenne Club and his cattle baron friends, now seen through the haze of years, and a romanticizing of the life they and their heroic ranch hands led.

The two leading protagonists of Wister's early western fiction are the picaros Specimen Jones and Lin McLean. The first is featured in a collection of stories Wister began for *Harper's* in 1893

16. Frances Kemble Wister Stokes, *My Father, Owen Wister* (Laramie, Wyo. 1952), p. 14; Owen Wister, *The Virginian* (New York, 1902), p. viii.

17. Stokes, *Owen Wister Out West*, pp. 33, 35, 39, 112, 118.

and published as *Red Men and White* in 1895, and the second is the subject of an episodic novel which bears his name, written in 1895 and 1896 and published in 1897. Jones is a likable vagabond, "seasoned by the frontier," who has tried a little of everything: "town and country, ranches, saloons, stage-driving, marriage occasionally, and latterly mines." "He had," Wister notes, "exhausted all the important sensations, and did not care much for anything any more. Perfect health and strength kept him from discovering that he was a saddened, drifting man." After six years of wandering through Arizona, Jones and a friend enlisted in the army on an impulse, but Specimen's "frontier personality . . . was scarcely yet disciplined into the military machine of the regulation pattern."[18] During his army tenure Jones manages, among other things, to mistake the general of his troop for a peddler and arrest the governor of his territory to save him from a particularly ticklish legislative struggle. He achieves certain small successes but primarily serves as a humorous foil to more respectable figures. Actually, the Specimen Jones stories are whimsical salutes to the frivolity of a nomad.

If Jones is a drifter, Lin McLean is a will-o'-the-wisp. Lin "came in the country about seventy-eight . . . and rode for the Bordeaux Outfit most a year, and quit." He then "blew in at Cheyenne till he was broke, and worked over on the Platte," "rode for Balaam awhile on Butte Creek," and later "drifted to Green River . . . and was around with a prospecting outfit on Galena Creek by Pitchstone Canyon." A contemporary of Lin's, aware of his habits, once predicted that "he'll wake about noon tomorrow in a dive, without a cent. . . . Then he'll come back on a freight and begin over again."[19]

But although Lin is a perpetual adolescent, a fool for women, and a hopeless vagabond, he possesses qualities of honesty and frankness which serve to contrast him favorably in Wister's mind with certain members of the "city crowd." In "How Lin McLean Went East," which appeared in *Harper's Monthly* in 1893 and was reprinted with slight changes as Chapter 3 of *Lin McLean*, Wister used his picaresque "son of the sagebrush" to expose flaws in the sham civilization of the East and to hold up the virtues of a frontier life.

18. Owen Wister, *Red Men and White* (New York, 1895), pp. 47, 149.
19. Owen Wister, *Lin McLean* (New York, 1897), pp. 8, 134.

In the midst of his wanderings Lin had an impulse to return to Swampscott, Massachusetts, his old home, to see his brother Frank and visit his parents' grave. At the station in Boston he greeted his brother enthusiastically, but "Frank McLean's heart did not warm" to the "long, brown fellow" from the West. Frank "saw he was being made conspicuous. He saw men and women stare in the station, and he saw them staring as he and his Western brother went through the streets." He thought "of the refined friends he should have to introduce his brother to; for he . . . now belonged to a small club where the paying-tellers of banks played cards every night, and the head clerk of the Parker House was president. . . . For the twentieth time Frank shifted a sidelong eye over his brother's clothes."

When Lin inquired about Swampscott, Frank replied that it was a "dead little town"; and when Lin announced his plans to "take a look at the old house," Frank responded, "Oh, that's been pulled down since—I forgot the year they improved that block." Eventually Frank caught sight of one of the members of his club staring at Lin with "diverted amazement on his face," and the strain became too great. "Lin," he blurted out, "while you're running with our crowd, you don't want to wear that style of hat, you know":

> [Lin] stopped dead short, and his hand slid off his brother's shoulder. "You've made it plain," he said evenly, slanting his steady eyes down into Frank's . . . "Run along with your crowd, and I'll not bother yu' more with comin' round and caus' yu' to feel ashamed. . . . I guess there ain't no more to be said, only one thing. If yu' see me around on the street, don't yu' try and talk, for I'd be liable to close your jaw up, and maybe yu'd have more of a job explainin' that to your crowd than you've had makin' me see what kind of a man I've got for a brother."

The next morning Lin took a train for Swampscott, where he noticed that the grave of his parents had been left untended. From there he "blew in" to New York, hoping for some amusement, but left with nothing but "a deep hatred for the crowded, scrambling East." He bought a train ticket for Green River, Wyoming, and after four days, when "civilization was utterly emptied out of the world, and he saw a bunch of cattle, and, galloping among them, his spurred and booted kindred, his manner took on that alertness a horse shows on turning into the home road." "No sir!" he mused,

"Yu' can blow in a thousand dollars like I did in New York, and it'll not give yu' any more home feelin' than what cattle has put in a stock-yard. Nor it wouldn't have in Boston neither. Now this country here (he waved his hand towards the endless sage-brush), seein' it once more, I know where my home is, and I wouldn't live nowhere else."[20]

Frank McLean has become so caught up in the trappings of civilization that he has lost the qualities that in Wister's eyes made a man "civilized"—reverence for family ties, sense of tradition, and loyalty to kindred—but Lin exhibits these qualities and senses the selfishness that lies beneath Frank's superficial polish. In this gift for stripping away the veneer of civilization and catching the true gist of a man's nature, Lin, for Wister, is representative of his "spurred and booted kindred." "Celluloid good-fellowship passes for ivory with nine in ten of the city crowd," the erstwhile Philadelphian later wrote, "but not so with the sons of the sagebrush. They live nearer nature, and they know better."[21]

It must have amused Wister to depict the great seriousness with which Frank McLean reacted to his club, the solemn ties he felt toward an association of clerks and bank tellers. To his delight in the unspoiled western wilderness Wister added a certain upper-class condescension toward men of commerce: he reserved some of his harshest prose for the "fetid commercial bores" he saw invading the West. "Every state in the Union seems to spawn them," he wrote in 1891, "and they infest every mile of railroad in operation. . . . The faces, the minds and the talk of these commercials in the Pullman cars are inferior to those in the conductor who takes the tickets and the brakeman who swings the lamp." This is reminiscent of Remington's remarks about the encroachments of industrial America upon the West, and indeed Wister noted after a conversation with Remington in 1893 that the illustrator "used almost the same words that have of late been in my head, that this continent does not hold a nation any longer but is merely a strip of land on which a crowd is struggling for riches."

"I am a thin and despondent man," Wister wrote after meeting Remington, "and every day compel myself to see the bright side of things because I know that the dark side impresses me unduly."[22]

20. Ibid., pp. 33–35, 36, 37–38, 40.
21. Wister, *The Virginian*, p. 22.
22. Stokes, *Owen Wister Out West*, pp. 97–98, 181.

If so, Wister was remarkably self-disciplined, for if Remington's "romantic" phase, as evidenced in such works as *John Ermine*, may be said to depict the dark, tragic side of the American West, Wister's writings in the same period emphasized those aspects of the western experience which were brightest for the future of the region and for America. This difference in tone between Remington and Wister can be seen by a comparison of Remington's *Men with the Bark On* with Wister's collection of stories *The Jimmyjohn Boss*, both of which were published in 1900. Though Dean Drake, the hero of *The Jimmyjohn Boss*, is a product of older, wilder times, he has the ability to adapt himself to the oncoming civilization from the East that Remington's protagonists lack. He suggests in his person a possible synthesis of the two regions and points in the direction of Wister's American colossus of Rhodes, the Virginian, who was meant to straddle the gulf between East and West.

Drake had been "raised on miscellaneous wickedness"; "a look at my insides would be liable to make you say your prayers," he confessed to a companion at one point. At nineteen, Drake is already a ranch foreman and exhibits a toughness and wisdom which indicate the depths of his training in the hard ways of the West. He had intended to enforce a no-drinking rule on his ranch, but a peddler smuggled liquor in to the cowboys, who in their stupor plotted to kill Drake. On a tip from the Chinese cook, Drake escaped, secured aid from the nearest ranch, and waited with his allies while the drunkards regained their senses and asked for their jobs back, whereupon he assigned them to other ranches to "stir [them] in with decenter blood." Throughout his perilous situation Drake demonstrates what Wister termed that "say-nothing strength that gets there." "The Lord helps those who help themselves," he notes after escaping from the ranch. "I've prospered. For a nineteen year old I've hooked my claw fairly deep here and there. As for to-day—why that's in the game too. It was their deal. . . . A joker dropped into their hands. It's my deal now, and I have some jokers myself." Here Drake demonstrates a keen sense of the mores of a world where one tried to anticipate wickedness and, if necessary, did the enemy one wicked turn better.

Yet Drake has a vision of a more civilized way of life, which accompanies his darker thoughts. "Some day, when I'm old," he says at one point, "I mean to live respectable under my own cabin and vine. Wife and everything."[23] He whistles light opera tunes, understands a smattering of Chinese, and develops a friendship with a New England schoolteacher named Bolles, whose presence symbolizes for Wister the more palatable aspects of eastern civilization, such as mildness, culture, and morality.

Dean Drake is a pivotal figure in the development of Wister's protagonists. More rogue than gentleman, he nevertheless demonstrates an ability to admire a man such as Bolles, who has never lived by his gun. This ability, which enabled Drake to transcend the level of a picaro, is spelled out by another Wister hero two years later: "I used to despise an Eastern man because his clothes were not Western. I was very young then. . . . A Western man is a good thing. And he generally knows that. But he has a heap to learn. And he generally don't know that."[24] This is the Virginian, and the symbolic qualities of that renowned horseman of the plains, can best be seen in terms of the heroic phase of Wister's fiction, representing the resolution in his mind of the quarrels with his heritage that had led him West in the first place.

A series of events enabled Wister to reintegrate himself with his boyhood East in the years after 1897. With the publication of the Lin McLean stories he had become an acknowledged success as a writer and was able to avoid "creeping back to the displeased law with my tail between my legs." "As far as the public goes," he noted, "I'm popular enough to have moved that purveyor of mere popularity *The Youth's Companion* to write me unsolicited for a story." Wister had always been painfully aware that his promise at Harvard (he had graduated summa cum laude) had not been measured in performance: he had had to resort to social connections to find work at Lee, Higginson and with the law firm of Ralston and Rawle. Now he could hold his head up with Proper Philadelphia and enjoy the rarefied air of its clubs and gatherings with a sense of a vocational foundation underneath.

In addition, after a long and not always peaceful bachelorhood, Wister married his cousin, Mary Channing Wister, in 1898. Not until that year, Wister's daughter maintains, was her father "at ease with himself." Even after "giving up the unpalatable grind of

23. Owen Wister, *The Jimmyjohn Boss* (New York, 1900), pp. 6, 9, 51, 61.
24. Wister, *The Virginian*, p. 498.

the law and devoting himself to writing," Wister was "restless and unhappy. . . . The satisfaction and peace of mind of at last having his own house must have been a blessing . . . his wife's steady nerves and health made all serene around her." Late in life Wister himself was to say in reference to his long companionship with Roosevelt: "There is but one piece of spiritual good fortune that surpasses having had the friendship of a great man, and that is to have had a perfect marriage."[25]

In January of 1902 the Wisters, accompanied by their three young children, returned to Charleston, South Carolina, where they had honeymooned, and spent the winter and most of the spring there. Wister had most of *The Virginian* still to complete, including the crucial task of weaving previously published short stories into novel form. The effect of his surroundings was unmistakable. "Of Charleston at the time," Wister later wrote, "the ancient Charleston of fine traditions and fierce prejudices, something still was left. . . . The ladies . . . shut firmly out certain things that are more than welcome today, such as publicity in the social columns, and conversations about the stock market and such other matters, which they deemed proper in a man's office, and not in a drawing room." Here was the old Philadelphia of his youth, which he had once thought stifling and now found charming. As he "pegged away at the Virginian," he "wandered and meditated and looked across the dreamy empty rivers to their dreamy, empty shores and the grey-veiled live-oaks that were all of a piece with the wistful silence." In this romantic atmosphere all of Wister's dreams about the possibilities of America seemed to take shape. "Full of echoes," he wrote, "this little, coherent, self-respecting place was also full of life; retaining its native identity, its English-thinking, English-feeling, English-believing authenticity holding on tight to George Washington and the true American tradition." That tradition, for Wister, had become once again related to an upper-class way of life. "What an oasis in our . . . desert of mongrel din and haste," he noted, his sense of the past returning with a vengeance. Wister had found the "real America" in Wyoming; he now found the "true American tradition" in old Charleston. His task in *The Virginian* was to insure that the two were not incompatible.[26]

25. Stokes, *Owen Wister Out West*, pp. 13, 201–02; Wister, *Roosevelt, The Story of a Friendship*, p. 58.

26. Ibid., pp. 100, 103.

In the "heroic" phase of Wister's response to the West his themes are historically oriented and his protagonists romantically portrayed. He departed radically from his previous vow to tell the truth about the West in *The Virginian*, which claimed to "present faithfully Wyoming between 1874 and 1890" but did nothing of the kind. One critic maintains that "it is strange that Wister could have called his *Virginian* an historical novel of the cattle-country when there is not one scene set on the range among the cattle, and when the cowboys seem throughout to spend their days in playful pranks, in love-making, in thief-hunting, in anything except work." Two others, in the course of their description of cowboy life in the Old West, have implied that *The Virginian* is not representative of Wyoming at any time.[27]

The courtship of Molly Wood and the Virginian, around which most of Wister's novel revolves, is highly contrived. Few women at all lived in the Wild West, and cowboys on ranges almost never saw them. The social life of cowpunchers consisted for the most part of blowouts in saloons, not of quiet walks in peaceful valleys, but the Virginian (a ranch foreman) has uncommon amounts of free time and is able to court Molly in a slow and leisurely fashion. Although in 1895 Wister had said of cowboys, "War they made in plenty, but not love; for the woman they saw was not the woman a man can take into his heart," by 1902 "truth" had apparently become a secondary concern. The Wisters' return to Charleston, the scene of their honeymoon, had doubtless brought back a whole flood of romantic memories, and the Virginian's gentle initiation of Molly Wood (Mrs. Wister was also called Molly) into the rites of marriage was a reenactment of scenes dear to Wister's heart. The Victorian courtship of the cowpuncher and his sweetheart also awakened in Wister a sense of his own background: he wrote his mother that he thought it "essential that the hero should meet the Great Aunt."[28]

Wister's most significant departure from "reality" was the deliberate idealization of his hero. In the first western story he wrote, "Hank's Woman," published in *Harper's Monthly* in 1892, the

27. E. Douglas Branch, *The Cowboy and His Interpreters* (New York, 1926), p. 192; Joseph B. Frantz and J. Ernest Choate, Jr., *The American Cowboy, The Myth and the Reality* (Norman, Okla., 1955), esp. chaps. 1, 4, 6, and 8.

28. Owen Wister, "The Evolution of the Cowpuncher," *Harper's Monthly* (September 1895), quoted in Stokes, *Owen Wister Out West*, p. 258.

Virginian is portrayed as a standard picaresque figure with a certain indefinable presence. He "indulges himself in several months' drifting" and states that he is not ready for "any such thing as a fam'ly yet. . . . Not till I can't help it." Although the Virginian "was unfathomable,"[29] little is made of the strong and silent aspects of his personality; in Wister's early stories he remains a picaro. By 1902, however, Wister had apparently lost all recollection of his earlier model, for the Virginian now advances resolutely toward his goals, has all the qualities of a gentleman, and eagerly learns Shakespeare, Jane Austen, Browning, and Thackeray from his sweetheart Molly Wood.

According to Mody Boatright, the Virginian is a "folk hero," in that he possesses "prowess and cleverness," qualities which are deemed "universally heroic" in the American imagination. "Prowess, when accompanied by the virtues of bravery, skill and loyalty, is a romantic ideal, aristocratic in its indifference to material gain, and accessible only to those who have economic security or are indifferent to it." "Cleverness," on the other hand, "is the middle classes' weapon against the aristocracy, realistic and often cynical."[30] These qualities can be seen in many American literary heroes of the nineteenth and twentieth centuries—Leatherstocking, Huck Finn, Jay Gatsby, and Holden Caulfield, for example—but a more illuminating discussion of heroism in *The Virginian*, for present purposes, would center on the cowboy protagonist's role as a cultural hero. The term "cultural" incorporates social change, whereas "folk" implies an idealized native consensus of a persistent nature. Americans have had different success models at different times in their history, and their cultural heroes are products of trends and changes in the social and economic structure of the nation. The interaction between the idealized traits of Wister's horseman of the plains and the aspirations of Americans at the close of the nineteenth century is particularly significant.

The Virginian's "manliness" is a quality to which a 1902 reader could warmly respond. It has been suggested that Roosevelt and Remington, as well as Wister, were attracted to the masculine

29. Wister, "Hank's Woman," reprinted in *The Jimmyjohn Boss*, pp. 252, 253, 254, 257, 259, 261.

30. Mody C. Boatright, "The American Myth Rides the Range," *Southwest Review, 36* (Summer 1951), pp. 157–65, esp. p. 157.

aspects of the West for personal reasons, but the individual needs of each were strongly related to tensions within American culture at the last quarter of the nineteenth century. The triumph of industrial enterprise paradoxically produced a heightened consciousness of women as delicate flowers and men as their defenders against the evils of a strange new world, resulting in a nationwide assertion of masculinity. The Virginian's manliness is never in question: a shade over six feet, he is referred to as a "giant," and although he is gentle and polite to women, they are quick to sense his power. Molly Wood eventually abandons her civilized heritage in Vermont to marry the Virginian, because, as she confides to Grandmother Stark, "I wanted a man who was a man."

Wister's contemporaries must also have applauded the manner in which the Virginian rose from humble origins to become a captain of industry. Part of the success ethic of the post-Civil-War generation was self-help, and as a young man the Virginian "found out what he could do, and settled down and did it." He "put his savings in banks," because he "had to work right hard gathering them in," and he chose not to live off his earnings in the cattle bonanza but bought land as an insurance for the future. At the novel's close the ex-dirt farmer is "an important man, with a strong grip on many various enterprises." The Virginian's adaptability to industrialization, a far cry from Remington's feeling that cowboys and the industrial West are incompatible, is one indication of Wister's strong desire to integrate the Old West and the new order of the East in the person of his horseman of the plains. As the Virginian articulates the doctrines he practices, he extends his self-help philosophy to a larger view of life. "It may be," he reflects, "that them whose pleasure brings yu' into this world owes yu' a living. But that don't make the world responsible. The world did not beget you. I reckon man helps them that helps themselves." In a bet, in a card game, in "all horse transactions and other matters of similar business," the same rule applies: "a man must take care of himself." Competition is the essence, and the best man wins.

It might seem that the Virginian holds up a kind of inverse morality as the only expedient in a society where an honest man is all the law one can find for five hundred miles—he who lives best lives roughest, meanest, and trickiest—but in actuality another characteristic which must have endeared him to his readers was his

combining of an acute awareness of blackguardism with a gentlemanly response to it. On one occasion he says to the outlaw
Trampas, "We ain't a Christian outfit a little bit, and maybe we
have most forgotten what decency feels like. But I reckon we
haven't *plumb* forgot what it means," and he then forces Trampas
to withdraw his off-color remarks about the character of Molly
Wood ("Stand on your laigs, you pole-cat, and say you're a liar!").
In a rough world of rough men the hero is distinguished by his
graciousness, civility, and reserve. The narrator of *The Virginian*
finds that "here in flesh and blood was a truth which I had long believed in words, but never met before. The creature we call a
gentleman lies deep in the hearts of thousands that are born without a chance to master the outward graces of the type."

Late nineteenth-century Americans revered the "rugged indi-
vidualist," but matters of decorum were highly prized, even among
the shadiest entrepreneurs. "The inner-directed business and banking entrepreneurs of this buccaneering age were only too eager to
conform to the strict Victorian code of manners when they entered
the drawing-rooms of society," notes one student of the business
community. It was as if the world of manners formed a counter-
weight against the world of business, reassuring the businessman
that virtue still existed.

Though he has come into contact with a good many of the "dark
places in life," the Virginian is careful not to reveal them. Even in
delirium, he addresses Molly as "Miss Wood," and "ma'am," and his
ravings, Wister notes, "did not run into intimate, coarse matters."
Unlike some of his cronies, he does not boast of his sexual exploits,
and in matters of dress he is so careful that when Molly brings him
to Vermont to meet her family, "Bennington was disappointed. To
see get out of the train merely a tall man with a usual straw hat, a
Scotch homespun suit of a rather better cut than most in Bennington—this was dull." "I have made one discovery," Molly says to her
hero. "You are fonder of good clothes than I am."[31]

Finally, the Virginian is a "good American." Impressed with
their technological and financial triumphs yet annoyed by crowded
conditions in their cities and an influx of immigrants from southern
and eastern Europe, Americans in the nineties were aggressive

31. Wister, *The Virginian*, pp. 4, 12, 17, 49, 111, 261, 270, 337, 372, 399, 497, 498,
502.

patriots whose zeal sometimes surpassed their tolerance. The heredity and veterans' societies that grew by leaps and bounds in this period often marked their patriotism with an air of exclusiveness and nativism.[32] The Virginian, for one, is not above an occasional nativist or racist salvo: he sings a song deriding the intelligence of Negroes ("I never went to college, but I'se come mighty nigh—I peeked through de door as I went by"); calls Germans "Dutchmen," Jews "Hebes," and doesn't consider Indians humans. For the most part, however, his Americanness is reflected in the breadth of his experience and the range of his background. Born in Virginia, at twenty-four he had seen Arkansas, Texas, New Mexico, Arizona, California, Oregon, Idaho, Montana, and Wyoming. By twenty-nine he has been East and confessed that a western man has a heap to learn, and his "various enterprises" will apparently increase his prestige and widen his scope.[33] Wister must have especially cherished this quality, which symbolized his attempt to combine the best features of nature and civilization, rugged individualism and gentlemanliness, past and present, and West and East into a more perfect whole. He suggests in the marriage of Molly and the Virginian that the "true American" traditions of the eastern seaboard will constantly be revitalized as they pass westward, creating an even stronger and more unified nation.

Wister's effort to reaffirm the spirit of the Old West thus emerged most clearly in his attempts to demonstrate that some of its heroes could thrive in the twentieth century. Although "the horseman, the cowpuncher, the last romantic figure upon our soil" will never come again, for "he rides in his historic yesterday," the beat of his hardy life could pound through the ages. "His wild kind," Wister wrote in 1902, "has been among us always . . . a hero without wings."[34] Behind the figure of the Virginian lay a vision of a twentieth-century America that could include old Charleston, the new industrial East, and the spirit of the Wild West.[35]

32. Wallace Evan Davies, *Patriotism on Parade* (Cambridge, Mass., 1955), passim.

33. Wister, *The Virginian*, pp. 62, 498.

34. Wister, preface to the 1902 edition of *The Virginian*, pp. viii, ix.

35. "I had found in Charleston," wrote Wister, "many people, whether urban or rustic, who were the sort of people I was . . . *Americans;* with whom I felt just as direct a national kinship as I felt with the Western cowpunchers" (Wister, *Roosevelt*, p. 247; italics Wister's).

Perhaps Wister sensed that hundreds of Americans of his day had similar visions: the reassertion of the traditions of an older America in a modern context; the revival of old social patterns in a technological age; a balance between the world of their fathers and the world they found their children growing up in. And, for a time, these visions seem to approximate reality. A month after the publication of *The Virginian,* Wister received a letter from the President of the United States. "[The Virginian] is a remarkable novel," it read. "If I were not President, and therefore unable to be quoted, I should like nothing better than to write a review of it. I have read it all through with absorbed interest and have found myself looking forward to taking up the book again all through the time I have been at work."[36]

Theodore Roosevelt, socialite and cowboy, had climbed the eastern political ladder to the White House; in so doing, he had convinced the American populace that he was also a man of the West. Americans had accepted men with the bark on and responded to the challenge of a hardy life: cartoons of the times pictured Roosevelt as a cowboy far more than as a socialite. Wister was fortunate enough to dramatize the full acceptance of the cowboy as one of America's own; as his novel climbed to the top of the best-seller lists, he must have realized how many Americans had come to identify with the rude yet romantic life of his horseman of the plains. He had thousands of requests to write a sequel to *The Virginian* but turned instead to a portrait of old Charleston, whose atmosphere had helped to make him famous. When he looked again to the West for subject matter, his magic moment had passed, and where he had once found heroes, he now, like Remington, found victims of the march of civilization. In a conversation with Roosevelt in 1912 he revealed plans to write a novel on "the tragedy of the cowpuncher who survives his own era and cannot adjust himself to the [one] which succeeds it."[37] Such was to be Wister's own fate: the man who had seen the Cheyenne Club at its heyday was to celebrate the 100th anniversary of the Philadelphia Club in 1934 with a withering blast at the New Deal.

36. Letter from Theodore Roosevelt to Owen Wister, June 7, 1902, Wister Papers.
37. Wister, *Roosevelt,* p. 319.

Part III: East and West in the Decade of Consensus

Remington, Roosevelt, and Wister were all individuals with unique psychological systems, but their backgrounds contained similar regional and genealogical characteristics. As writers on the West, moreover, they were heirs and contributors to a particular tradition of eastern literary responses to the wilderness beyond the Mississippi. The initial western journey of each man cannot be understood without an understanding of his particular adolescent experiences in the East, and his response to the West is equally indecipherable without a knowledge of his experiences beyond the Mississippi and the attitudes he brought to bear upon them.

Though some attention has already been given to the fluctuating economic trends, shifting status patterns, and the changing literary themes that accompanied the rise of industrial America, the chronology of the three men's careers and the impact their response to the West made upon their eastern contemporaries dictate that further consideration be given to the East they left behind. By 1885 all three men were on the plains or in the Rockies, but by 1895 each had returned East on a permanent basis. None had published an account of the West prior to 1885, but each had become a widely successful exponent of western life by 1902. In their youth all three had experienced the impetus of urbanization and industrialization, and together they had been able to explore in their young manhood the ramifications of a counterurban and counterindustrial existence. In so doing, they came to grips with two large manifestations of the dual nature of nineteenth-century American civilization: the complex of factors (such as ethnic heterogeneity, metropolitan living, and corporate enterprise) associated with the East, and its counterpoint, the image of an ethnically homogeneous, rural, and individualistic West.

Beginning approximately with the outbreak of the Spanish-American War in 1898 and extending certainly through Roosevelt's two presidential administrations and possibly through that of Taft, the United States enjoyed "a time of sureness and unity, at least on the surface of . . . life." Historians, according to one student of the early twentieth century, have found the ten-odd years after 1898 "a period of general agreement and confidence," a decade when "ultimate values and goals could be taken for granted," for Americans "believed so deeply in a consensus on these matters that they could not imagine a serious challenge." In particular, "the writers of best sellers" and "the men elected to national office" did not question "the wide and slightly vague consensus which held together moral certainty and progressive change." Wister, as a best-selling novelist, Remington, as the nation's leading illustrator, and Roosevelt, as, among other things, "the model for right-thinking American youth," become closely identified with this "consensus."[1]

Eastern Americans of the 1898–1909 period responded to the western writings of Roosevelt, Wister, and Remington largely in terms of the counterpointed images of East and West.[2] As the prodigals returned East and assumed positions of prominence, they brought with them a series of selected sense impressions which their public popularized into a cohesive, if simplistic image. The implications of this image were subsequently examined by a populace curiously anxious to find it attractive, and a strong desire on the part of Americans of the 1900s to strike a "conventional balance between East and West"[3] is found at the heart of the "consensus" of the ten-odd years after 1898. Consideration of Roosevelt, Remington, and Wister as image-makers for a particular generation thus leads eventually to a fuller understanding of that generation's conception of American civilization.

1. Henry F. May, *The End of American Innocence* (New York, 1959), pp. 18, 21, 28, 29, 107.

2. The term West, as used in this and succeeding chapters, represents a rural, egalitarian, individualistic subculture that was, on the one hand, noneastern and, on the other, identifiably American.

3. May, *The End of American Innocence,* p. 47.

7. The Rough Riders: Regiment of True Americans

Sunday, the 22nd of May, in 1898 was a memorable day in the history of San Antonio, Texas. The First Volunteer United States Cavalry assembled in squadron formation on the grounds of the Exposition building, a mile from the center of town, to hear a reading of the articles of war. Colonel Leonard Wood majestically presented each captain with a copy of the articles, and the troops listened as "the stately passages were pronounced in solemn sentences." Lieutenant Colonel Theodore Roosevelt wore his gravest expression as the articles were read, and when it came his turn to speak, his eyes blazed as he announced to the men that marching orders had been received and they were to prepare to embark for Cuba.

A great cheer rose from the troops, and Roosevelt and Wood "embraced like schoolboys." Twenty picked voices from the ranks broke into the strains of "How Firm a Foundation," and the rest of the regiment joined in the chorus. A trumpeter took up the refrain, and the singing could be heard for a mile around. At the conclusion of the first selection A. R. Perry, famed as the "best bronco buster in the regiment," stepped forward and began "Onward Christian Soldiers" in his resonant tenor. "Brothers, we are treading where the saints have trod," he sang. "We are not divided, all one body we," and his companions, their emotions now at the breaking point, filled the dusty air with the sounds of their sobs. Together they launched with Perry into the chorus, and in their minds' eye they saw the cross of Jesus next to the American flag at the head of their ranks as they marched against the Spanish.[1]

1. The standard accounts for the formation and training of the Rough Riders in their pre-Cuba phase are Edward Marshall, *The Story of the Rough Riders* (New York, 1899); Theodore Roosevelt, *The Rough Riders* (New York, 1902); and Clifford F. Westermeier, *Who Rush to Glory* (Caldwell, Idaho, 1958). Here see Marshall, p. 44; Roosevelt, p. 46; Westermeier, p. 79.

The triumphant processions of the Rough Riders and their brother volunteer regiments—the Second Volunteer U.S. Cavalry (Torrey's Rocky Mountain Riders) and the Third Volunteers (Grigsby's Cowboys) from their base camps in Texas, South Dakota, and Wyoming—to Florida marked the crest of a wave of fanfare and hoopla that had begun with the War Department's decision on April 25 to raise three regiments of mounted riflemen to fight the Spaniard. As the Rough Riders arrived at the San Antonio railroad station prior to embarking, they saw that the cars had been decked in red, white, and blue bunting, with signs praising each state and territory that had contributed to the formation of the regiment. Girls in white dresses lined up to be kissed, threw posies at the trains, and snipped off the soldiers' buttons as souvenirs. As the regiment crossed the Deep South on its way to Tampa, it was often forced to halt in order to receive gifts. Women baked pies and cakes, knitted socks, and offered pitchers of milk for the boys in brown. A carefree engineer slammed on his brakes upon noticing a Negro farmhand pulling a wagon filled with watermelons, and the volunteers helped themselves. Former members of the Confederacy buried an old hatchet and opened their hearts to the Rough Riders, some of whom were Yankees. It seemed as if the whole nation was echoing the First U.S.'s battle cry: "Rough, tough, we're the stuff, We want to fight and we can't get enough."[2]

The concept of employing cowboys and other inhabitants of the Wild West as cavalrymen was not entirely new: Roosevelt, as part of his search for new challenges in 1886, had conceived the notion of organizing a cowboy troop to fight against Mexico, whose relations with the U.S. had become somewhat strained. "I have not the least idea there will be any trouble," he wrote Henry Cabot Lodge in August, "but as my chances of doing anything in the future worth doing seem to grow continually smaller, I intend to grasp at every opportunity that turns up." Roosevelt's desire to do something worth doing was considerably stronger than America's desire to fight the Mexicans, and a short time later he confessed that his anxieties occasionally led him to foolhardiness. "If a war had come

2. Roosevelt, *The Rough Riders,* pp. 52–53, 142–43, 145; Marshall, *Story of the Rough Riders,* p. 19.

off," he informed Lodge, "I would surely have had behind me as utterly reckless a set of desperadoes as ever sat in the saddle."[3]

By 1898 America seemed more seriously inclined toward international involvement, and the forthcoming crusade against Spain awakened Roosevelt's old notions of glorious belligerency. At thirty-eight, however, he was more prudent than at twenty-six, and when President McKinley offered him the colonelcy of a prospective volunteer regiment, he declined it, pleading insufficient military experience. Leonard Wood, a former Indian fighter and McKinley's chief army medical adviser, thus received command of the First Volunteers, with Roosevelt as Lieutenant Colonel. This seemed to satisfy Roosevelt's ambition without jeopardizing his image or impeding the war effort, and so the first regiment of cowboy volunteers came into being.

Publicity and myth have contributed to misconceptions about the Cuban campaign. At the outbreak of the war Wood's and Roosevelt's regiment of volunteers was merely one of three units that were simultaneously forming, but while the national press waxed enthusiastic over the Rough Riders and their "vigorous, manly, dashing young leader," the Second and Third Volunteer U.S. Cavalries, under the respective leadership of Colonels Jay Torrey and Melvin Grigsby, suffered from hard luck and lack of publicity. Wood's and Roosevelt's connections in the War Department assured the First Volunteers of actually taking part in the Cuban campaign, but Grigsby's and Torrey's units were destined to spend the whole of 1898 camped at Chickamauga, Georgia, and Jacksonville, Florida.[4] Moreover, the now famous "charge up San Juan Hill" was actually directed against "Kettle" Hill, a flanking outpost, and contributed far less to America's victory than Admiral Cervera's decision to sail out of Santiago and face four U.S. battleships; Roosevelt clearly did not ride at the head of his troops as they swarmed up Kettle Hill; and "the Americans made a mess of their war effort ... the real explanation of the quick American military success lay in the even more incredible inefficiency and blundering of the

3. Roosevelt to Lodge, August 10, 1886, and August 20, 1886, quoted in Hagedorn, *Roosevelt in the Bad Lands,* pp. 413, 415.

4. See Westermeier, *Who Rush to Glory,* for the best account of Torrey's Rocky Mountain Riders and Grigsby's Cowboys.

Spaniards."[5] But newspaper war correspondents, who in 1898 served not only as reporters of recent developments in the progress of the war itself but also as publicity agents for the war effort, searched for ways to give the daily routine of men in uniform a relevance to the civilian population; they subordinated the uneventful tasks of the regulars and volunteers to the acknowledged greater glories of America's crusade on behalf of bleeding Cuba and found heroism where we might find tedium or pathos. And of all the lives dedicated to the cause of righteousness, none were more potentially heroic than those of the Rough Riders.

From their birth the First Volunteers had been blessed with a lieutenant colonel who seemed incapable of staying out of the limelight. Since his return to New York in 1886 Roosevelt had made a futile but well-publicized run for Mayor, secured an appointment to the Civil Service Commission under President Harrison in 1889 and a cherished nonpartisan reappointment under Cleveland in 1893, become president of New York's Board of Police Commissioners in 1895, and initiated a term as Assistant Secretary of the Navy under McKinley in 1897. While attempting to climb this eastern political ladder, Roosevelt had continued to stress his interest in the West, writing his life of Benton, *The Winning of the West,* and his articles on "Ranch Life and the Hunting Trail" between 1886 and 1896. The extent to which he had managed to cultivate his image as a man of East and West can be seen in the *Daily Oklahoma State Capital's* reaction to his appointment as Colonel Wood's second in command: "Secretary of Navy Roosevelt was himself a cowboy early in his life and is willing to take desperate chances. He does not know the meaning of fear. It is foreign to his composition." In the earliest dispatches concerning the formation of cowboy regiments Roosevelt's name was not mentioned, but as soon as the Denver *Republican* coined the phrase "Rough Riders," the alliteration was too tempting to resist, and the First Volunteers became "Teddy's Terrors" and "Roosevelt's Rough Riders" forevermore. "Colonel Wood," the New York *Press* commented, "is lost sight of entirely in the effulgence of Teethadore."[6]

5. C. Vann Woodward in John M. Blum et al., *The National Experience* (New York, 1963), p. 506.

6. See William H. Harbrough, *Power and Responsibility* (New York, 1961), and Blum, *The Republican Roosevelt,* for Roosevelt's political career; *Daily Oklahoma State Capital* (Guthrie, Okla.), May 4, 1898.

The Rough Riders consisted of twelve troops—five from New Mexico Territory, three from Arizona Territory, two from the Indian Territory, one from Oklahoma Territory, and one from "New York and the Eastern States"—but it was this last troop, K, which aroused the most attention and generated the most publicity. Although only 34 of the 99 men from K troop whose addresses were available came from the East, with only 17 from New York City proper and only 2 who gave metropolitan men's clubs as residences,[7] the impression persisted that Troop K of the Rough Riders was a collection of "swells," who had left their clubs to follow Roosevelt, carrying their dress suits in their hands. War correspondent Edward Marshall, in his *Story of the Rough Riders*, which appeared in 1899, gave "an idea of K Troop":

> Woodbury Kane was a polo player of note, and a hard rider on the hunting field. He came of a fighting family; played football at Harvard.
>
> Craig Wadsworth was one of the "fighting Genesee Wadsworths," whose name had always been among the foremost in annals of the country in war. He had led the Genesee Valley hunts for some years, and at other times had led many a German in New York ballrooms.
>
> William Tiffany was a nephew of the late Mrs. August Belmont, and a grandnephew of Commodore Perry. He spent several years on the plains of Montana.
>
> Reginald or "Reggie" Ronalds was the son of Mrs. Pierre Lorrilard Ronalds, who is the best known American in London, is a great friend of the Prince and Princess of Wales, and has a voice that has held Europe and America under its spell for two generations. Ronalds once played tackle on a famous Yale football team.
>
> Dudley S. Dean, captain of the Harvard football team of '91, was in charge of the business of the Mexican Central R.R. at Las Vegas, New Mexico, up to the time when he resigned and came North to enlist.
>
> Horace Devereaux, from Colorado Springs, was the leader of one of Princeton's most famous football teams.

---

7. "Muster-Out Roll" for First Volunteer United States Cavalry, reprinted in Roosevelt, *The Rough Riders*, pp. 238–69.

Marshall lists four more Harvard graduates, two more Yale athletes, two "famous clubmen," and one "well-known polo player" before turning to other matters. "I devote considerable space to these men," he tells us, "in order to illustrate the extraordinary materials of which the regiment was made."[8]

In fact, the Easterners in the Rough Riders created a stir far disproportionate to their number. The press, particularly its western representatives, had a field day with the "dudes" from K Troop when they arrived in San Antonio on the 10th of May to begin training. "The Texas cowboys who have the pleasure to mess with this party of New York 'high rollers' will have an enjoyable time so long as they are in camp," the *Daily Express* noted. "Ninety percent of them carry a large wad in their side pockets with which to play a little game of draw and large bank accounts behind them. Some of them have their 'men' with them to care for their uniforms and top boots at a salary of $60 a month." The Denver *Evening Post* suffered from regional self-consciousness: "The New York swells," it pointed out, "who enlisted in the 1st regiment of U.S. volunteer cavalry had to leave their valets at home. They are probably nice fellows and all that, but it must be remembered that every man sent by New Mexico as a member of that regiment is just as good as the best New York swell." And the Las Vegas, New Mexico, *Daily Optic* was the most apprehensive of all: it noted that "there is some local fear expressed since forty of the New York 400 have gone to San Antonio . . . that the simple manners and customs of the New Mexico cowboy may be contaminated and his morals deteriorated by contact with these New Yorkers."[9]

For the most part, however, the Easterners in the Rough Riders were looked upon as celebrities rather than dudes or corrupters of the morals of youth: their presence served to heighten the "American" qualities of the regiment and to increase its fanfare. The prevalent image of the Rough Riders in the local and national newspapers of 1898 and in those histories of the unit written immediately after the war was that of an institution that helped bring the most perfect specimens of manhood from both East and West under the glorious roof of patriotism. Just as the Rough Riders' trip through

8. Marshall, *Story of the Rough Riders*, pp. 28–30.

9. San Antonio *Daily Express*, May 11, 1898; Denver *Evening Post*, May 11, 1898; Las Vegas *Daily Optic*, May 16, 1898.

the South had healed old sectional wounds through the balm of a national crusade, so the regiment itself, in the minds of contemporaries, proclaimed in its composition the merging of good Americans from both sides of the Mississippi.

Essential to the Rough Riders' image as a meeting place of East and West was harmony between the clubmen of Troop K and the cowboys of the other twelve troops, and commentators on the regiment therefore set out to describe the ease with which dude and plainsman became acclimated to one another. The Denver *Evening Post* testified to this in verse form:

We was somewhat disappointed, I'll acknowledge, fur to see
Sich a husky lot o'fellers as the dandies proved to be,
An' the free an' easy manner in their bearin' that they had
Sort o' started the impression that they mightn't be so bad.
There was absence of eye-glasses, an' of center parted hair,
An' in social conversation they was expert on the swear,
An' the way they hit the grub-pile sort o' led us to reflect
That our previous impressions mightn't prove so damn correct.

And the Chicago *Tribune,* in July 1898, took up the theme of compatibility from the Easterners' point of view:

They scoffed when we lined up with Teddy,
    They said we were dudes and all that;
They imagined that "Cholly" and "Fweddie"
    Would faint at the drop of a hat.
But let them look there in the ditches,
    Blood-stained by the swells in the van,
And know that a chap may have riches,
    And still be a man!

But it remained for the Santa Fe *New Mexican,* in describing the arrival of the Rough Riders in San Antonio, to merge East and West in the First Volunteers. "Some [of the men]," the *New Mexican* commented, "wore the broad-brimmed hat and had the bronzed cheek of the plains, and others bore the unmistakable stamp of the student and club man, but these latter were athletes and trained sportsmen. All mingled with easy good-fellowship."[10]

10. "Teddy's College Terrors," Denver *Evening Post,* May 21, 1898; "The Dudes Before Santiago," Chicago *Daily Tribune,* July 12, 1898; Santa Fe *New Mexican,* May 11, 1898.

War correspondents and historians of the Cuban campaign echoed the refrain. Edward Marshall, in recalling the induction of New York swells into the First Volunteers, remembered that "the comic paragraphers had a deal of fun over the enlistment of these men—these petted ones of fortune who were going to war—but the comic paragraphers stopped saying funny things when the petted ones of fortune, later, stood up like the real men they were and took, without whimpering, their doses of steel medicine on the battlefields of Cuba." On this same subject Richard Harding Davis was even more vehement:

> Some of the comic paragraphers who [made fun of] the members of the Knickerbocker Club and the college swells of the Rough Riders organization . . . ought, in decency, since the fight at Guasimas to go out and hang themselves with remorse. For the same spirit that once sent these men down a white-washed field against their opponents' rush-line was the spirit that sent Church, Channing, Devereux, Ronalds, Wrenn, Cash, Bull, Larned, Goodrich, Greenway, Dudley Dean, and a dozen others through the high hot grass at Guasimas, not shouting, as their friends the cowboys did, but each with his mouth tightly shut, with his eyes on the ball, and moving in obedience to the captain's signals.[11]

Davis' statement hints at one of the peculiarities of corespondents who stressed the unique composition of the First Volunteers. The same individuals who were quick to point out the adaptability of clubman and cowboy to one another also exhibited a fascination for the upper-class Easterner as dude and swell. Thus the Chicago *Tribune,* which was to emphasize the bravery and masculinity of the "swells" after the battle at Guasimas, noted in an article on the Rough Riders in camp that "the Fifth Avenue recruits . . . were rather bored . . . as none of them could secure passes. William Tiffany has been coming into town to eat dinner, but he had to eat three meals at the mess table today. He found the bacon and bread hard to swallow, and was hungry and unhappy when the bugle sounded 'lights out' and he had to retire to his harsh gray blanket." Even Marshall, while most anxious to stress the "good-fellowship"

11. Marshall, *Story of the Rough Riders,* p. 33; Richard Harding Davis, *The Cuban and Porto Rican Campaigns* (New York, 1898), pp. 151–52.

of the fashionable members of K Troop, showed an equal delight in their upper-class habits: "Colonel Wood ordered all superfluous baggage left behind, telling the men that they could take with them only such necessaries as they could find room for in their blanket rolls. Hundreds of boxes were sent by express that day to Western ranches and Eastern mansions. Kane, Tiffany, and Ronalds sheepishly admitted that their rejections included the swallow-tailed coats and low-cut vests of full dress suits."[12]

The presence of fashionable Easterners in the Rough Riders unquestionably gave the regiment a stature and newsworthiness which greatly enhanced its popular appeal; indeed, the sight of a New York swell going off to war in his dress suit was often news in itself. But equally attractive to the press and the public was the presence of cowboys in the First Volunteers and the consequent image of a cavalry of bronco busters riding hard on the Spanish. As early as 1895 Albert McIntire, the governor of Colorado, had conjured up such a vision in noting that he had "an idea which, in case of trouble will be placed into practice and will astonish the world and make the name Colorado known in army literature for some time to come. Colorado will have absolutely the best cavalry troop in the whole army, barring none. It will be made up of cowboys and range men who are accustomed to being in the saddle day and night and who know no fear. . . . absolutely nothing human, except an immense force, could withstand their onslaught." In January of 1898 Colonel Melvin Grigsby, later of the Third Volunteers, saw the relevance of a cowboy troop to the Cuban campaign: "while watching cowboys riding their broncoes in the streets of Pierre [South Dakota], the idea first came to me that these rough and bronzed riders of the plains, used to camp life in all kinds of weather, and expert shots with a rifle and revolver, would make gallant soldiers and daring fighters, in case the government should be drawn into war with Spain and need volunteers to be sent to Cuba."[13]

The legislative effects of such sentiments appeared in an April amendment to the Volunteer Army Bill of 1898. Through the efforts of Colonels Grigsby and Torrey and Senators James Kyle of

12. Chicago *Daily Tribune*, May 18, 1898; Marshall, *Story of the Rough Riders*, pp. 42, 43, 48–49.

13. Albert McIntire, "Cowboys and Dynamite," in Denver *Rocky Mountain News*, December 22, 1895; Otto L. Sues, *Grigsby's Cowboys* (Salem, S.D., 1900), pp. 1–2.

South Dakota and Francis Warren of Wyoming, the Army Bill was amended to include the organization of "companies, battalions, or regiments, possessing special qualifications and regulations." With the raising of three regiments of mounted riflemen "equipped and armed by the United States for this special service," the cowboy as cavalryman had come into being.[14]

In practice, the idea was a miserable failure. The tangled underbrush in the jungles around Santiago made riding nearly impossible; the limited mobility of a man on horseback made him an easy target for sharpshooters. Horses accustomed to the drier heat of the Southwest and the northern plains suffered greatly in the steam bath of the tropics; many died of heat prostration or contracted diseases and had to be killed. Warfare took the form of trench raids and ambushes; the Rough Riders' "charge" up Kettle Hill was in fact a slow, painful inching on their stomachs. The only effective use of horses in the Cuban campaign was that of baggage transports and silent companions for lonely war correspondents, and the only cavalry action that took place was on the sands of the Rough Riders' post-Cuba base at Montauk Point, Long Island, where Roosevelt and a few bronco busters rode up and down the beaches to blow off steam.[15]

Nevertheless, the cowboys had ample opportunity to exhibit the flush of their manhood and the spirit of their patriotism. "The four troops of mounted riflemen being organized in New Mexico for service in Cuba," the Santa Fe *New Mexican* boasted, "will in many respects be the most noted volunteer squadron ever enlisted. . . . The primary object of the organization of such a body of soldiers is to teach the civilized world that America possesses a class of men who, when . . . brought face to face with the enemy, never quit fighting until victory or death comes."[16] The presence of cowboys in the Rough Riders not only served, in the minds of their followers, to announce to the world the unique qualities of men of the western plains, it served to further identify the "wild riders and riflemen" as America's own.

In this vein, newspaper correspondents and other commentators of the times focused upon the cowboy volunteers both as products

14. Sues, *Grigsby's Cowboys*, pp. 4, 7.
15. See R. H. Davis, *The Cuban and Porto Rican Campaigns*, pp. 218–23; Roosevelt, *The Rough Riders*, pp. 141–44, 146, 224.
16. Santa Fe *New Mexican*, April 28, 1898.

of the western experience and as sons of the American heritage. "The cowboys," said the commander of the U.S. Army, "are able in a pre-eminent degree to take care of themselves, and always know where they are: why, you cannot lose one of them, no, not even in a blizzard." A correspondent for the Denver *Evening Post* called the western representatives of the Rough Riders "tall, well-built, athletic fellows, bronzed from exposure," and the Guthrie, Oklahoma, *State Capital* went so far as to claim that "every one [of the recruits from Oklahoma Territory] is stalwart in stature, strong and hardy in constitution, of rugged character and accustomed to an outdoor frontier life. Everyone of them is a fine horseman and all are familiar with firearms. Many of them have been in service in the Indian campaign in the West and there is about them a sturdy self-reliance, characteristic of the true Westerner." Even Roosevelt dusted off some of his earlier comments about men of the West to describe his Rough Riders: "They were a splendid set of men . . . tall and sinewy, with resolute, weather-beaten faces, and eyes that looked a man straight in the face without flinching. They included in their ranks men of every occupation; but the three types were those of the cow-boy, the hunter, and the mining prospector."[17]

The cowboy volunteer's westernness made him no less an American. While the Denver *Evening Post* noted that recruits for Colonel Torrey's Second Volunteers were "distinctively Western men with sunburned faces, and the spirit of independence and ability to take care of themselves that is peculiar to life in the West," the *Rocky Mountain News* from the same city announced that "great patriotic interest and pride have been felt by the people of [Wyoming] in the crack cavalry regiment being organized by Colonel Torrey. If given an opportunity all feel that it will immortalize the courage, the manhood and the patriotism of that distinctive type of western civilization, 'the cowboy.'" And the Cheyenne, Wyoming, *Sun-Leader* soared to even greater heights of patriotism, if not of prose:

> We are proud that our hardy and brave citizens of the country decided to enlist in their country's defense and glory in the . . . assurance that they will be the principal feature of the

17. Cheyenne, Wyo., *Sun-Leader*, quoting General Nelson A. Miles, March 10, 1898; Denver *Evening Post*, May 7, 1898; Guthrie, Okla., *State Capital*, May 9, 1898; Roosevelt, *The Rough Riders*, p. 15.

United States army. . . . Torrey's regiment will go down in history with Napoleon's Scotch guards. How honest, natural and patriotic it is to fly to the defense of your country with the garb of the ranch . . . which clothes a fond heart that beats at this time only that the blood it impels through the veins of true Americans may be shed in defense of the country's honor.[18]

Just as followers of eastern members of the Rough Riders were zealous in their attempt to emphasize the rougher and tougher qualities of their "curled darlings," so western columnists were anxious to emphasize the gentlemanliness of the cowboy volunteers. Colonel Torrey had exhibited certain fears that cowboys were still thought of as desperadoes in the East; while in Washington he noted that "here in the east you think no cowboy is fit for decent company. This is a great error. . . . All we want is a chance to show what we are made of and I think we will surprise the people of the east." The Cheyenne *Sun-Leader* picked up this theme, pointing out the "gentlemanly and refined conduct" of "Torrey's husky, skillful and brave riders . . . showing that the . . . western lads come from homes of purity and refinement not to be excelled in any city." Otto Sues, the historian of Colonel Melvin Grigsby's Third Volunteers, reaffirmed the *Sun-Leader's* remarks. Speaking of public reaction to Grigsby's regiment, he noted:

people who had never been outside of their native burg, and who judged the cowboys entirely by what they had read in yellow-covered literature, came out of curiosity to see the men who picked their teeth with a bowie knife and snuffed candles with the bullet from a six-shooter. . . . The yellow covers were greatly surprised to find that "Grigsby's boys" were orderly, well-behaved, gentlemanly and intelligent; that even the "long-haired pards" who were with the regiment were as well up on current topics and gentlemanly behavior as the best of the spectators.

And that old friend of the volunteers, the Denver *Evening Post,* wrote that "although Col. Melvin Grigsby's cowboys come from

18. Denver *Evening Post,* May 16, 1898; Denver *Rocky Mountain News,* May 29, 1898; Cheyenne, Wyo., *Sun-Leader,* May 31, 1898.

the far west and are considered by some people to be rough, they have shown themselves to be gentlemanly and chivalrous on all occasions."[19]

From this documentation of the aristocratic lineage and hearty good-fellowship of the eastern volunteers and the self-reliance and gentlemanliness of those from the West, it was only a brief step to a general characterization of the Rough Riders as an organization which contained superpatriots from all parts of the nation and incorporated the best features of East and West, North and South. "All Easterners and Westerners, Northerners and Southerners, officers and men, cowboys and college graduates, wherever they came from, and whatever their social position," Roosevelt wrote of his regiment, "possessed in common the traits of hardihood and a thirst for adventure."[20]

Throughout his eight-month sojourn with the unit Roosevelt was to find instances where the Rough Riders awakened in him or others the spirit of patriotic consensus. Passing through the South on his way to Tampa, he noted:

> everywhere the people came out to greet us and cheer us. . . . We were travelling through a region where practically all the older men had served in the Confederate Army, and where the younger men had all their lives long drunk in the endless tales told by their elders. . . . The blood of the old men stirred in the distant breath of battle; the blood of the young men leaped hot with eager desire to accompany us. . . . Everywhere we saw the Stars and Stripes, and everywhere we were told, half-laughing, by grizzled ex-Confederates that they had never dreamed in the bygone days of bitterness to greet the old flag as they now were greeting it, and to send their sons, as now they were sending them, to fight and die under it.

In an improvised hospital in Cuba Roosevelt was touched by the wounded's breaking into a chorus of "My Country 'tis of Thee"; and as Rough Riders from the East and West were buried together in the jungle, he mused: "There could be no more honorable

---

19. Guthrie, Okla., *State Capital,* quoting Colonel Jay L. Torrey, May 5, 1898; Cheyenne, Wyo., *Sun-Leader,* May 31, 1898; Sues, *Grigsby's Cowboys,* p. 12; Denver *Evening Post,* June 25, 1898.
20. Roosevelt, *The Rough Riders,* p. 19.

burial than that of these men in a common grave—Indian and cowboy, miner, packer, and college athlete—the man of unknown ancestry from the lonely Western plains, and the man who carried on his watch the crests of the Stuyvesants and the Fishes, one in the way they had met death, just as during life they had been one in their daring and their loyalty." And the San Antonio *Daily Express* carried Roosevelt's thoughts to their loftiest implication. In characterizing "Teddy's Bold Warriors" before their departure from Cuba, it cried: "This is democracy as Washington, Jefferson, and the other fathers of the republic dreamed of and gave their best thought and best blood to establish, and this is the democracy for which the highest and the lowliest, the rich and the poor, the young and the old, are ready to fight side by side and if need be mingle their blood in one common stream of patriotic sacrifice."[21]

Significantly the same heroic qualities emphasized in Wister's *Virginian* were attributed to the Rough Riders. The volunteers were manly (the Santa Fe *New Mexican* called them "fine specimens of physical manhood"), self-reliant ("The battalion chief of a newly raised American regiment," Roosevelt said, "has positively unlimited opportunities for the display of individual initiative"), gentlemanly ("During our entire time of service," noted Roosevelt, "I never heard in the officers' mess a foul story or a foul word"), and, being "good Americans," impressively patriotic.[22] The unquestioned righteousness of their cause swept aside social distinctions and regional jealousies; and the tone of the decade was reflected in the poems and songs which sprang up in praise of the Rough Riders as they prepared to embark for Cuba. The last stanza of a poem written on the outbreak of the war by Sam Cary Meek, a New Mexico Civil War veteran, is particularly suggestive:

Let patriots from the East and West, and from the North and South,
Make them dance to deadly music, from our cannon's mouth,
And give the Cubans liberty; baptized in patriots' blood,
To bequeath to their posterity; a birthright born of God.[23]

21. Ibid., pp. 52–53, 107, 109; San Antonio *Daily Express*, May 11, 1898.
22. Santa Fe *New Mexican*, May 2, 1898; Roosevelt, *The Rough Riders*, pp. 43, 47.
23. Meek's poem "We are Coming, Governor Otero!" appears in the April 29, 1898, issue of the Santa Fe *New Mexican*.

Here the merging of regions in a patriotic American cause is coupled with what might be called righteous wrath. This state of mind was echoed by one general of the Cuban campaign, who said, "This is God Almighty's war, and we are only His agents."[24]

Such wrath easily spilled over into nativistic antagonisms in 1898. In the same breath that one song asks the volunteers to "save from foul disgrace and famine prisoned mother, wife, and maid," it implores Americans to "smite to earth the Spanish coyote." Meek speaks of Spain as "a nation of murderers" with "brutish passions"; in other songs the Spaniards are referred to as "dirty Dons," "vultures," and "bloody Dagoes." The *Daily Oklahoma State Capital,* in commenting on a rumored invasion of Texas by Spanish-controlled elements in Mexico, claimed that "if all the Spaniards who inherit the land of 'God and Liberty' should take it into their crazy heads to cross over the Rio Grande on a hostile mission, what few of them that ever found their way back would cross the river sadder and wiser men. . . . Away back in 1836 Texas suffered an invasion by way of the Rio Grande. The bones of 75 percent of the invaders were left to bleach on the prairies. . . . A handful of patriots did the work and today the descendants of these same men —pure American stock—can lick the whole Spanish outfit." In this same vein a "loyal" New Mexican complained in a telegram to the New York *World* that "Roosevelt's cowboy regiment is liable to be a fake," since "a large proportion of the applicants for enlistment are foreigners, while the cowboy element is purely native born."[25]

One can sense beneath the patriotic pronouncements associated with the formation of the Rough Riders a certain amount of anxiety concerning the components of the "true America" with

24. The general's remark is quoted in Davis, *The Cuban and Porto Rican Campaigns,* p. 97; for another discussion of the "new patriotism" ushered in by the crusade of 1898, see Paul H. Buck, *The Road to Reunion* (Boston, 1937), pp. 298–307. "The outbreak of the war with Spain," writes Buck, "advertised the fact that the people of the United States were a nation. . . . The Spanish-American war . . . completed the revolution in sentiment through which the generation had passed. For a time all people within the country felt the electrifying thrill of a common purpose" (p. 306).

25. See Westermeier, *Who Rush to Glory,* pp. 146, 147, 149, 152; Guthrie, Okla., *State Capital,* May 4, 1898; Edward J. Murray, quoted in the Las Vegas *Daily Optic,* May 17, 1898.

which they were so often linked. True Americans were democrats; hence the volunteer units became symbols of democracy. True America bred gentlemen in the full flush of their manhood who knew how to help themselves; thus the wildest cowboy became a gentleman, the most fastidious dude a "real man." But all this hero-making was not accomplished without a few stresses and strains, and certain commentators felt a compulsion not only to reassert the glories of American culture but to seize upon its unique elements and hold these up as proof of the United States' unquestioned international superiority. In their eyes the cowboy as cavalryman became a symbol of American accomplishment: "There can be no question as to the accuracy of his marksmanship or his ability to show even the Cossacks of the Don tricks in fancy riding. . . . Ten or twelve hundred cowboys mounted and armed could lead a charge that would forever remain an incident in the history of modern warfare. . . . They are the best shots to be found in any country—experts everyone of them—and in a charge would sweep every living thing before them, leaving only death and destruction in their path."[26]

The chauvinistic glorifications of "America's own" is paralleled in other attitudes that are both products of consensus and manifestations of anxiety, such as a sense of the superiority of the Anglo-Saxon peoples and of the white race. "To occupy my spare moments," Roosevelt wrote in describing the Rough Riders' journey from San Antonio to Tampa, "I was reading Demolins' 'Supériorité des Anglo-Saxons.' " He then launched into a discussion of Demolins' thesis that in the non-English-speaking countries "militarism deadens the power of individual initiative, the soldier being trained to complete suppression of individual will, while his faculties become atrophied in consequence of his being merely a cog in a vast and perfectly ordered machine." "I can assure the excellent French publicist," Roosevelt noted, "that American militarism, at least of the volunteer sort, has points of difference from the militarism of Continental Europe." He then proceeded to point out that the Anglo-Saxon "is in no danger whatever either of suffering from unhealthy suppression of personal will, or of finding his faculties of self-help numbed by becoming a cog in a gigantic and

26. Cheyenne, Wyo., *Sun-Leader*, April 7, 22, 1898.

smooth-running machine. If a battalion chief wants to get anything or go anywhere he must do it by exercising every pound of resource, inventiveness, and audacity he possesses."[27] Roosevelt was highly critical of some of the inefficiency exhibited in running the Cuban campaign, yet he was equally capable of using "the endless confusion and delay" as a foil to exhibit the "opportunities for individual initiative" inherent in the American system. In the face of Remington's feeling that the war against Spain dramatized the conquest of man by the machine, Roosevelt's conclusion is an extraordinary one.

Equally extraordinary but characteristic was Roosevelt's and his contemporaries' attitude toward those Americans not of the white race. Of the Indians in his regiment Roosevelt took pains to note that "they lived on terms of complete equality" with their white comrades; that only "one or two of them needed rough discipline"; and that "vindictive though the hatred between the white man and the Indian is when they stand against one another in what may be called their tribal relations, men of Indian blood, when adopted into white communities, are usually treated precisely like anyone else."[28] The very fact that Roosevelt felt compelled to mention this indicates his consciousness of race, if not his condescension. While racism assuredly took much stronger forms than this in the decade after Cuba, the intention here is less to chastise Roosevelt than to point out the intimate connections between a series of attitudes which clustered around the concept of patriotism at the opening of the twentieth century.

Brigaded with the Rough Riders in Cuba was the Tenth Regular Cavalry, a Negro unit. The Tenth Cavalry was just to the rear of the Rough Riders as they crawled up Kettle Hill, and in advance of them at the earlier battle of Guasimas. Its troops were veterans, most of them career soldiers, and they took the heaviest doses of Spanish fire at Kettle Hill, losing eleven out of twenty-two officers.

27. Roosevelt, *The Rough Riders*, pp. 47–48. A delightful combination of belligerency and Anglo-Saxon supremacy appears in the remarks of a British war correspondent in Cuba, Sir Bryan Leighton, who allegedly said to "a travelling Russian, Prince X": "You see, Prince, the great result of this war is that it has united the two branches of the Anglo-Saxon people; and now that they are together they can whip the world, Prince! they can whip the world!" (quoted in Roosevelt, *The Rough Riders*, p. 192).

28. Roosevelt, *The Rough Riders*, pp. 20, 22, 24.

Another Negro regiment, the Ninth Cavalry, which was in a different brigade from the Rough Riders, was also on the scene at San Juan Hill and claimed the honor of being the first to reach the Spanish trenches. In fact, the scene at San Juan Hill is best described by Roosevelt as one of "great confusion . . . the different regiments being completely intermingled—white regulars, colored regulars, and Rough Riders."[29]

It seems strange that in the accounts of the campaign around Santiago so little mention is made of the Ninth and Tenth Regulars—and that often inaccurate. One New York paper, according to Richard Harding Davis, wrote, in describing the "charge": "Inspired by the example of the Rough Riders, the Sixth and Ninth Regulars charged the hill with undaunted courage"—an account which Davis considered "extremely unfair to the regulars." Moreover, in the photographs, paintings, and sketches of the Cuban campaign the Ninth and Tenth cavalries are never pictured. Roosevelt, in his account of the action around Santiago, gives credit to the Negro regulars, but in a rather backhanded fashion:

> No troops could have behaved better than the colored soldiers had behaved so far; but they are, of course, peculiarly dependent upon their white officers. Occasionally they produce noncommissioned officers who can take the initiative and accept responsibility precisely like the best class of whites; but this cannot be expected normally, nor is it fair to expect it. With the colored troops there should always be some of their own officers; whereas, with the white regulars, as with my own Rough Riders, experience showed that the non-commissioned officers could usually carry on the fight by themselves if they were once started, no matter whether their officers were killed or not.[30]

At one point of the battle around San Juan Hill, Roosevelt describes how the innate superiority of the white race manifested itself under pressure:

> None of the white regulars or Rough Riders showed the slightest sign of weakening; but under the strain the colored in-

29. Ibid., pp. 129, 139.

30. R. H. Davis, *The Cuban and Porto Rican Campaigns*, p. 238; Roosevelt, *The Rough Riders*, pp. 143–44.

fantrymen (who had none of their officers) began to get a little uneasy and to drift to the rear. . . . This I could not allow, as it was depleting my line, so I jumped up, and walked a few yards to the rear, drew my revolver, halted the retreating soldiers, and called out to them that I . . . would shoot the first man who on any pretense whatever, went to the rear. . . . This was the end of the trouble, for the "smoked Yankees" . . . flashed their white teeth at one another, as they broke into broad grins, and I had no more trouble with them, they seeming to accept me as one of their own officers.

"In return," Roosevelt notes in his most beneficent tones, "the Rough Riders, although for the most part Southwesterners, who have a strong color prejudice, grew to accept them with hearty good-will as comrades, and were entirely willing, in their own phrase, to 'drink out of the same canteen.' "[31] For superpatriots this was a most gracious gesture.

The Cuban campaign had demonstrated the inadequacy of cavalry techniques in modern warfare and had ushered in the horrifying possibilities of a major war in a technological age. As Remington had seen in his week on the battleship *Iowa,* the worst aspect of "modern" war was not loss of life but loss of identity in a huge, impersonal, machine-made environment. It had revealed the incredible inefficiency and ill-preparedness of the American armed services, a fact that Roosevelt was never to forget. It had dramatized the drudgery of camp routine and the dependence of the fighting man on necessities such as proper food and shelter. It should have wearied America once and for all of any more patriotic missions and caused her citizens to treat the returning servicemen as victims rather than heroes. But it only created the impression that all the things America went to war for—all the components of American patriotism—were eminently relevant.

Once the United States had come to the aid of bleeding Cuba and driven the Spaniard from the New World, she was secure in her righteousness. The cowboys and clubmen of the Rough Riders who had demonstrated their mettle in a glorious charge up San Juan Hill deserved to be called true Americans, and Theodore Roose-

31. Roosevelt, *The Rough Riders,* pp. 144–45.

velt, in the words of Edward Marshall, had become "the most magnificent soldier I have ever seen." "It was as if," said Marshall of Roosevelt, "that barbed-wire strand had formed a dividing line in his life, and that when he stepped across it he left behind him in the bridle path all those unadmirable and conspicuous traits which have often caused him to be justly criticized in civic life, and found on the other side of it, in that Cuban thicket, the coolness, the calm judgment, the towering heroism, which made him . . . the most admired and best beloved of all Americans in Cuba."[32]

Thus, while Remington dragged his weary self back to New Rochelle and countless members of the Second and Third volunteers, who had never seen action, were ravaged by yellow fever, the Rough Riders returned to a glorious homecoming at Montauk Point. Lond Island Sound was "dotted with the white hulls of welcoming yachts," and as the transport *Miami* approached, carrying newly promoted Colonel Roosevelt and his men, "these sent up a deafening scream of welcome from their steam whistles." As the *Miami* neared the pier, a band struck up "When Johnny Comes Marching Home Again," and the Rough Riders responded with their cheer: "Rough, tough, we're the stuff." With the "first glimpse of Roosevelt on the bridge of the ship, the crowd on shore went mad." As the "famous New York hero" walked down the gangplank with General Joseph Wheeler, an ex-Confederate cavalry commander, "ten thousand cheers went up."[33]

The stay at Montauk was an idyl after the tortuous weeks in Cuba. Roosevelt took two or three hours off from his routine paper work to gallop down to the beach and bathe in the surf, or else go for "long rides over the beautiful rolling plains" with his cowboy and socialite companions. "Galloping over the open, rolling country, through the cool fall evenings," he noted, "made us feel as if we were out on the great Western plains." When a grand parade scheduled for the Rough Riders in New York City was canceled, a bronco-riding contest was held among the troops. And on Sunday, September 13, some three months and three weeks after their convocation at San Antonio, the First Volunteers held their final meeting. Roosevelt accepted a replica of Remington's "Bronco Buster"

32. Marshall, *Story of the Rough Riders,* p. 104.
33. Ibid., pp. 239–41.

from the troopers. In the Colonel's final speech, which disappointed neither his men nor an expectant public, he said:

> I am proud of this regiment, because it is a typical American regiment, made up of typical American men. The foundation of the regiment was the 'Bronco Buster,' and we have him here in bronze. The men of the West and the men of the Southwest, horsemen, riflemen, and herders of cattle, have been the backbone of this regiment, as they are the backbone of their sections of the country. Besides the cowpuncher, this regiment contains men from every section of the country and from every state within the Union. . . . This demonstrates that Uncle Sam has a nobler reserve of fighting men to call upon, if the necessity arises, than any other country in the world."[34]

Roosevelt returned to Sagamore Hill and began plans for his successful campaign for governor of New York in 1899. In the course of that campaign he commissioned Remington to paint "The Charge Up San Juan Hill," which pictures the Colonel at the head of his troops, mounted on his war pony and brandishing his sword. In the background are the Rough Riders, breathing fire and pushing pell-mell at the enemy. The painting indicated that Roosevelt's political acumen had not been dulled by his military success, and it helped to remind the public of his heroic deeds while subtly implanting certain images which had no basis in fact. But no one cared whether Roosevelt actually rode up the hill, whether the Rough Riders charged or crawled, or whether the hill was San Juan or Kettle. All the memories of America's splendid little war flooded Remington's canvas, and Roosevelt was shrewd enough to capitalize on the spirit of the times.

As for the Rough Riders, they in turn reminded themselves and the nation of their valiant crusade against the infidel by staging a reunion in Las Vegas, New Mexico Territory, in June 1899. The Santa Fe Railway was reportedly besieged with requests for accommodations as the volunteers poured in from all over the West. Governor Roosevelt sent word that he would attend, and an elaborate three-day program was arranged. Governor Otero of New Mexico praised the regiment's desire "to keep warm the fires of

34. Roosevelt, *The Rough Riders*, p. 224; Marshall, *Story of the Rough Riders*, p. 252.

patriotism and nourish the love of country and devotion to its flag, which has ever marked the true American." Parades, band concerts, bronco-busting contests, and a baseball game highlighted the ceremonies, which concluded with a display of fireworks depicting the Battle of San Juan.[35]

The violence and drudgery of Cuba had become a glorious cavalry charge, and the dismounted cowboy crawling through the underbrush had evolved into a dashing rider on a fiery horse. In the shade of San Juan Hill the cowboy became a patriot and a hero, and three years after the Rough Riders' first reunion Owen Wister elevated him to semipermanent status in that capacity. The consensus that accepted the cowboy and clubman as "true Americans," that made Roosevelt the most revered President since Lincoln, and that eulogized the Rough Riders had as its foremost axiom a delicate balance between old tradition and new technology, and the delicacy of this balance dictated that the consensus was not long to endure. But while Roosevelt reigned, it endured, influencing all phases of American life.

35. Westermeier, *Who Rush to Glory*, pp. 254–56.

8. Technocracy and Arcadia: Conservation under Roosevelt

The crusade on behalf of Cuba might have been a "splendid little war," but it was also a demonstration of some of the difficulties inherent in an attempt to make some order out of the chaos of rampant industrialism. The lesson of the war experiences to Roosevelt and the others was twofold: America possessed both the technological might and the patriotic spirit to exert leadership in the twentieth-century world, but she was considerably less competent in making efficient use of her technological strength than in harnessing the forces of consensus for expeditions against her enemies. The war operations, Roosevelt noted, were noteworthy for their "buoyant and lighthearted indifference to detail"; the aid any individual battalion chief received in the administering of his tasks was "of the most general, not to say superficial, character."[1] "It is not necessary," the former Rough Rider said in his first annual message to Congress in 1901, "to increase our army beyond its present size at this time. But it is necessary to keep it at the highest point of efficiency." Similarly, in announcing new policies governing the regulation of corporations, labor legislation, immigration restriction, and agriculture, Roosevelt noted that he would be guided by the principle that "the old laws and customs which had almost the binding force of law were once quite sufficient. . . . Since the industrial changes which have enormously increased the productive power of mankind, they are no longer sufficient."[2]

Roosevelt must have felt himself peculiarly suited to lead America into the industrial age. His eastern experiences in the nineteenth century had clustered around the relation of industrialism to an organized system of power and status groupings, and at the open-

1. Roosevelt, *The Rough Riders*, pp. 47–48.
2. Roosevelt, *Works, 15* (National Edition, 20 vols. New York, 1926), 87, 122. Unless otherwise noted, subsequent references to Roosevelt's *Works* for this chapter are from the National Edition.

ing of the twentieth century he and a number of his upper-class colleagues became involved with the federal government, which was confronting similar problems. The government had remained largely indifferent to the extraordinary developments in industrial enterprise during the nineteenth century, but Roosevelt and his peers had taken note of certain trends which accompanied industrialization and responded to these trends in an active fashion. Financial success had become equated with social success, and, more importantly, technological expertise had become associated with financial triumphs. As a result, during the seven years of Roosevelt's presidency there was an increased participation on the part of the federal government in the sphere of industrial enterprise. In particular, the Roosevelt administrators introduced the concept of an elite into the governing process itself, coming to believe in a government of administrative experts that attempted to convey to the public the ends of industrial living.

Even while Roosevelt and the others were attempting to connect their nineteenth-century eastern experiences with the problems America faced in the twentieth century, however, they were in turn influenced by the powerful countereastern image that many of their contemporaries had come to associate with the American West. Just as commentators on the Rough Riders anxiously sought to make gentlemen of cowboys and cowboys of gentlemen, so the Roosevelt administrators committed themselves to a brisk restructuring of federal policy to deal more efficiently with a technological society, while at the same time insisting that such a restructuring revitalized those twentieth-century symbols of a nontechnological, Arcadian America. The leaders of the Roosevelt conservation movement, in particular, combined a faith in technocratic efficiency with a delight in the image of a nontechnological, nonurban, noncorporate, nonelitist—in short, a noneastern—society.

To the Roosevelt policymakers "conservation" came to mean concern not only for the nation's forest but for all its natural resources and public lands. Gifford Pinchot, Chief of the Forest Service under Roosevelt, termed conservation "the foresighted utilization, preservation, and/or renewal of forests, waters, lands and minerals," and, in terms of legislation, the Roosevelt conservationists primarily concerned themselves with land and water projects. The Newlands Act, passed in 1902, financed irrigation projects in the arid areas of the West through a Reclamation Fund composed of proceeds from the sale of public lands in thirteen states and three territories west of the Mississippi. A Public Lands Commission created by Roosevelt in 1903 recommended the withdrawal from entry of public domain resource lands for purposes of study and reclassification, a task which was begun in 1905. And in 1907 Senator Francis G. Newlands of Nevada, the author of the Newlands Act, sponsored a bill to appoint a permanent body to coordinate the activities of all federal water resources agencies, including the construction of new projects.[3]

The Newlands Bill died in the Senate, but conservationists had already directed their energies to a reorganization of the executive to further their interests. In his first annual message Roosevelt had called for a transfer of the Bureau of Forestry (later the Forest Service) from the Department of Interior to that of Agriculture, and a general centralizing of those agencies dealing with forest reserves. "The present diffusion of responsibility," he noted, "is bad from every standpoint. It prevents that effective cooperation between the government and the men who utilize the resources of the reserves, without which the interests of both must suffer."[4] Finally, in 1905, the Bureau of Forestry consolidated such functions as protection, mapping and description of timber, and tree farming in a single agency, under the jurisdiction of the Department of Agriculture.

The centralization of this particular agency in the years 1901–05 typifies the growing interest of the Roosevelt administration in executive agencies with specialized functions. Generally, after an appointed commission of "experts" concerned with a specific phase of conservation had filed reports that pointed to outdated laws or techniques concerning their subject, legislation was recommended to increase the power of the commissions in the interests of efficiency and expertise. Conservationists remained confident in the efficiency and disinterestedness of public enterprise, and their faith in administrative agencies of the executive branch demonstrated their commitment to the governing capabilities of an educated

3. Gifford Pinchot, *Breaking New Ground* (New York, 1947), p. 505.
4. Roosevelt, *Works, 15,* 103.

elite. Roosevelt sponsored the transfer of the forests from Interior to Agriculture because, according to one account, "the Forestry Bureau had the trained personnel to conduct the work of protection and conservation scientifically." In arguing for his Ohio River Bill, Newlands said that he hoped "to see a commission of experts that will have the power to initiate both investigation and construction and with ample funds to complete its projects, not a commission that will have to wait on the tardy initiative of Congress as to projects the details of which it is incapable of dealing with." The chairman of the Oregon Conservation Commission wrote Newlands that "the great difficulty in this country . . . lies in the fact that the views of experts are of little value, and that a slap-dash-haphazard way of going at anything will produce results." And late in his second administration Roosevelt moaned: "I am afraid all modern legislative bodies tend to show their incapacity to meet the new and complex needs of the times."[5]

The function of such decision-making governmental structures was not new to Roosevelt and his colleagues. Indeed, institutions which consolidated power in the hands of a few "experts" had been developed by upper-class members of the business and financial elites in the 1870s and 80s. Metropolitan men's clubs were collections of men whose power and prestige in business and social circles were unquestioned and who sought to further their interests by close association with one another. Corporations had learned that their most successful response to industrialization was consolidation; centralized boards of directors made decisions which affected vast sums of capital and huge holdings. Boarding schools, Ivy League universities, and exclusive college clubs provided sons and potential sons of the Establishment with a precise training in social expertise. All of these institutions recognized the need for a commitment to the new industrial order, whether in the consolidation of business enterprise or in the creation of self-perpetuating social elites. As long as the vast majority of Americans were white, Protestant, Anglo-Saxon, and of rural antecedents, these institutions could be assimilative as well as exclusive; only when a sizable

5. Newlands in *Congressional Record*, 60th Cong., 1st Sess., p. 391; Joseph Teal to Francis G. Newlands, February 26, 1916, Newlands Papers, Yale University; Roosevelt to Dan T. Moore, January 9, 1909, Theodore Roosevelt Papers (Harvard College Library).

number of successful individuals were found to be of different ethnic and religious origins was the stability of Establishment organizations threatened.

The Roosevelt conservationists simply enlarged the sphere of influence of this professionalist approach to industrialism. In their eyes the federal government was as much a self-perpetuating Establishment institution as a large corporation or an exclusive university, and the long-range purpose of legislative innovations was the preservation of "the stability of the institutions upon which the welfare of the whole country rests."[6]

The intimate connection between "stability" in an industrial society and the "welfare" of the populace was in fact a crucial concept for these decision-makers and a logical outgrowth of their nineteenth-century experiences. Since the majority of Americans could not cope with the complexities of the twentieth century and yet needed more than ever the benefits of stable institutions, the role of the technical elite in modern society assumed vast importance. The elite were viewed as interpreters and solvers of the problems of urbanization and industrialization, experts upon whom the majority of citizens were dependent for guidance in a chaotic world. Hence the federal government, in the person of these experts, should take a more active part in the lives of individual citizens for the public good. The reorganization and strengthening of the executive, legislation to increase the powers of the federal government, and the new policies of efficiency and expertise thus became means of strengthening and stabilizing traditional aspects of the American heritage. As such they drew their strength not only from technological knowledge but from moral conviction, and represented the degree to which the needs and goals of a privileged set of individuals in the late nineteenth-century East had become identified with the aspirations of the nation.

Certain aspects of the East had been found wanting, however, even by its social and occupational leaders, and the West had consequently emerged as an attractive counterimage. This phenomenon was to greatly affect responses to the conservation movement, which was primarily directed at western portions of the continent. Al-

6. Roosevelt, *Works,* 22 (Memorial Edition), 452.

though exponents of conservation often spoke of the intimate connection between their policies and a new industrial order, at other
times they likened the movement to a quest to restore to Americans
the benefits of a preindustrial age and reasserted some of the tenets
of a nontechnological America.

The giant corporation seemed to threaten the well-being of many
Americans in the latter decades of the nineteenth century. Popu-
lists inveighed against trusts and railroad magnates, and cartoonists
pictured corporations as giant octopi entangling and crushing the
small entrepreneur. The term "monopoly" became particularly
nasty, and the Roosevelt conservationists, for all their commitment
to consolidation and elitism, were quick to label their movement
antimonopolist. Newlands suggested that the proceeds from the
leasing of coal and iron deposits be turned over to the Reclamation
Fund to "continue the beneficent work of home building and the
creation of a self-respecting industrious yeomanry throughout the
entire country," and noted that "if we adopt that provision . . . it
seems to me we will have advanced quite a way in the direction of
curbing and restraining monopolies." In advocating government
regulation of the price of coal, he spoke of the possibility of the
gradual concentration and consolidation of coal lands "in the hands
of great corporations, a system which will inevitably end in monopoly and in the oppression of the people. . . . It seems to me, at all
events, that we can prevent the monopoly of the past." The "so-
called conservation policy," Newlands said in summation, involved
"the careful study" of all the public domain "for the purpose of
determining . . . what restrictions shall be placed upon private
ownership in order to prevent monopoly."[7]

Pinchot felt even more strongly the intimate connection between
the conservation movement and an antimonopolist tradition. One
of the "three great purposes of Conservation policy" was "to see to it
that the rights of the people to govern themselves shall not be con-
trolled by great monopolies through their power over natural resources." "Monopoly on the loose," Pinchot wrote, "is a source of
many of the economic, political, and social evils which afflict the

7. Newlands, in Arthur P. Darling, ed., *The Public Papers of Francis G. Newlands*,
1 (2 vols. Cambridge, Mass., 1932), 95, 99, 100, 111. Darling's edition is distinct from
but overlaps much of the material in the Francis G. Newlands papers at Yale University.

sons of men. Its abolition or regulation is an inseparable part of the Conservation policy." "I believe in free enterprise," he continued, "freedom for the common man to think and work and rise to the limit of his ability, with due regard to the rights of others. But in what Concentrated Wealth means by free enterprise—freedom to abuse the common man—I do not believe. I object to the law of the jungle."[8]

Pinchot's concern for the common man was another traditional tenet of the Roosevelt conservationists. "I stand for the protection of the individual home-seeker," Newlands said in 1906. "I stand for individual homes in the West, and I stand for a policy which will give to the [home-seeker] at a reasonable price the necessities of life." Roosevelt echoed these words and took them a step further. "Most of the works contemplated," he said in reference to the Newlands Act, "are of national importance, involving . . . the securing of stable, self-supporting communities . . . the nation as a whole is of course the gainer by the creation of these homes." To combat monopoly, Roosevelt promised the renaissance of Newlands' "self-respecting industrious yeomanry." "The creation of small irrigated farms under the Reclamation Act," he noted, "is a powerful offset to the tendency of certain other laws to foster or permit monopoly of the land. . . . The constant purpose of the government in connection with the Reclamation Service has been . . . to put upon the land permanent home-makers, to use and develop it for themselves and for their children and children's children."[9]

The "individual home-seeker" to which Roosevelt and his colleagues were so devoted was none other than "that pre-eminently typical American, the farmer who loses his own medium-sized farm." To have the yeoman farmer replaced "by either a class of small peasant proprietors or by a class of great landlords with tenant-farmed estates," wrote Roosevelt, "would be a veritable calamity." "The growth of our cities," he continued, "is a good thing but only insofar as it does not mean a growth at the expense of the country farmer." Here in the midst of the twentieth century was an appeal on the part of the conservationists to the older visions of a rural Arcadia. "The government should part with its

8. Pinchot, *Breaking New Ground*, pp. 506, 507, 509.

9. Newlands, in Darling, *The Public Papers of Francis G. Newlands, 1,* 103; Roosevelt, *Works, 15,* 194, 314, 445.

title only to actual home-makers," Roosevelt noted, in a passage that might have been attributed to Henry George, "not to the profit-maker who does not care to make a home. Our prime object is to secure the rights and guard the interests of the small ranch-man, the man who ploughs and pitches hay for himself. It is this small ranchman, this actual settler and home-maker, who in the long run is most hurt by permitting thefts of the public land."[10]

Closely allied to conservation in the eyes of the Roosevelt policy-makers was the preservation, theoretically at least, of a rural way of life. To that end Roosevelt recommended the establishment in 1908 of a Commission on Country Life to "direct the attention of the Nation to the problems of the farmer, and to secure the neces-sary knowledge of the actual conditions of life in the open coun-try." "No nation," Roosevelt wrote in a letter announcing the formation of the Country Life Commission, "has ever achieved permanent greatness unless this greatness was based on the well-being of the great farmer class, the men who live on the soil; for it is upon their welfare, material and moral, that the welfare of the nation ultimately rests." The "conservation of natural resources," Roosevelt felt, "underlies the problem of rural life"; progress in conservation paved the way for the progress in the "other material question of . . . importance now before the American people"— "the strengthening of country life."[11]

In seeking to strengthen the position of the farmer in a tech-nological society, the commission of experts on country life, of which Pinchot was a member,[12] resorted to the same techniques and employed the same rhetoric as the crusaders for conservation. They consistently advocated educating the farmer in modern busi-ness techniques: some of the "remedies suggested by the Commis-sion," according to Pinchot, included "better organization among

10. Roosevelt, *Works, 15,* 441, 448.

11. Roosevelt, letter to L. H. Bailey, August 10, 1908, reprinted in L. H. Bailey, ed., *Report of the Commission on Country Life* (New York, 1911), pp. 41–46. Hereafter cited as CLC Report.

12. The other members included Bailey, a professor at the New York State College of Agriculture; Henry Wallace, editor of *Wallace's Farmer;* Kenyon L. Butterfield, from Massachusetts Agricultural College (now the University of Massachusetts); Wal-ter H. Page, editor of *World's Work;* Charles S. Barrett, president of the Farmers Cooperative and Educational Union; and William A. Beard, of *Great Western* maga-zine.

farmers, [which means] better business"; in transmitting the report of the Commission to Congress in February 1909, Roosevelt noted that "the object of the Commission on Country Life is to . . . call [the farmer's] attention to the opportunities for better business and better living on the farm"; and the report of the Commission itself suggested that "the farmer must have exact knowledge of his business and of the particular conditions under which he works," insisted upon "really scientific and self-perpetuating agriculture," and called for "fresh blood, clean bodies and clear brains" from the farms "that can endure the strains of modern urban life."[13] At the same time, however, the Commission borrowed the conservationists' enthusiasm for the Arcadian aspects of rural America. Heeding Roosevelt's reminder that "we were founded as a nation of farmers, and in spite of the great growth of our industrial life it still remains true that our whole system rests upon the farm," the commissioners proclaimed their goal as "the development . . . of a new and permanent rural civilization." Such a civilization, buttressed by legislative innovations in conservation, would be free from the old western bugaboos: "speculative holding of lands; monopolistic control of streams; wastage and monopolistic control of forests; and restraint of trade."

The Commissioners on Country Life were quick to align themselves with the small farmer and the independent homeowner. "Unless the people be aroused to the danger to their interests," they cried in referring to water power, "there will probably be developed a monopoly greater than any the world has yet seen." "The farmer," they maintained, "must own both the water and the land if he is to be master of his own fortunes. One of the best elements of any population is the independent home-owning farmer, and the tendency of government . . . should be towards securing the ownership of the land by the man who lives on and tills it. . . . We need such an attitude of government . . . as will safeguard the separate and individual rights of the farmer, in the interest of the public good."[14]

Utopia for the Country Life Commissioners was not unlike that of the conservationists: the "new rural society" would include a balance between country and city, West and East, presided over by

13. Pinchot, *Breaking New Ground*, p. 342; CLC Report, pp. 21, 25, 31, 85.
14. CLC Report, pp. 10, 30, 61–62, 70, 71–72, 79.

a beneficent government of paternalists. "All people are bettered and broadened by association with those of far different environment," the Commission pontificated. "There is as much need of a new attitude on the part of the townsmen as on the part of the farmer. . . . There should be more frequent social intercourse on equal terms between the people of the country and those of the city." Above all, the development of an ideal society which blended the rural and urban Americas was "largely . . . a question of guidance." The exercise, the Commissioners felt, "of a wise advice, stimulus, and direction from some central national agency . . . extending over a series of years, could accomplish untold good, not only for the open country, but for all the people and for our institutions."[15]

The technocratic paternalists of the Roosevelt administration found themselves allied in their quest with groups whose purposes were directly opposed to theirs. "Those who came to the support of conservation," Samuel P. Hays writes, "were [often] prone to look upon all commercial development as mere materialism, and upon conservation as an attempt to save resources for use rather than to use them wisely. . . . An exclusively hardheaded economic proposition, therefore, became tinged with the enthusiasm of a religious crusade to save America from its materialistic enemies." Such groups as the Daughters of the American Revolution, the General Federation of Women's Clubs, and the American Civic Association "viewed with alarm the way in which industrialism, in a short space of fifty years, had altered American society," and "looked upon conservation as an antidote to changes they resisted." Worshipers of the self-sufficient entrepreneur, they thrilled to Roosevelt's desire to safeguard the interests of the "man who ploughs and pitches hay for himself." Repulsed by the sprawling metropolis, they seized upon the preservationist aspects of conservation policy and called for city parks, recreation areas, and national forests. Since they saw everywhere "conspicuous consumption of huge fortunes, and a headlong worship of the almighty dollar,"[16] Newlands' and Pinchot's campaign against concentrated wealth aroused them. In short, whereas the Roosevelt conservationists were fully committed to the furtherment of business techniques in a technological

15. Ibid., pp. 148–49.
16. Samuel P. Hays, *Conservation and the Gospel of Efficiency* (Cambridge, Mass., 1959), pp. 141, 145.

age, many of the groups they appealed to viewed conservation as an antibusiness movement.

This alignment might seem paradoxical in view of the fact that Roosevelt, Newlands, and the other conservationists often stressed the need for immersion in and devotion to the industrial order. Perhaps they realized that the standard nineteenth-century platitudes which held up the virtues of a small-business, small-town, individualistic society would strike a responsive chord in the hearts of constituents, particularly those from the West. But it is more likely that the paternalistic notions of the Roosevelt conservationists included a belief that somehow the federal government could enact a balance between traditional and modern America. In this sense conservation legislation was intended to preserve the status of representatives of older America by insuring that they could adapt to the new times. Thus the Newlands Act, which protected the small homemaker from monopoly and oppression by the intrusion of a benevolent government into local affairs, clearly envisaged a society where each man could develop expertise without losing his identity or trampling upon someone else. Since industrialism, with its rapid technological changes and consequent social flux, threatened the maintenance of balanced progress, an enlightened government of experts was needed to insure that modern America somewhat resembled the nation from which it had sprung.

In the eyes of both the technocratic paternalists and the general public, the federal government in the Roosevelt administrations came to be seen as a moral force. Roosevelt spoke of the "square deal" in domestic affairs and of "gentleman's agreements" in foreign policy. Pinchot waxed eloquent about the "general good." And a Chicago conservationist stated that "the moral tone which the conservation movement has given to the entire country has perhaps been more effective for the general good of the American people than any one thing in our generation." This morality in government was perfectly consistent with a consensus of values which affirmed equality of opportunity, the right of the common man, and the democratic political process, while at the same time upholding an open-class society with acknowledged leaders, correct practices, and certain social barriers. In reorganizing the structure of the government, the technocratic paternalists were attempting to insure the "stability of American institutions" in what they recognized as a changing age. In appealing to traditionalist patterns of behavior, such as self-reliance, and eulogizing traditional success models, such as the yeoman farmer, they were articulating America's need to reassert the common elements of her heritage. More moral functions they could not have imagined.

The Roosevelt conservationists held sway only briefly; indeed, many of their assumptions about the role of the federal government in local affairs were challenged as early as the Taft administration. And more importantly, the whole tenor of American culture changed radically shortly after Roosevelt and the rest had vanished from the scene. The balance between old and new, moral and practical, aristocrat and common man disintegrated, and with it went the series of unalterably right principles which lay at the core of the decade of consensus.[17] Thus the years immediately after the First World War may be seen as a period of cultural deintegration, in which one can point to single aspects of the Roosevelt consensus that remained intact and to others that disappeared.

One can, for example, recognize the methods of the technocratic paternalists in the business fetish of the 1920s, but their notion of the government as a positive, moral force has vanished. And with this piecemeal legacy come disparate notions of the character of Roosevelt's conservation crusade and of the reform movement with which it has often been linked—Progressivism. While the Roosevelt conservation movement has been viewed both as a link in the American chains of individualism and social justice and as a corporate, collectivist approach to the problems of science and technology, Progressivism has been termed both a middle-class recoil from the economic and social problems of industrial America and a conspiracy to preserve power and prestige in the hands of major economic interests.[18] Each of these interpretations has a certain

17. See May, *The End of American Innocence,* for a discussion of what he calls the "certainty of moral values" that buttressed decision-makers in the Roosevelt era.

18. Some of the relevant historical treatments of conservation are Roy M. Robbins, *Our Landed Heritage* (Princeton, N.J., 1942); Hays, *Conservation;* Richard Hofstadter, *The Age of Reform* (New York, 1955); George E. Mowry, *The Era of Theodore Roosevelt* (New York, 1958); and on Progressivism, Gabriel Kolko, *The Triumph of Conservatism* (New York, 1963). Some of the difficulties in relating the conservation movement to Progressivism are apparent in Hays, who concludes that since Roosevelt's "ultimate scheme of values was firmly rooted in an agrarian social order," he "had great respect" for Thomas Jefferson, whom Roosevelt called in his *Naval War of 1812* "perhaps the most incapable executive that ever filled the presidential chair."

validity, for it is possible to find in Progressive rhetoric and policy both positive and negative approaches to industrialism, both confidence and distrust in corporate structures, both elitism and egalitarianism. The Roosevelt administrators may have recognized that one logical extension of rapid industrialization was a new American ethos built upon science and technology, fully urbanized, symbolized by large corporate structures, and ruled by an educated elite, but they were less capable of recognizing that this ethos was far removed from the rural, individualistic, agrarian, egalitarian one of their fathers. Being children of one world and parents of another, they chose to try to combine the two; since the worlds were ultimately incompatible, however, any balance between them was naturally of the most tenuous sort. Nevertheless, in the ten years after the Spanish-American War men thought that this balance could be achieved.

Thus, to set the attitudes of conservationists and other decision-makers of the decade of consensus off against such standard political demarcations as liberalism, conservatism, reform, or reaction is less helpful than to characterize these men in terms of their reactions to twin patterns of behavior that they had encountered in their lifetimes: one associated with a rural and agrarian, the other with an urban and industrial, culture. In a sense the central task of Roosevelt and his colleagues was to reconcile the presence in America of the East and the West. The former of these regions symbolized an urban, corporate, elitist way of life, and the latter a rural, individualistic, egalitarian one, but they could merge in a triumphant reassertion of the "Americanism" that inhabitants in both those regions shared. The war of 1898 had served as a great moral crusade to demonstrate the innate superiority associated with one's being an American, and conservation policies of the Roosevelt administrations attempted to reshape the role of the federal government in order to cope more adequately with the East while preserving the virtues of the West. Moreover, throughout the period imaginative attempts to relate the experience of the West to that of the East and to the American consensus were expressed by those eastern men of the West—Frederic Remington, Theodore Roosevelt, and Owen Wister.

9. Roosevelt, Remington, Wister: Consensus and the West

"In 1885," Owen Wister wrote in the preface to his fifth volume of western stories,

> the Eastern notion of the West was "Alkali Ike" and smoking pistols. No kind of serious art had presented the frontier as yet. . . . Then, Mr. Roosevelt began to publish his vivid, robust accounts of Montana life. But words alone, no matter how skillfully used, were not of themselves adequate to present to the public a picture so strange and new. Another art was needed, and most luckily the man with the seeing eye and shaping hand arrived. A monument to Frederic Remington will undoubtedly rise some day; the artist who more than any one has gathered up in a grand grasp an entire era of this country's history, and handed it down visible, living, picturesque, for coming generations to see.

Roosevelt, Remington, and his humble self, Wister felt, had produced the kind of serious response to the West which had helped to transform it, for his eastern friends, from a borderland of savagery and civilization to "an entire era of this country's history."[1]

The western theme as expressed by Wister and his colleagues bears only a slight resemblance to earlier eastern views, which focus on those aspects of the western experience that seemed in opposition to the social order. The strength of the Leatherstocking Tales, for example, lies in the attractiveness of Natty Bumppo's anarchism, which his abundant natural environment reinforces, but Roosevelt, Remington, and Wister picture the West not as an alternative to civilization but as a particular kind of civilization, a "grim, harsh land," filled with "men with the bark on," where "a man must take care of himself." Rather than drawing distinctions between the presence and absence of organized society, they distinguish between two types of social orders—one agrarian, rural,

1. Owen Wister, *Members of the Family* (New York, 1911), p. 15.

egalitarian, and ethnically and racially homogeneous (West), and the other industrial, urban, elitist, ethnically heterogeneous, and racially mixed (East). Since they view life in the West within the wide-ranging, fluctuating, and elusive social context of late nineteenth- and early twentieth-century America, they adopt a more "serious" and detailed approach than Cooper, Irving, and Parkman.

Roosevelt, Remington, and Wister gave careful attention to the hates, dreams, and misfortunes of Westerners as well as to their values and prejudices, because each of them sensed that to come to grips with the western experience was to encounter certain aspects of American culture which the rush of industrialism threatened to sweep away. The were motivated to "westernize" themselves, in a way that earlier writers and tourists were not, by their individual dissatisfactions with their eastern heritage. Each sought for something in the West with which he could identify, and that search lent his experiences a greater significance. Idiosyncratic as their searches were, however, they can be seen to have a common cultural foundation in the state of economic and social flux that marked the latter portions of the nineteenth century.

The Roosevelt generation's sense of instability led to a general search for stabilizing forces in a fluctuating age. Businessmen sought to explain the presence of panics and depressions by a pendulum theory of economics: the national economy, they hoped, rose and fell at regular intervals and was thus ultimately predictable. Sociologists such as William Graham Sumner discussed the ever-varying American social scene in terms of rigid patterns of behavior which emphasized the interrelation of classes and the balance of nature. Members of the eastern upper class attempted to preserve their status and prestige by forming self-perpetuating, stabilizing, elitist institutions. But economic depression (the panic of 1893), violence (the Pullman strike), "mongrelization" (the heavy influx of immigration in the late eighties and nineties), and a whole host of other problems associated with an urban and industrial civilization constantly threatened stability.

Eventually individuals of Remington's and Wister's generation attempted to turn, like prodigal sons, to their fathers for security and guidance. In some cases this reassertion of a rural, egalitarian, Anglo-Saxon heritage took the form of wistful attempts to replace industrial society with an agrarian-based utopia; in others it manifested itself in a neo-Jacksonian indictment of the "undemocratic" corporation; in still others it burst out in patriotism, xenophobia, and racism. These reactions were perhaps the most noisy but by no means the only late nineteenth-century attempts to find security through a revivification of the past: the "400" and the *Social Register* attempted to equate prestige, stability, and one's family tree; exclusivist business and social organizations sought to retain power in a changing age; boarding schools and colleges were conceived of as guardians of traditional values; and while Charles Francis Adams "settled on railroading," his brother Henry began a close investigation of his family traditions and his country's early history.

The "Wild" West came, in this view, to represent the stage of civilization in America before the advent of industrialization, and as such it was both romantic and potentially tragic. Its virtues (self-reliance, "hardiness," and the like) were heroic because they suggested to Easterners of Roosevelt's generation the glories of their past, while harmonizing with their present aspirations. Yet the western kind of rugged individualism was threatened by the march of technological progress, and Remington's and Wister's contemporaries were excessively aware of the dire future in store for that America once the armies from the East reached its borders.

As the nineteenth century drew to a close and the problems of urban living became more complicated, Easterners turned with increasing attentiveness to the writings of those individualists who had encountered the western experience. After 1885, as Wister said, art of the frontier became increasingly serious business. Contemporary criticism of Roosevelt, Remington, and Wister emphasized more and more the relevance of a western way of life to eastern Americans. Though early reviews often reflect the older eastern conception of the West as a wilderness filled with strange inhabitants, as the nineteenth century moves toward its conclusion, that attitude is increasingly accompanied by a sense that the West may symbolize the last stages of preindustrial America, about to pass into oblivion. Twentieth-century reviews have entirely dropped the notion of the West as a strange wilderness and emphasize its historic and "American" qualities.

Accompanying this change in attitude toward the region is a differing response to the writers themselves. Early reviewers tend to picture Roosevelt, Remington, and Wister as chroniclers of strange happenings. As the image of the West takes on a more historic quality, the trio of writers is seen as commentators on a dying civilization, historians of America. And finally, as the spirit of the West becomes infused with other attempts to reassert American traditions in the decade of consensus, Roosevelt, Remington, and Wister are seen as patriotic-spirited "good Americans."

Neither Remington nor Wister appeared substantially in print before 1895, although William A. Coffin remarked in *Scribners* for March 1892 that "Eastern people have formed their conceptions of what the Far-Western life is like more from what they have seen in Mr. Remington's pictures than from any other source," and the New York *Tribune* in 1894 called Wister "an American Kipling . . . [who] is doing for the far West very much what Mr. Kipling did for the far East." With these brief exceptions, reviewers centered their attention on the western writings of Roosevelt in the ten years after 1885.

Initially, these commentaries tended to picture Roosevelt as an expert on a relatively unknown portion of American life. The New York *Times* reminded its readers in 1888 that "Mr. Roosevelt writes . . . of a grazing country, with but here and there spots of farm land. Through the region settlements are sparse," and followed this up a year later with the statement that "though there be more than a century separating the early pioneer of Kentucky from the ranchman of to-day, there is still the living bond of human sympathy between them," for "both have had to fight their way through the wilderness." "Men died of hunger and thirst" in Roosevelt's West, the *Times* noted, "just as they did when Boone starved in the wild woods. The social element does not change. Just as it is today on the border land of civilization, so was it in 1774." As late as 1893 the *Nation* observed in a review of *The Wilderness Hunter* that "our country still has the unexplored places, the peculiar life, and strange characters, not to be found in the earth's older regions, which belong to a nation's youth . . . and Mr. Roosevelt has seen and written of these."[2]

"Wilderness" and "strange" are words often used to describe the West in the early reviews of Roosevelt's work, coupled with "sav-

2. William A. Coffin, "American Illustration of To-day," *Scribners, 11* (March 1892), 348; New York *Tribune*, July 1, 1894; New York *Times*, November 30, 1888 (review of *Ranch Life and the Hunting Trail*); New York *Times*, July 7, 1889 (review of *Winning of the West*); *Nation, 57* (September 14, 1893), 200.

age" and "barbarous" to denote such western inhabitants as the
cowboy, and "practical" and "experienced" to characterize Roosevelt. The standard early review of *Ranch Life and the Hunting
Trail* and *The Wilderness Hunter*, both of which had appeared by
1888, pictures Roosevelt as well-suited to characterize the traps and
pitfalls of western life to those eager young gentlemen of the East
who would try ranching in the wilderness. "The business of ranching has, for some occult reason," *The Dial* maintained, "a special
charm for the gilded youth of the Eastern states; and Mr. Roosevelt
seems to have followed it . . . for some years before his fancy led
into politics." As such, the *Times* pointed out in an 1888 review of
Ranch Life and the Hunting Trail, "Mr. Roosevelt has had full
practical experience of what he writes about. . . . To be a cowboy,
[he] tells the ambitious young gentleman of the East, is by no means
an easy task." In particular, as the *Tribune* noted, to be a cowboy
meant to submit oneself to a life "that was in nearly all respects an
intelligent barbarism." The "continuous and exhausting labor" of
ranching promoted among the cowboys "a sort of reckless fatalism,"
which found satisfaction in "barbarous and crude forms of dissipa-
tion." "The cowboy," concluded the *Tribune*, is "a pretty rough
character," whose "overwrought quickness on the trigger" can only
"be regarded indulgently" when one considers that his wilderness
environment subjects him to "a servitude of the hardest kind."

The image of "young gentlemen" going West on a lark implies
a conception of the West as an uncivilized wasteland, fit for a
"gilded youth's momentary indulgences. The characterization of
the cowboys as rough, crude, and reckless harmonizes with Parkman's portraits of coarse trappers and Irving's description of sinister backwoodsmen. Consistent with these attitudes is the picturing
of Roosevelt as one who "has both felt the delights and the troubles
of a free, independent life."[3] For the most part, the West remained
in these reviews simply a region void of civilization, with the
pleasures and pains which accompanied society's absence.

Almost simultaneously with the closing of the frontier in 1891
and the publication of the Turner thesis two years later, however,
came a slight shift in attitude—a sense that whatever peculiar char-

3. *Dial, 15* (September 16, 1893), 149; New York *Times*, November 30, 1888, and
July 7, 1889; New York *Tribune*, October 14, 1888 (review of *Ranch Life and the
Hunting Trail*).

acteristics life on the "border-land of civilization" took, that life was passing from view and, as such, had begun to take on a historical importance that required closer study. For example, the *Atlantic Monthly* for 1895 saw Roosevelt's writings on the West as "rescuing from forgetfulness" much that was worth knowing of the "extremes of human condition" which "touch without intervening social grades" on the American continent. "Civilization here borders upon primeval savagery," the *Atlantic* mused. "Distinguishable types among the human strata of our frontier change and fade like forms seen in a dissolving view." The "representative figures" of this "strange and transitory mess" have been preserved in "Mr. Roosevelt's sketches from real life," for "no one has known this sociological variety better, has had more facilities for observing it, or was fitter to describe its features." In particular, "Mr. Roosevelt's cowboy" is the last of those "original wilderness hunters" who "have become creatures of vague remembrance"; and in "a little while" even "the semi-nomadic horseman of the cattle range" will "ride away into oblivion and night."

Roosevelt had had the good fortune, as *Overland* pointed out in 1896, to be "working on a ranch during the days of Frontier tragedies" and thus to be "thrown into daily contact with the border desperadoes and the Indians." "What Mr. Roosevelt had described," continued *Overland*, "will tomorrow be a mere tradition." And the *Nation*, which only four years earlier had characterized Roosevelt's West as "unexplored," its life "peculiar," and its inhabitants "strange," found in 1897 that "the days of the cattle kings, the cowboys, and the great roundups may be nearly over"; hence "their story . . . marks a stage in the development of the country that cannot be ignored." In this light, "there is probably no one better able to deal with the subject than Mr. Roosevelt."[4]

The New York *Times*, which in 1893 expressed pleasure at Roosevelt's portrait of "that part of the United States, though relatively small, which is still a wilderness," reversed its field as civilization threatened to render the Old West obsolete. In 1894 it chided those "rather aristocratic dwellers on the Atlantic coast" who deemed in earlier times "frontier people as somewhat akin to barbarians"; lamented that "there is even to-day, in large cities, a

4. *Atlantic Monthly*, 75 (June 1895), 829–30; *Overland*, 28 (November 1896), 604; *Nation*, 64 (February 4, 1897), 92.

population prone to regard the remote West in the same light";
and called the West "an integral part of the mighty American Republic." In 1896, in a review of Roosevelt's *Ranch Life and the
Hunting Trail,* the *Times* noted that "if the cattle country of the
West is fast being curtailed . . . the greater, then, must be the
interest felt in the nomadic, or pastoral conditions of former years."
Roosevelt's cowboy has evolved in these reviews from a "pretty
rough character" to a "rational, understandable human being,"
and from a reckless fatalist who "earned wages laboriously, and
spent them foolishly" to a "strong, self-reliant, and manly" individual with "many estimable traits."[5] Similarly, the *Times* saw a lesson in Roosevelt's *Wilderness Hunter:* "the possession of no other
qualities by a nation can atone for the lack of that vigorous manliness which the chase cultivates," and applauded Roosevelt for
"wisely setting himself the task of stimulating a love of country in
the rising generation."[6] Thus in the minds of eastern reviewers
Roosevelt himself had evolved from a practical expert on cattle
ranching and a teller of strange tales into first a chronicler of a
phase of American civilization and finally a patriot who saw the
legacy of a western experience in some of the ideals of modern
America.

In his ultimate role Roosevelt was lauded by *Forum* in 1896 for
his "noble and patriotic" *Winning of the West.* In a lengthy review
which set the tone for forthcoming paeans to the Rough Riders,
Forum thanked Roosevelt for "a history that enlarges . . . comprehension of the character of the nation . . . by unfolding . . . the
heroic and noble deeds of the generations that have preceded."
"Roosevelt," the review continued, "has seen that the history of the
West is the history of the movement of a people which cannot be
understood except in connection with the similar movements that
have characterized the Aryan race, and especially the English portion of it . . . Mr. Roosevelt is never weary of pointing out to us the
part the West has played in making the American nation what it is.
. . . He is a man and an American, and nothing that is human and
American is alien to him."[7]

5. New York *Times,* December 30, 1894 (review of *Winning of the West*); and
October 17, 1896 (review of *Ranch Life and the Hunting Trail*).
6. *Times,* August 6, 1894 (review of *The Wilderness Hunter*).
7. *Forum, 21* (July 1896), 570–72, 576.

Roosevelt as superpatriot captured the imagination of many eastern reviewers after 1898, and his image as a man of the West became increasingly identified with his "Americanism." He became the supreme Rough Rider, the foremost member of that regiment of true Americans. The *Nation* cynically remarked that "Colonel Roosevelt has been selected [to run for Governor of New York] largely from his distinction as the head of the Rough Riders," and the *Dial*, in reviewing Roosevelt's account of the cowboy volunteers, noted that "other regiments have been more famous in history, but none illustrates so thoroughly the possibilities of modern newspaper advertisement as this." The *Critic*, however, sounded a more dominant note:

> In [Roosevelt's book] the regiment stands and moves and lives before us as a unit—while all its individual members—from the Northwest and Southwest, the Eastern universities and the Clubs of New York—are sketched . . . with their brilliant courage in the dash up the hill, and their uncomplaining fortitude. . . . It is a long list of interesting men that their Colonel describes in these pages, with [a] hearty appreciation of true manhood. . . . The book demonstrates . . . what manner of men this country can produce when duty calls . . . how truly we are one people, how, in critical moments, all distinctions disappear, all barriers are thrown down. It vindicates, above all, the principle of equality, which has raised American manhood to a height where even those least favored by fortune or circumstances are self-reliant, self-respecting men."[8]

As early as 1893, the sense of the West as manly, egalitarian, self-reliant, and Aryan, and thus the focus of true America, had been expressed in scholarly form by Frederick Jackson Turner in his "Significance of the Frontier." In a letter to Turner a year later, Roosevelt said that he thought the "pamphlet on the Frontier . . . struck some first class ideas" and "put into definite shape a good deal of thought which has been floating around rather loosely"; he added in an 1896 letter to Turner, "I think it will be a good thing for this country when the West, as it used to be called, the Centre, as it really is, grows so big that it can no more be jealous of the

8. *Nation, 67* (October 13, 1898), 282; *Dial, 27* (November 16, 1899), 363–64; *Critic,* 35 (September 1899), 862.

East."[9] And in those instances when the ex-ranchman was not overly eager to connect his western experiences to the glories of the American past, his reviewers often helped him out. "Self-reliance" may have had a personal meaning to Roosevelt in Dakota, but to the *Nation* it was one of those traits associated with "the development of the country."

Remington's western writings appeared a full decade later than Roosevelt's first effort, and hence few reviewers used the term "wilderness" to characterize the West of *Pony Tracks* and *Crooked Trails*. However, the New York *Tribune* for 1895 noted that "the pony tracks led us into many strange and stirring scenes." The *Bookman* in the same year commented on "the vigour and occasional crudeness of the better class of people to be met in the West" and called Remington's experiences "strange and adventurous." In the next breath the *Bookman* picked up the vanishing West theme by pointing out that Remington "has roamed everywhere ... where the American may still revel in the great red-shirted freedom which has been pushed so far to the mountain wall that it threatens soon to expire somewhere near the top"; and the *Times,* for the same year, appreciated in Remington's stories "what is so delightful: a nearness to the true primitive condition of man, which is the purely physical one."

By 1898 reviewers had made a clear connection between Remington's work and the passing of a phase of America. The *Dial* called Remington "the delineator par excellence of the Indian, the cowboy and the greaser" and felt that "the sharp realism of his pictures will make them of positive historical value to future generations, when the types and phases of American character he chooses to portray have disappeared from the shifting stage of our national life." The *Times* noted that "the city and town-confined man who reads this book will marvel at the life Mr. Remington spreads out before him," pointing out that "the stories recall days now largely passed ... which still live and find a welcome place in story."[10]

9. Theodore Roosevelt, letters to Frederick Jackson Turner, February 10, 1894, and December 15, 1896, in E. Morison, *Letters of Theodore Roosevelt, 1,* 363, 571.

10. New York *Tribune,* October 31, 1895 (review of *Pony Tracks*); *Bookman,* 2 (October 1895), 150; New York *Times,* August 11, 1895 (review of *Pony Tracks*); *Dial,* 25 (October 16, 1898), 265; New York *Times,* October 29, 1898 (review of *Crooked Trails*).

In the midst of the decade of consensus Remington's *John Ermine of the Yellowstone* exhibited his hatred of the "cards and custards" of eastern civilization by demonstrating the selfishness and hypocrisy of the attitudes of white characters toward his Indianized hero. At the close of the novel John Ermine is pictured as a victim of the "march of white humanity" across the western plains: the white soldiers are particularly anxious to initiate Ermine into their community, take his hair out of braids, and teach him army phrases, but the moment he does not conform to his "station" and aspires after Katherine Searles they reject him and eventually attempt to kill him. Reviewers, with their own general commitment to white supremacy and worship of the Anglo-Saxon tradition, were baffled by Remington's tragedy. The *Times* contrasted *John Ermine* with the *Virginian,* calling it "a much nearer approach to the reality of life on the Western prairies than was to be found in Mr. Wister's entirely satisfying presentation of it from the romantic point of view." "[Remington] is to blame," the *Times* continued, "for the fact that any half fair reader's sympathy will be all on the side of John Ermine, even though he will be a little dubious himself as to the wisdom of pretty Katherine's satisfying romantic interests by actually marrying a long-haired scout. . . . Poor Ermine's civilization would not stand the test . . . his experience seems inevitable."[11] It is as if the reviewer actually felt that the "reality" of life in "civilized" America made Ermine's and Katherine's infatuation necessarily unrealized, and that the yearning proper Miss Searles had for the scout was simply an indulging of her "romantic' instincts. In asserting this, the *Times,* in the final analysis, turned its back on Ermine just as the white soldiers did; his "civilization" would not stand the test.

The *Lamp,* in a 1903 review of *John Ermine,* exhibited a similar response. "When at a critical period [Ermine] comes under the influence of a mysterious hermit who works purposely upon the white nature of his pupil," the *Lamp* maintained, "one . . . concludes that the situation is being reasonably unfolded and that the all-conquering Anglo-Saxon blood will assume its place. . . . Here is the chance to efface early association and allow innate nobility, heroism, and devotion [to come through]." "But," noted the *Lamp,* "the girl received John Ermine's homage as impertinence. In his

11. New York *Times,* December 13, 1902 (review of *John Ermine*).

humiliation white blood and heredity do not count. John Ermine is Indian, all Indian. . . . He dies practically a savage; his early training has won." The review called *John Ermine* "an interesting variant on the frontier novel" and labeled Remington "of stern stuff" for his sense of Ermine's social limitations.[12] It could no more sense the indictment of white civilization in Ermine's tragedy than Remington himself could sense the inconsistency between this indictment and his own racist attitudes.

Eastern reaction to the writings of Wister followed similar patterns. Since Wister did not appear in print to any sizable extent until after 1893, many of the reviews of his early writings, *Red Men and White* (1895) in particular, had begun to sense that Wister's West was passing into history. William Dean Howells, in a review of *Red Men and White* in *Harper's Weekly* for 1895, spoke of the "wicked world of the border" and the "desperadoes, red savages, white semi-savages, gamblers, and ranchmen" which "have never been done so well as Mr. Wister has done them"; and William Morton Payne, in the *Dial* for 1896, saw one of the "morals" of Wister's stories as "the danger to our civilization resulting from the lawlessness of the frontier." But more characteristic of contemporary reaction to *Red Men and White* was the *Tribune's* sense "that these tales of [Wister's] are really records of certain phases of American life, records of rough social phenomena which are passing from the plains and mining towns west of the Mississippi and have in some gone quite out of sight."

The *Tribune* still thought of western society as "rough" and Wister's cowboy Lin McLean as "queer," but felt that Wister was a painter of "camp life and Western adventure as they actually have been known among our cowboys, frontiersmen, and 'greasers.'" The *Nation*, reviewing *Lin McLean* in 1898, picked up this theme. "When America is so old," it noted, "that native heroes . . . have become epical and legendary, the cowboy will doubtless be the centre of an imposing cycle. Mr. Wister's Western sketches are valuable contributions to the tradition. Already the figure [of McLean] has the imaginative charm of a vanishing type."[13]

12. *Lamp*, 26 (Feburary 1903), 58.

13. William Dean Howells, review of *Red Men and White*, in *Harper's Weekly*, *39* (November 30, 1895), 1133; William Morton Payne, in *The Dial*, *20* (March 16, 1896), 173; New York *Tribune*, June 23, 1895, and November 17, 1895; *Nation*, *66* (May 26, 1898), 407.

Wister's image as a historian of the Old West was even more clearly associated with his patriotic qualities, in the minds of his readers, than that of Roosevelt or Remington. *World's Work,* in a review of the *Jimmyjohn Boss,* made a characteristic connection between the passing of Wister's West and the spirit of "real" America. "Wister," it wrote, "has exploited the essential spirit of frontier Wyoming and Arizona, the cattle people and the cattle country, with the plains and mountains where they lived, all wholly American of our blood and soil." In the same paragraph that it spoke of "cowboys and Indians and soldiers, and hard women of that lynch-law belt now gone," *World's Work* pointed out that "Mr. Wister's work expresses . . . what precious little other American fiction tries to express—Americanism." "To catch the deeper meaning of our life," the review concluded, "one's path must be toward that Western verge of the continent where all white men are American-born, because there only are the culture and conservatism of the East, the chivalry and the fire-eating spirit of the South, and the broad unhampered gambler's view of life native to raw Western soil, all transmuted into a democracy of no distinctions."[14]

Lindsay Swift, in the *Saturday Evening Post* for 1902, labeled Wister's *Virginian* "intensely American in its knowledge of un-exhausted conditions of human existence, and its bold proclamation of the dogma of the right to master and prevail under the beneficent reign of equal opportunity." Frank Jewitt Mather of *Forum* in the same year noted that "the transplanted Virginian and actual cowboy . . . is indubitably of heroic make . . . sure of his own mind and his own deed," and Hamilton Mabie of the *Ladies Home Journal* called *The Virginian* "distinctively American," Wister's West an environment which "developed the elemental qualities of manhood," and "the hero of this tale of the vanished frontier" a "real man."

In general, contemporary critics of *The Virginian* were quick to respond to the same heroic qualities that newspaper correspondents saw in the Rough Riders. Several reviews agreed with Mabie's conception of the Virginian as a real man: Hamblen Sears of the *Book Buyer,* for one, stated in 1902 that the horseman of the plains "is no pasteboard type to hang the rags of plot and passion

14. *World's Work,* 5 (November 1902), 2794.

on. . . . Mr. Wister knows how to set up his man on his own legs in all his lithe, tiger-like build." The Virginian was also gentlemanly ("Owen Wister's Virginian is a gentleman under a coat of roughness," noted the *Atlantic*), "American" ("genuinely patriotic without being maudlin," said the *Bookman*), and, of course, self-reliant (as *Forum* phrased it, "sure of his own mind and deed"). Edward Clark Marsh, writing near the end of the decade of consensus, made a full and graphic statement of the relations between Wister's fiction and that decade's ideals. "Where is our classical record of life on the Western frontier, in the fleeting period of its cowboy domination which forms the most romantic episode in American history?" Marsh asked, and then answered:

> Few would dispute that it is in the novels and tales of Owen Wister. . . . The unnamed hero is indeed the type of the cowpuncher, the classic form of him; but the type is at the same time a highly individualized man. . . . He is all himself, with his quiet manner, his self reliance, his Southern drawl. . . . Mr. Wister . . . is American through and through, and believes in it. It can quite safely be said that no living American writer of fiction is more completely indigenous than Mr. Wister. It may further be claimed that the Americanism embodied in his books is of the kind in which we may, before a world audience, feel some pride.

In summation, Wister, in "setting forth a phase of life which is to be found only in the United States," and in giving artistic embodiment to "a species of man fast passing into a remembrance," had, for the New York *Times*—and doubtless many others—"come pretty near to writing the American novel."[15]

Contemporary reaction to Remington, Roosevelt, and Wister in the late nineties and 1900s indicates the degree to which the Wild West had become firmly associated with the American heritage. Those aspects of the western experience that they emphasized

15. Frank Jewitt Mather, Jr., in *Forum*, *34* (October 1902), 223–24; Hamilton W. Mabie, in *The Ladies Home Journal*, *19* (August 1902), 15; Hamblen Sears in *Book Buyer*, *25* (October 1902), 250–51; H. W. Boynton in *Atlantic Monthly*, *90* (August 1902), 282; Edward Clark Marsh, "Representative American Story Tellers, VI. Owen Wister," *Bookman*, *27* (July 1908), 458–66.

struck vibrant chords in the hearts of their readers. As technological and financial triumphs, coupled with a vast increase in population of an increasingly mixed ethnic nature, made white Anglo-Saxon America, in the eyes of the native-born, both the glorious and most threatened nation in the world, the role of masculinity, individualism, and gentlemanliness became of crucial interest, and the fact that Roosevelt, Remington, and Wister examined such topics in a rapidly passing western context meant that both their writings and that context would be considered all the more significant. Thus the trio of writers took part in, as it were, a regional round-robin: their eastern heritage both drove them West and enabled them to respond to the western experience in such a way as to make it attractive to their eastern contemporaries, who came to envisage an integration of East and West in a twentieth-century America that contained the best of both.

That Wister, Remington, and Roosevelt, in this sense, came full cycle can be seen from their comments on one another as the turbulence of the nineties gave way to the illusory calm of the decade of consensus. In 1895 Roosevelt called Wister "a teller of tales of strong men" and suggested that he dealt with "the great problems of American existence and the infinite picturesqueness of our life as it has been and is being led here on our own continent":

> Grim, stalwart men stride through Wister's pages. It is this note of manliness which is dominant through the writings of Mr. Wister. Beauty, refinement, grace are excellent qualities in a man, as in a nation, but they come second . . . to the great virile virtues—the virtues of courage, energy, and daring: the virtues which beseem a masterful race—a race fit to fill the forests, to build roads, to found commonwealth, to conquer continents, to overthrow armed enemies. It is about the men who can do such deeds that Mr. Wister writes.

And by 1907 Roosevelt could state about Remington what he had implied about Wister:

> I regard Frederic Remington as one of the Americans who has done real work for this country, and we all owe him a debt of gratitude. . . . It is no small thing for the nation that such an artist and man of letters should arise to make permanent

record of certain of the most interesting features of our national life . . . [Remington] is, of course, one of the most typical American artists we have ever had, and he has portrayed a
most characteristic and yet vanishing type of American life.
The soldier, the cowboy and rancher, the Indian, the horses
and the cattle of the plains, will live in his pictures and bronzes
for all time.[16]

Wister was equally enthusiastic about the contribution Roosevelt and Remington had made to an understanding of the West
in its American perspective. As early as 1891 he felt that "Roosevelt
had seen the sagebrush true, and felt its poetry," and was a "pioneer
in taking the cowboy seriously." In 1894 Wister wrote Roosevelt
that he liked the "manliness and simplicity" of *The Wilderness
Hunter,* and in 1895 he congratulated Roosevelt on his *American
Ideals,* which one critic called a mass of "braggadocio and condescension." "I have the happiness to hold a firm belief in the American," Wister noted, and later called Roosevelt the "moral leader
of the United States." On Remington, Wister surpassed himself.
In 1897, standing "before many paintings of the West . . . the whole
mystic pageant of American soil; the only greatly romantic thing
our generation has known, the last greatly romantic thing our
continent holds; indeed the poetic episode most deeply native that
we possess," Wister wrote: "When Remington came with only a
pencil, I forgot the rest. . . . No words of mine can tell you how
Remington has been a poet here." And by 1902, Wister's "American heart" was smote all the more with the indigenous qualities of
Remington's work. "Remington has taken the likeness of the modern American soldier," he wrote, "and stamped it upon our minds
with a blow as clean-cut as is the impression of the American eagle
upon our coins in the mint. . . . Remington is drawing the most
picturesque of the American people. . . . Remington is not merely
an artist; he is a national treasure."[17]

16. Theodore Roosevelt, "A Teller of Tales of Strong Men," *Harper's Weekly, 39*
(December 21, 1895), 1216, and "An Appreciation," *Pearson's, 18* (October 1907), 394.
17. Theodore Roosevelt, letter to Owen Wister, April 20, 1894; Owen Wister, letter
to Theodore Roosevelt, February 27, 1895, quoted in Wister, *Roosevelt,* pp. 36, 38;
Wister, *Roosevelt,* p. 367; Wister, "Concerning the Contents," preface to Remington's
Drawings (New York, 1897); Wister, preface to Remington's *Done in the Open, Current Literature, 33* (December 1902), 651–56.

Even the misanthropic Remington could occasionally stir himself to praise his western colleagues. In 1899 he wrote to Wister:
"You have an air tight cinch on the West—others may monkey but
you arrive with a horrible crash every pop"; and he sent back one
of Wister's stories for *Harper's* in 1900 with the notation: "It
doesn't need illustrating—it's all there—I wouldn't want to inter-
fere." The same year Remington called one of Wister's stories
"great" and noted that "what we do along such lines can have no
comparison. I'm a snare drum and you are an organ."[18] It was characteristic of Remington that he responded to Wister in the same
breezy, whimsical, subjective manner that he responded to everyone else about him. Remington either liked something because it
was "true" or "all there," or disliked it because it was "damn rot."
He attempted to judge himself and his contemporaries solely by his
personal artistic standards; nevertheless, his peers' sense that the
West was a phase of the nation's history conditioned his response
in spite of himself.

Ultimately, even Roosevelt, Remington, and Wister, who had
formed friendships with one another early in life and solidified
them as each became famous, fell increasingly into conventional-
ized nostalgic and patriotic prose to characterize themselves and
one another as the twentieth century advanced. Besides dusting off
their noblest and most chauvinistic phrases to describe each other,
the trio identified themselves as "good Americans." "It would be a
mistake to nominate me for President," Roosevelt noted in 1916,
"unless the country has as its mood something of the heroic."
"They say my writings are very American," wrote Wister in 1908.
"They ought to be. I have been on this soil, ancestrally speaking,
since the Merion settlement in Pennsylvania, more than two hundred years." "I hated Europe," with its "collars, cuffs and foreign
languages," Remington confessed to Perriton Maxwell in 1907, to

18. Frederic Remington, letters to Owen Wister, 1899–1901, quoted in N. Orwin
Rush, "Frederic Remington and Owen Wister, the Story of a Friendship," in K. Ross
Toole et al., eds., *Probing the American West* (Santa Fe, N.M., 1962), pp. 154–57;
McCracken, *Frederic Remington,* pp. 34–36. Of the friendships between the three
men, that of Roosevelt and Remington appears to have been the least close. Roosevelt
wrote a handful of letters to Remington in the 1895–1909 period, most of which were
very brief (see E. Morison, *Letters*). No replies from Remington could be found in
the Remington papers at Ogdensburg, New York, or in the Roosevelt collection at
Harvard, although they surely existed at some point.

which Maxwell responded: "[Remington's] has always been a praiseworthy egotism. He is proud of his Americanism."[19]

As critic after critic sang *The Virginian's* praises, spoke of the Americanness of Roosevelt and Remington, and reveled in the fond memories of the western experience, the decade of consensus came to agree with Wister that the West was "the poetic episode most deeply native we possess." As such the cowboy took his place in a long line of inspiringly anarchistic American heroes, cartoonists reminded the public that a former Rough Rider occupied the White House, and Remington "immortalized himself" in bronze and silently counted his $25,000 a year salary. In their extraordinary desire to retain a piece of the past in a world oriented toward some frightfully technological future, Americans of the 1900s tried to balance their awareness of the implications of a complex industrial society with their hopes that that society might not turn out to be so complicated. The Theodore Roosevelt administration showed a keen understanding of what living in modern America entailed, and it planned accordingly; yet this pragmatic approach to twentieth-century realities was often coupled with vivid rhetorical assertions of the relevancy of older experiences to changing times. The New York *Times* admired the "sharp realism" of Remington's paintings, but also found "entirely satisfactory" Wister's delineation of "the only greatly romantic thing our generation has known." Eventually critics of Roosevelt and the others found themselves asking their readers to believe that the West, that land of hardy native-born gentlemen who believed in the ideals of democracy, was the "true America," while accepting its vanishing into history.

The West that the trio had helped to implant in the American imagination was no more an oasis in the urban desert than its cowboy inhabitants were gentlemen, however, and older America eventually became a feeble patriarch as the solid framework of principles and attitudes which had buttressed the decade of consensus rotted and crumbled. Morality, in its testy old age, appeared as

19. Quoted in Dixon Wecter, *The Hero in America* (New York, 1941), p. 359; Wister, quoted in *Bookman*, 27 (July 1908), p. 466; Perriton Maxwell, "Frederic Remington, A Painter of the Vanishing West," *Current Literature, 43* (November 1907), p. 525.

prudery; the gentleman's world of Anglo-Saxonism degenerated into squalling nationalism and xenophobia; the technocratic paternalists gave way to an administration which believed that "the business of government is business"; and small-town America became Main Street.

For those of the decade of consensus who survived, the times became increasingly painful. Remington, beleaguered by civilization's advances, ate and drank himself to death. Roosevelt, almost blind and infirm, made a pitiful attempt to revive the spirit of his Rough Riders in a volunteer regiment in 1917 and found polite but firm rebuffs on all sides. And Wister, who felt himself an "old-timer" in 1910, suffered through the twenties, the depression, and the New Deal. In 1933 he declined an invitation to visit Wyoming, saying that "too many ghosts are there for me. . . . I don't want to see any of that country again. Too much nostalgic for past happenings." One of his obituaries in 1938 noted that "one turns in vain to a majority of American histories of literature to find him as much as mentioned; while even most of the exceptions do little more than comment glancingly in one sentence upon the *Virginian,* and nearly all but dismiss it as the relatively respectable ancestor of a whole host of widely romanticized cowboy fictions."[20]

To modern eyes the numerous attempts to balance East and West in the 1890s and 1900s may seem as self-assured and contrived as the stiffest of Edwardian collars. Nevertheless, the search in America for an understanding of industrial and urban life, with its consequent countersearch for an alternative to that life, remains our irrevocable link to the generations of Roosevelt, Remington, and Wister. Countless commentators of the 1960s have investigated with great seriousness the task of eastern living, and countless Americans, in turn, have exhibited a strong attraction for fantasy versions of the Wild West, in the form of popular novels, motion pictures, and radio and television serials. The President of the United States in 1958 named Westerns as his favorite literary genre; in 1964 *The Virginian* appeared as a television series; and Remington's paintings still command impressive sums at urban art auctions.

20. Wister, letters to Robert V. Johnson, November 16, 1910, and to "Mr. Hancock," September 2, 1933, quoted in University of Wyoming Library Associates, *Fifty Years of the Virginian* (Laramie, Wyo., 1952), pp. 7, 8; London *Times,* July 27, 1938, obituary of Owen Wister.

It was the Roosevelt generation that first called attention to a dilemma in American culture which is still present: how to come to terms with metropolitan living while demonstrating the relevancy of alternative existences. The search for freedom from a corporate and technological world still manifests itself in the arena of national politics, as when in the flush of Barry Goldwater's triumph at the Republican Convention in 1964 pride-filled delegates rose to denounce the "Eastern Establishment," whose yoke they had momentarily cast off. Perhaps such attempts to resist the tide of corporate professionalism are as fallacious as earlier desires to implant the yeoman farmer in the midst of technocratic America, but they represent the same reluctance on the part of Americans to wholly embrace an urban and industrial society without positing alternatives to it.

References

This section is divided into two parts: the first a discussion of primary source material, and the second an attempt to place each of the chapters in the context of related secondary works. These references do not constitute a complete bibliography; they should be supplemented by the footnotes. Only those works published from 1900 on include publishers.

PRIMARY SOURCES

Chapter 1

There has not been a quantitative study of changes in the composition of the eastern upper class in the last quarter of the nineteenth century. The primary sociologist of the eastern upper class, E. Digby Baltzell, has been forced in his analyses of the relation between social stratification and urban institutional structures in the late nineteenth and early twentieth centuries (*Philadelphia Gentlemen* [Glencoe, Ill., Free Press, 1958] and *The Protestant Establishment* [New York, Random House, 1964]) to rely on an intuitive correlation between membership in the *Social Register* and attendance at certain prestigious educational and vocational institutions as his criterion for upper-class status. Baltzell has arbitrarily chosen the *Social Register* as an "index of upper-class status"; eighteen private schools as "leading" centers of educational prestige; Harvard, Yale, Princeton, and the University of Pennsylvania as "elite" universities; and certain metropolitan men's clubs, such as the Union and Somerset in Boston, the Union and Knickerbocker in New York, and the Philadelphia and Rittenhouse in Philadelphia, as the "most distinguished" of their kind in the metropolitan Northeast.

Like any scholar who attempts to identify a series of interrelated institutional structures with a hierarchical theory of social groupings, Baltzell has been criticized for imposing his own values upon his sociological model. But in one sense his choices are a helpful guide to assessing social change in the late nineteenth- and early twentieth-century East. If one correlates membership in the *Social Register* for the years 1887 to 1900 with registration lists for the aforementioned schools, colleges, and clubs, certain names reappear with monotonous regularity. Whether or not one is willing to accept Baltzell's characterization of these names as a "primary group of prestige and power," his model nevertheless aids in the uncovering of a remarkably cohesive educational and vocational pattern among a relatively small number of families.

Thus my nonquantitative attempt to evaluate the effect of social change upon an identifiable set of individuals and families focuses upon the educational and social institutions which Baltzell and others have associated with the upper class. Of the New England private schools, St. Paul's, Andover, Exeter, and Groton provided the most data. Joseph Howland Cott, *Memorials of St. Paul's School* (New York, 1891), and Owen Wister, "St. Paul's School: Retrospect and Prospect" (unpublished pamphlet, 1935), are contemporary memoirs of an Episcopalian boarding school in the 1870s and 80s, while the *Phillips Academy Alumni Directory* for 1906 and 1907 (Andover, Mass., 1907) and *A Catalogue of the Members of Pi Alpha Epsilon of Phillips Academy, Andover* (New Haven, 1897) shed light on the kinds of individuals who attended Andover in the last years of the nineteenth century. Post-Civil-War life at Exeter is described in Charles Henry Bell, *Phillips Exeter Academy in New Hampshire* (Exeter, 1883), while *A Catalogue of the Officers and Students of Phillips Exeter Academy* (Boston, 1883) and the *Alumni Directory of Phillips Exeter Academy* (Exeter, 1926) present valuable sociological data on Exeter in the late nineteenth and early twentieth centuries. The mores of Groton in this period are ably illustrated in *Groton School 1884–1902* (Groton, Mass., 1903)—a series of articles written by twenty-five Groton upperclassmen, one of whom was Quentin Roosevelt, son of the President. Frank D. Ashburn's *Fifty Years On: Groton School 1884–1934* (privately printed, New York, 1934) is valuable as both a history and a source book.

The relationship of New England private schools to the exclusive social clubs and fraternal orders at Ivy League universities can be determined by a technique used by Baltzell: the correlation of *Social Register* membership with college and club attendance for the forty-odd years after 1870. In some cases information on club membership has not been made public but is available upon request. See undergraduate catalogues for the years 1870–1910 for Harvard, Yale, Princeton, and the University of Pennsylvania, as well as membership lists for the following clubs for those years: at Harvard, The Hasty Pudding-Institute of 1770, Porcellian, A.D., Fly, Spee, and Delphic; at Yale, Fence Club, Zeta Psi, St. Anthony

Hall, and Delta Kappa Epsilon (fraternities), and Skull & Bones and Scroll & Key (senior societies); at Princeton, Ivy, Cottage, Colonial, and Cap and Gown (eating clubs); and at the University of Pennsylvania, Delta Psi (St. Anthony Hall), Delta Phi (St. Elmo's), Zeta Psi, and Phi Kappa Sigma (fraternities). Compare membership in these institutions with private school attendance and *Social Register* membership (after 1887) for a sampling of individuals.

The same correlative technique may be used in an analysis of metropolitan men's clubs. Compare *Social Register* membership with private school and college affiliation for members of the following metropolitan clubs for the 1887–1910 period: in Boston, the Union and Somerset; in New York, the Union, Century, Metropolitan, and Knickerbocker; in Philadelphia, the Philadelphia and Rittenhouse.

Social Register membership may also be correlated with vocation and, if possible, income for the same period. Since *Social Register* applications seek information about an individual's private school, college, and clubs, a number of comparisons may be made at once. As a guide to the extent to which newly acquired wealth impressed the *Register*, compare *Registers* for Boston, New York, and Philadelphia with lists of income distribution for those cities, such as *The Rich Men of Philadelphia, Income Tax of the Residents of Philadelphia and Bucks County for the Year Ending April 30, 1865* (pamphlet, Philadelphia, 1865), Gustavus Myers, *History of the Great American Fortunes* (3 vols. Chicago, Charles H. Kerr, 1911), Ferdinand Lumberg, *America's 60 Families* (New York, Vanguard Press, 1937), M. Y. Beach, "Wealth and Wealthy Citizens of New York," reprinted in Henry W. Lanier, *A Century of Banking in New York* (New York, George H. Doran, 1922), and Wellford I. King, *The Wealth and Income of the People of the United States* (New York, Macmillan, 1915).

Chapter 2

James Fenimore Cooper's writings have been collected in *The Complete Works of J. Fenimore Cooper* (32 vols. New York, Putnam's Leather-Stocking Edition, ca. 1893). Most important of these for a study of Cooper's relation to the dialectic of eastern society and western wilderness are the Leatherstocking Tales, including *The Deerslayer, The Last of the Mohicans, The Pathfinder, The*

Pioneers, and *The Prairie.* Allan Nevins has collected and abridged these five novels in a one-volume edition entitled *The Leatherstocking Saga* (New York, Pantheon, 1954). Cooper's Littlepage Trilogy, consisting of *Satanstoe, The Chainbearer,* and *The Redskins,* also deals with the interactions of East and West.

Of the western writings of Washington Irving, *Astoria* and *The Adventures of Captain Bonneville* appear in the several sets of Irving's works, the standard of which is the author's Uniform Revised Edition (New York, 1860–61). Oklahoma University Press has reprinted *Bonneville* with an introduction by Edgeley W. Todd (Norman, 1961); reproduced Irving's narrative (John F. McDermott, ed., *A Tour on the Prairies* [Norman, 1955]); and collected Irving's western journals (John F. McDermott, ed., *The Western Journals of Washington Irving* [Norman, 1944]). Stanley T. Williams, Irving's modern biographer, and B. D. Stimson have combined in another edition of *A Tour on the Prairies,* entitled *Washington Irving on the Prairie, or A Narrative of a Tour of the Southwest in the Year 1832* (New York, American Book Co., 1938).

A convenient collection of Francis Parkman's works is the Memorial Edition (Boston, Little Brown, 1905). Since Parkman's writings pursue recurrent psychological themes, any student of Parkman should be familiar with the body of his work. Parkman's western writings completed before 1865 are *The Oregon Trail, The Conspiracy of Pontiac,* and *Pioneers of France in the New World. Vassal Morton,* a novel published in 1856, is also instructive. The most authoritative source of Parkman's western journeys is Mason Wade, ed. *The Journals of Francis Parkman* (2 vols. New York, Harper, 1947). Wilbur Jacobs' edition of Parkman's *Letters* (2 vols. Norman, University of Oklahoma Press, 1960), and contemporary memoirs by O. B. Frothingham (*Proceedings of the Mass. Historical Society* [1894]), and Edward Wheelwright (*Publications of the Colonial Society of Mass., 1* [1894]) provide additional source material, as does Charles H. Farnham's *Life of Francis Parkman* (Boston, Little, Brown, 1900).

Eastern writings on the West for the 1865–85 period are numerous and of uneven quality. The following works are intended as a guide, not a full compilation: Samuel Bowles, *Across the Continent* (Springfield, Mass., 1865); Demas Barnes, *From the Atlantic to the Pacific* (New York, 1866); Silas Seymour, *Incidents of a Trip through the Great Platte Valley, to the Rocky Mountains and Laramie Plains* (New York, 1867); Charles L. Brace, *The New West* (New York, 1869); Samuel Bowles, *Our New West* (Hartford, Conn., 1869); Samuel Bowles, *The Switzerland of America* (Springfield, Mass., 1869); William Barrows, *Twelve Nights in the Hunters' Camp* (Boston, 1869); Henry E. Davies, *Ten Days on the Plains* (New York, 1871); N. P. Langford, "The Wonders of the Yellowstone," *Scribners Monthly*, 2 (May 1871), 7–16; Clarence King, *Mountaineering in the Sierra Nevada* (Boston, 1872); Charles E. Harrington, *Summering in Colorado* (Denver, 1874).

See also J. T. Reister, *Sketches of Colorado* (Macon, Mo., 1876); Richard T. Dodge, *The Plains of the Great West* (New York, 1877); Mrs. Frank Leslie, *A Pleasure Trip from Gotham to the Golden Gate* (New York, 1877); E. T. Coleman, "Mountains and Mountaineering in the Far West," *Alpine Journal*, 7 (August 1877), 233–42; Mrs. Caroline C. Churchill, *Over the Purple Hills, Sketches of Travel in California* (Chicago, 1877); Anna Gordon, *Camping in Colorado* (New York, 1879); William H. Rideing, *A-Saddle in the Wild West* (New York, 1879); I. Winslow Ayer, *Life in the Wilds of America* (Grand Rapids, 1880); Rossiter W. Raymond, *Camp and Cabin: Sketches of Life and Travel in the West* (New York, 1880); Benjamin F. Taylor, *Summer-Savory Gleaned from Rural Nooks in Pleasant Weather* (Chicago, 1880); J. W. Buel, *Heroes of the Plains* (St. Louis, 1881); Caroline H. Dall, *My First Holiday* (Boston, 1881); General J. S. Brisbin, *The Beef Bonanza* (Philadelphia, 1881); Alfred T. Bacon, "Ranch Cure," *Lippincott's Magazine*, 28 (1881), 90; Bacon, "Colorado Roundup," *Lippincott's Magazine*, 28, 622; G. Thomas Ingham, *Digging Gold among the Rockies* (Philadelphia, 1882); William H. Bishop, "Southern California," *Harper's Monthly*, 65 (October 1882), 713–28.

See also George R. Buckman, "Ranches and Ranchers of the Far West," *Lippincott's Magazine*, 29 (May 1882), 26–35; J. A. Butler, "Some Western Resorts," *Harper's Magazine*, 65 (August 1882), 341; Benjamin F. Taylor, *Between the Gates* (Chicago, 1883); Ernest Ingersoll, *Knocking Round the Rockies* (New York, 1883); George O. Shields, *Hunting in the Great West* (New York, 1883); Mary E. Blake, *On the Wing: Rambling Notes of a Trip to the Pacific* (Boston, 1883); Herman Happt, *The Yellowstone Park* (New York, 1883); Almon Gunnison, *Rambles Overland: A Trip*

Across the Continent (Boston, 1884); Clarence A. Miller, "A City in the Old West," *Overland, 4* (October 1884), 334–43; Elizabeth Custer, *Boots and Saddles* (New York, 1885); Ernest Ingersoll, *The Crest of the Continent* (Chicago, 1885); Alice Rollins, "Ladies' Day at the Ranch," *Harper's Magazine, 71* (June 1855), 3–17; Rufus F. Zogbaum, "A Day's Drive with Montana Cowboys," *Harper's Magazine, 71* (July 1885), 188–93.

Chapter 3

The sources for a study of the adolescence of Remington, Wister, and Roosevelt present striking contrasts. The Frederic Remington Papers, which are located in the Remington Art Memorial in Ogdensburg, New York, and have to some extent been duplicated on microfilm in the New York Public Library, are a researcher's nightmare. Virtually none of Remington's letters are dated, and although several can be determined to have been written in the West, the majority of these are entirely routine. (See above, Chap. 3, pp. 54–60). According to Mrs. Catherine Taggert, curator of the Memorial since 1959, no indexes for the collection existed before that date. Although such indexes are being drawn up for the Ogdensburg collection, the New York collection as of 1966 remained chaotic. In addition to letters from Remington to his wife, there are several letters to Remington from various persons, most notably Poultney Bigelow, Roosevelt, and Wister. None of Remington's replies to Roosevelt have been located; his letters to Wister may be found in the Owen Wister papers in the Manuscript Division of the Library of Congress. Remington's letters to Bigelow are in a collection of Remington's correspondence at St. Lawrence University, which also contains letters to Eva Caten and John Howard, an Ogdensburg lawyer who accompanied Remington on two of his trips to the Southwest and Mexico. The St. Lawrence collection contains over 100 letters, none of which are particularly helpful. Remington was apparently an inefficient correspondent; he was certainly a terse and uninformative one.

The remainder of the Ogdensburg collection consists of scrapbooks containing sketches, newspaper clippings, and invitations: notable among the last are two formal requests for the Remingtons' presence at dinner at the White House during Roosevelt's presidency. In general, the Remington Papers are not helpful in understanding his youth: no boyhood letters survive; if the young Remington kept diaries, they have disappeared; and the collection contains no letters from Frederic to his parents, or vice versa.

The Owen Wister papers in the Library of Congress are more extensive and considerably more manageable. Besides the Wister family's personal correspondence from 1865 to 1934, the papers include diaries, financial statements, pamphlets, scrapbooks, and manuscripts of Wister's books, as well as typescript copies of some of the western journals. (The full western journal collection is in the Western History Research Center at Laramie, Wyoming.) For this chapter the Wister family correspondence was particularly informative, especially letters from Owen to Mrs. Owen Jones Wister, his mother, for the 1865–84 and 1885–96 periods, and from Mrs. Wister to Owen for the same time span. Another collection of Wister correspondence may be found in the New York Public Library.

Theodore Roosevelt was a particularly articulate and self-conscious youth. Besides his voluminous letters to his family, friends, and acquaintances, which have been selected and edited by Elting E. Morison and others (*The Letters of Theodore Roosevelt* [8 vols. Cambridge, Mass., Harvard University Press, 1951]), Roosevelt kept several diaries, some of which have been published as Theodore Roosevelt's *Diaries of Boyhood and Youth* (New York, Scribners, 1928), the remainder of which may for the most part be found in the Theodore Roosevelt Papers at the Harvard College Library, the best source of Rooseveltiana. The Roosevelt collection in addition includes volumes of letters—catalogued by year as well as by correspondent—manuscripts, drawings, scrapbooks, and notes, all in excellent order. Any student of Roosevelt's youth should begin there. Numerous friends and acquaintances of T. R. have published accounts of his adolescent days, and one full-length book (Carleton Putnam, *Theodore Roosevelt* [New York, Scribners, 1958]), has been devoted to Roosevelt's "formative years."

The relative lack of printed material on Remington and Wister has to some extent been compensated for by the kindness of informed persons. Robin McKown, whose *Painter of the Wild West: Frederic Remington* (New York, Messner, 1959), though intended as a partially fictionalized work for juvenile readers, is the most reliable biography of Remington yet written, has fortunately preserved her notes, which include the typescripts of Remington letters, as well as old photographs and news items from Canton and Ogdensburg and from acquaintances of the Remington family, most notably G. Atwood Manley, the grandson of Gilbert E. Manley, who purchased the *St. Lawrence Plaindealer* from Colonel Seth Remington in 1873. Mrs. McKown has given me complete access to her notes, which have proved a valuable supplement to the small amount of information found in the Remington papers.

Similarly, my access to the material contained in the Owen Wister Papers has been rendered more useful by personal interviews with Mr. Owen Jones Wister and Mrs. Frances Kemble Wister Stokes, who made every effort to enhance my understanding of their father's youth. Ten of Wister's letters have been published by Mrs. Stokes in a pamphlet entitled *My Father, Owen Wister, and Ten Letters Written by Owen Wister to his Mother during his First Trip to Wyoming in 1885,* published in honor of the 50th anniversary of *The Virginian's* appearance by the University of Wyoming Library Associates (Laramie, 1952). A final revealing source of Wister's childhood is his article "Strictly Hereditary," *Musical Quarterly,* 22 (January 1936), 1–7.

Chapter 4

The most extensive source of information on Roosevelt's years in Dakota is Hermann Hagedorn's collection of notes for his *Roosevelt in the Bad Lands* (Boston, Houghton Mifflin, 1921), which has been deposited in the Theodore Roosevelt papers at the Harvard College Library. Hagedorn's notes include lengthy interviews with several Dakotans who accompanied Roosevelt on his many ventures to the Badlands, including William Sewall, his foreman on the Elkhorn ranch, William Merrifield and Sylvance Ferris, his partners on the Maltese Cross ranch, Lincoln Lang, a neighbor of Roosevelt's, and Jack Willis, his guide on a bighorn sheep hunt in the Rocky Mountains. Recollections of Roosevelt's years in Dakota by contemporaries should be compared with his own accounts in "Hunting Trips of a Ranchman," "The Wilderness Hunter," "Ranch Life and the Hunting Trail," and "An Autobiography," in Vols. 1, 2, 4, and 22 of his *Works* (Memorial Edition, 22 vols. New York, Scribners, 1923). These works, together with "Game Shooting in the West" and "Good Hunting" (in Vol. 1), "Outdoor Pastimes of an American Hunter" (Vol. 3), "A Book-Lover's Holidays in the Open" (Vol. 4), and "The Winning of the West" (Vols. 10–12), form the basis for a critical examination of Roosevelt's writings on the West. Both biographical and critical studies of Roosevelt's West are enhanced by his numerous letters from Dakota in the years between 1881 and 1886, some of which have been reprinted in Morison, *Letters,* some of which appear in Henry Cabot Lodge, ed., *Selections from the Correspondence of Theodore Roosevelt and Henry Cabot Lodge, 1884–1918* (2 vols. New York, Scribners, 1925), and the remainder of which are in the Theodore Roosevelt Collection at Harvard, as are Roosevelt's diaries for his Badlands years.

Chapter 5

Although Frederic Remington wandered incessantly through the West for a period of better than eight years, beginning in 1883, the longest period in which he based himself in any one locale was his stay in Kansas from March 1883 to the summer of 1885. For that reason it has been difficult to locate contemporary material for Remington's travels after 1885 from sources other than his own writings. On Remington in Kansas, Robert Taft's chapter in his *Artists and Illustrators of the Old West* (New York, Scribners, 1953) has been invaluable. It should be supplemented by an examination of the files of the *St. Lawrence Plaindealer* (Canton, N.Y.), from 1880–85, for occasional mention of Remington's activities, and the following Kansas newspapers for the years 1883–86: Peabody *Gazette,* El Dorado *Republican,* El Dorado *Walnut Valley Times,* and Kansas City *Tribune.* One other source of information on Remington in the West appears in Deoch Fulton, ed., *The Journal of Lieutenant Sydenham 1889–90 and His Notes on Frederic Remington* (New York, The New York Public Library, 1940). Lieutenant Alvin H. Sydenham, an officer in General Miles' cavalry troop at Fort Keogh, Montana, met Remington in November 1890, when the latter was following the cavalry as an artist-correspondent for *Harper's.*

Remington's writings have supplied the remainder of biographical information which appears in this chapter. The following have been especially useful: For Kansas, "Coursing Rabbits on the Plains," *Outing, 10* (May 1887), 111–21. For the Southwest, "A Rodeo at Los Ojos," *Harper's Monthly* (March 1894), pp. 516–27;

"An Outpost of Civilization," *Harper's Monthly* (December 1893), pp. 71–80; and "On the Indian Reservations," *Century, 38* (July 1889), 394–405. For the Great Plains, three articles in *Harper's Weekly:* "The Sioux Outbreak in South Dakota" (January 24, 1891), "Lieutenant Casey's Last Scout" (January 31, 1891), and "The Sioux War" (February 7, 1891), plus "Stubble and Slough in Dakota," *Harper's Monthly* (August 1894), pp. 451–57. *Collier's, 34* (March 18, 1905), "The Remington Number," contains "A Few Words from Mr. Remington," a brief and unsatisfactory autobiographical account of his years in the West.

Remington's western writings, which have received virtually no attention from scholars, remain in separate volumes. In chronological order, they are: *Pony Tracks* (New York, 1895)—a collection of articles from *Harper's Monthly* and *Harper's Weekly,* which has been reissued by the University of Oklahoma Press with an introduction by J. Frank Dobie (Norman, 1961); *Crooked Trails* (New York, 1898)—another collection of articles from *Harper's Monthly* and *Harper's Young People; Sundown Leflare* (New York, 1899) —a collection of five stories previously published in *Harper's Monthly; Stories of Peace and War* (New York, 1899)—three articles from *Harper's Monthly; Men with the Bark On* (New York, 1900)—a collection of articles previously published in *Harper's Monthly; John Ermine of the Yellowstone* (New York, Macmillan, 1902)—Remington's only novel; and *The Way of an Indian* (New York, Fox, Duffield, 1906)—a collection of stories which had previously appeared serially in *Cosmopolitan.*

Chapter 6

"Upon every Western expedition," Owen Wister wrote of his travels to the Northwest and Southwest between 1885 and 1900, "I kept a full, faithful realistic diary." These diaries, now termed Wister's "journals," were discovered in 1951 by Mrs. Frances K. W. Stokes and Owen Wister, Jr., and deposited in the University of Wyoming Library, with typescript copies in the Library of Congress. They form the major source of biographical information about Wister's western journeys, although they are seldom full, intermittently faithful, and hardly realistic. Some of the journals have been published in an edition by Mrs. Stokes entitled *Owen Wister Out West* (Chicago, University of Chicago Press, 1958), which must be used with care.

For a complete list of Wister's writings, see George T. Watkins, "Owen Wister Out West: A Biographical and Critical Study," (unpublished doctoral dissertation, University of Illinois, 1959), pp. 429–34. The following western writings of Wister have provided a base for the critical portions of this chapter and have illuminated the biographical portions: "Evolution of the Cowpuncher," *Harper's Magazine, 91* (September 1895), 602–17; *Red Men and White* (New York, 1896)—a collection of stories previously published in *Harper's Monthly; Lin McLean* (New York, 1897)—a novel based on more *Harper's Monthly* and *Harper's Weekly* stories; *The Jimmyjohn Boss* (New York, Harpers, 1900)—another collection of previously published stories; *The Virginian* (New York, Macmillan, 1902)—Wister's best known western novel, based on several previous stories which he had expanded and incorporated into the body of the narrative; and *Members of the Family* (New York, Macmillan, 1911)—a volume of western stories written for the most part before 1909. Wister's works have been collected in an eleven-volume edition published by Macmillan in 1928, which contains six volumes of western writings.

Chapter 7
Several of the sources previously cited in relation to Roosevelt and Remington are important in clarifying their role in the Cuban campaign. These include Morison's edition of Roosevelt's letters, the letters and diaries in the Theodore Roosevelt collection, some of which appear in Anna Roosevelt Cowles, ed., *Letters from Theodore Roosevelt to Anna Roosevelt Cowles, 1870–1918* (New York, Scribners, 1924), as well as letters from Remington to Eva Caten Remington (Remington Papers, New York Public Library), and Remington's collection of short stories, *Men with the Bark On.* Two of Remington's Cuban articles not published in that collection should also be consulted: "The Training of Cavalry," *Harper's Weekly* (April 2, 1898), and "Wigwags from the Blockade," *Harper's Weekly* (May 14, 1898).

Information about the Rough Riders and their sister volunteer regiments is based on five contemporary accounts: Richard Harding Davis, *The Cuban and Porto Rican Campaigns* (New York, 1898); Edward Marshall, *The Story of the Rough Riders* (New York, 1899); Theodore Roosevelt, *The Rough Riders* (New York, 1899); Otto L. Sues, *Grigsby's Cowboys* (Salem, S.D., 1900); and

Torrey's Rough Riders: A Historical and Biographical Souvenir of the Second United States as Volunteer Cavalry (Jacksonville, Fla., 1898). For contemporary reaction to the Rough Riders, see John G. Winter, Jr., "The Fight of the Rough Riders," *Outlook*, 60 (September 1898), 19–20; H. E. Armstrong, "Roosevelt as a Volunteer," *Independent*, 53 (September 1901), 2277–81; and the following newspapers for the year 1898: Albuquerque *Daily Citizen*, Boston *Evening Transcript*, Canton, N.Y., *St. Lawrence Plaindealer*, Cheyenne, Wyo., *Sun-Leader*, Chicago *Tribune*, Guthrie, Okla., *Daily Oklahoma State Capital*, Denver *Evening Post*, Denver *Republican*, Denver *Rocky Mountain News*, Las Vegas *Daily Optic*, New York *Times*, New York *Tribune*, New York *World*, Philadelphia *Bulletin*, San Antonio *Daily Express*, Santa Fe *New Mexican*, Sioux Falls, S.D., *Daily Argus-Leader*.

Chapter 8

Sources for a study of the social attitudes of conservationist policymakers are found in their private letters and diaries as well as in their public statements. In particular, the Francis Newlands Papers at Yale University Library, the Gifford Pinchot Papers at the Library of Congress, and the Theodore Roosevelt collection at Harvard University are extensive and informative. A contrasting of Roosevelt's letters to Pinchot with Roosevelt's inaugural addresses proved especially valuable. It is evident that although Roosevelt arrived at the notions of the federal government as "steward of the public welfare" quite independently of Pinchot and Newlands, he borrowed many of his notions about the implementation of the conservation program from them.

Congressional debates over the Newlands Act of 1902 and the proposed Newlands Bill of 1907 illustrate the rhetoric in which the technocratic paternalists clothed their proposals. The gap between the implications of conservationist legislation and the rhetoric with which that legislation was introduced is also apparent in official government publications, such as the *Report of the Inland Waterways Commission* (1908) and the *Report of the Commission on County Life* (1911). Roosevelt's public addresses, particularly those as governor of New York and as President, are suggestive; the best one-volume collection of these appears in Vol. 15 of the National Edition of Roosevelt's collected works (22 vols. New York, Scribners, 1925). Gifford Pinchot's autobiography, *Breaking New Ground* (New York, Harcourt Brace, 1947) is also valuable, though jaundiced and slipshod in places. Arthur B. Darling has edited a limited version of the Newlands Papers entitled *The Public Papers of Francis G. Newlands* (2 vols. Boston, Houghton Mifflin, 1932), which contains much important material for the years between 1898 and 1909. Roosevelt's *Autobiography* (Vol. 22 of the Memorial Edition of his works) contains informative chapters on the conservation movement.

Chapter 9

The following eastern magazines and newspapers were consulted for their reaction to the western writings of Remington, Roosevelt, and Wister during the 1885–1909 period: *Atlantic Monthly, Book Buyer, Bookman* (also briefly termed the *Lamp*), *Century, Collier's, Cosmopolitan, Craftsman, Critic, Current Literature, Dial, Everybody's, Forum, Harper's Monthly, Harper's Magazine, Harper's Weekly, Harper's Young People, Ladies' Home Journal, McClure's, Metropolitan, Nation, Outing, Outlook, Pearson's, Saturday Evening Post, Scribner's Success, World's Work, Youth's Companion,* Boston *Evening Transcript,* Boston *Globe,* New York *Journal,* New York *Times,* New York *Tribune,* New York *World,* Philadelphia *Bulletin,* Philadelphia *Inquirer, Christian Science Monitor* (Boston). For the comments of Remington, Roosevelt, and Wister on one another's writings, see, in addition to the above, letters from Roosevelt to Remington and Wister in Morison, *Letters,* and in the Theodore Roosevelt Papers; letters from Wister to Roosevelt and Remington in the Wister Papers and in the New York Public Library's collection of Wister letters; and letters from Remington to Wister in the Remington Papers, New York Public Library. No letters from Remington to Roosevelt apparently have survived.

Secondary Sources

Chapter 1

My effort to describe the formation of an Eastern Establishment is another in a series of attempts to examine social change in late nineteenth-century America through the methodological interaction of history and the social sciences. Since the 1950s historians have increasingly called upon the techniques of the behavioral sciences both as general methodological guidelines in the writing of social history and as aids in specific studies of cultural change. Pathbreakers in this respect are three interdisciplinary works of the 1950s: Erik Erikson, *Childhood and Society* (New York, Norton, 1950), David Potter, *People of Plenty* (Chicago, University of Chicago Press, 1951), and David Riesman, *The Lonely Crowd* (New Haven, Yale University Press, 1952). Erikson has emphasized the close relationship between the psychic structure of an individual and the configuration of environmental patterns in which his life evolves; Potter has drawn upon the acknowledged existence of such patterns to theorize about the "national character" of America; and Riesman has proposed that a correlation may be made between measurable manifestations of cultural change, such as a shift from a producer-oriented to a consumer-oriented economy, and changes in the kinds of qualities a culture deems "successful." Each of these works has implied that in a given historical period social change can be observed in extralegislative areas.

One of these areas has been seized upon by Richard Hofstadter in his *Age of Reform* (New York, Knopf, 1955). Hofstadter sees as one manifestation of the changes industrialism brought to eastern America a "status revolution" which realigned social groupings in terms of the dominant ethos of industrial enterprise. His model remains, whatever its limitations, an important and original interpretation of social life in the post-Civil-War era. For the historiographical implications of Hofstadter's study, see his "History and the Social Sciences," in Fritz Stern, ed., *The Varieties of History* (New York, Meriden, 1956). Critiques of Hofstadter, in addition to this chapter, are found in R. A. Shathein, "A Note on Historical Method," *Journal of Southern History*, 25 (1959), 356–65, and Richard B. Sherman, "The Status Revolution and Massachusetts Progressive Leadership," *Political Science Quarterly*, 78 (March 1963), 59–65.

Other historical treatments of nineteenth-century reform movements which draw upon the techniques of the social sciences include David Donald, "Towards a Reconsideration of the Abolitionists," in *Lincoln Reconsidered: Essays on the Civil War* (New York, Knopf, 1956); George E. Mowry, "The Progressive Profile," in his *The Era of Theodore Roosevelt* (New York, Harpers, 1958);

and Ari Hoogenboom, *Outlawing the Spoils* (Urbana, University of Illinois Press, 1961). Two general surveys of the relationship between history and the social sciences are Seymour M. Lipset and Leo Lowenthal, eds., *Culture and Social Character* (New York, Free Press of Glencoe, 1961), and Edward Saveth, ed., *American History and the Social Sciences* (New York, Free Press of Glencoe, 1964).

The changes in wealth, power, and status which marked the post-Civil-War decades have been studied in a number of contexts. George R. Taylor's *The Transportation Revolution* (New York, Rinehart, 1951) and Edward C. Kirkland's *Industry Comes of Age* (New York, Holt, Rinehart, and Winston, 1961) document changes in the American economy immediately prior to and after the Civil War, while Thomas C. Cochran, *Railroad Leaders, 1845–1890* (Cambridge, Mass., Harvard University Press, 1953), and G. R. Taylor and I. D. Neu, *The American Railroad Network, 1861–1890* (Cambridge, Mass., Harvard University Press, 1956), point to some of the principal areas in which fortunes were made. Two books by Edward Kirkland illuminate changing attitudes in the business community in this period: *Business and the Gilded Age* (Madison, University of Wisconsin Press, 1952), and *Dream and Thought in the Business Community* (Ithaca, Cornell University Press, 1956). The relation of industrialism to social attitudes in the late nineteenth century is also the subject of Richard Hofstadter, *Social Darwinism in American Thought* (Boston, Beacon Press, 1964), Irwin G. Wyllie, *The Self-Made Man in America* (New Brunswick, Rutgers University Press, 1954), and Sidney Fine, *Laissez-Faire and the General Welfare State* (Ann Arbor, University of Michigan Press, 1956).

The question of whether power became diversified or concentrated in the late nineteenth century has been debated at considerable length by sociologists and political scientists. As Edward Saveth points out, "the extent to which power is concentrated or diffused has been shown to be much influenced by the researcher's procedure" *(American History and the Social Sciences,* p. 274). E. Digby Baltzell, in *Philadelphia Gentlemen* (Glencoe, Ill., Free Press, 1958) and C. Wright Mills, in *The Power Elite* (New York, Oxford University Press, 1956), have tended to see a late nineteenth-century coalition of power in the hands of a patrician class, while Robert A. Dahl's "A Critique of the Ruling Elite Model," *Ameri-*

can Political Science, 52 (1958), 463–69, and N. W. Polsby, "The Sociology of Community Power: A Reassessment," *Social Forces* (March 1959), pp. 232–36, emphasize the diffusion of power among increasingly varied interest groups. My term Eastern Establishment suggests that the ruling elite model has some validity in the post-Civil-War East, provided one emphasizes that the coalition of Establishment institutions implied a certain amount of power diffusion.

The private preparatory school has received little attention by scholars, either in terms of its historical development or as a representative American institution. James S. McLachlan, "The Education of the Rich: The Origin and Development of the Private Prep School, 1778–1916" (unpublished doctoral dissertation, Columbia University, 1966), is the only available scholarly work on the New England private school. McLachlan presents a wealth of information in a lively and thoughtful fashion, but is forced by the scope of his study to give scant attention to the post-Civil-War boarding school as a depository of eastern patrician values. For narrative histories of some of the major New England private schools, see Arthur Standwood Pier, *St. Paul's School 1855–1934* (New York, Scribners, 1934), and Roger W. Drury, *Drury and St. Paul's: The Scars of a Schoolmaster* (Boston, Little, Brown, 1965); Claude M. Fuess, *An Old New England School* (Boston, Houghton Mifflin, 1917) and *Men of Andover* (New Haven, Yale University Press, 1928); Myron R. Williams, *The Story of Phillips Exeter* (Exeter, Phillips Exeter Academy, 1957); and Frank D. Ashburn, *Fifty Years On: Groton School 1884–1934* (privately printed, 1934) and *Peabody of Groton* (New York, Coward-McCann, 1944).

Histories of the Ivy League universities covered in this chapter include Samuel Eliot Morison, *Three Centuries of Harvard* (Cambridge, Mass., Harvard University Press, 1936), Thomas J. Wertenbarker, *Princeton 1746–1896* (Princeton, Princeton University Press, 1946), George Wilson Pierson, *Yale College: An Educational History 1871–1921* (New Haven, Yale University Press, 1940), and Edward P. Cheyney, *A History of the University of Pennsylvania, 1740–1940* (Philadelphia, University of Pennsylvania Press, 1940). Of these works only those of Morison and Pierson make a serious effort to relate the social structure of the universities to the changing demands of industrial America. Wertenbarker's study should be supplemented with Hardin Craig's *Woodrow Wilson at Princeton* (Norman, University of Oklahoma Press, 1960), which covers Princeton in the early years of the twentieth century.

Metropolitan men's clubs have received treatment in Baltzell, *Philadelphia Gentlemen* and *The Protestant Establishment* and in Mills, *The Power Elite*. Both these sources should be used with care, for they assume a cohesiveness among upper-class institutions in the twentieth century which has not been conclusively substantiated, although it may well have existed through 1940, as Baltzell claims. For a descriptive treatment of metropolitan men's clubs in the nineteenth and twentieth centuries, see Dixon Wecter, *The Saga of American Society* (New York, Scribners, 1937), pp. 252–88.

Although much has been written on the *Social Register* as an arbiter of social acceptance, it has not been fully treated as an institutional manifestation of class consciousness in an industrial society. Comments on the founding of the *Register* appear in Baltzell, *Philadelphia Gentlemen,* Wecter, *The Saga of American Society,* and Cleveland Amory, *Who Killed Society?* (New York, Harpers, 1960). The tendency of the last two works and others, such as Nathaniel Burt's *The Perennial Philadelphians* (Boston, Little, Brown, 1963), to substitute anecdote for analysis is one which has plagued historical studies of the American upper class. Edward Saveth's "The American Patrician Class: A Field for Research," in Edward Saveth, ed., *American History and the Social Sciences* (New York, Free Press, 1964), pp. 202–14, points out some analytical guidelines.

Chapter 2

Recent attempts to characterize the response of pre-Civil-War Easterners to the western experience have led to a debate over the components of the early nineteenth-century image of the West. The focus of the debate can be seen in a quotation from an antebellum eastern commentator on life in the wilderness. Cornelius C. Felton, a Harvard professor, in an 1842 review of Caroline Kirkland's *Forest Life,* lamented that in the West "manners are . . . of the most unrestrained sort . . . one is embarrassed . . . in a circle of these tree-destroying sovereigns," but found "compensation for these things" in the "activity" and "stir" of western life. Two students of antebellum American culture have used Felton's statement to promote conflicting views of mid-century relations between West and East. Henry Nash Smith, in *Virgin Land: The American West as Myth and Symbol* (New York, Vintage, 1959), finds a "covert class bias" in Felton and relates it to the notion that "writers who sought to deal with the . . . West continued for decades to waver between a direct response to their materials and the attitude of reserve or disapproval of Western coarseness dictated by the prevalent social theory" (*Virgin Land*, pp. 253, 259). On the other hand, Rush Welter, in "The Frontier West as Image of American Society: Conservative Attitudes before the Civil War," *Mississippi Valley Historical Review* (March 1960), reprinted in Saveth, *American History and the Social Sciences*, pp. 322–39, claims that Smith has badly paraphrased Felton, and that Felton's statement actually indicates that traditional eastern fears of the West had by the 1840s "metamorphosed into a tacit recognition (however reluctant) that the West embodies American political institutions in their most characteristic form." "In their reflections on the character of the people who took up land in the West and on the social situation in which they found themselves," Welter maintains, eastern conservatives "betrayed a grudging admiration for men and social institutions they would not otherwise have respected. Their relative tolerance in this respect helped to prepare the way for an idealization of the man of the West as the American hero and of western society as the model of our social implications."

Smith and Welter's debate has raged on, pitting such studies as Richard Chase, *The American Novel and Its Tradition* (Garden City, N.Y., Doubleday, 1957), Charles Sanford, *The Quest For Paradise* (Urbana, University of Illinois Press, 1961), A. N. Kaul, *The American Vision* (New Haven, Yale University Press, 1963), and Leo Marx, *The Machine in the Garden* (New York, Oxford University Press, 1964), which see contradictory attitudes toward the West as representative of deeper paradoxes within nineteenth-century American culture, against recent interpretations such as Edwin Fussell's *Frontier* (Princeton, Princeton University Press, 1965) and William Goetzmann's *Exploration and Empire* (New York, Knopf, 1966), which find beyond the physical and social ambivalence of the West a wholesale release of energies which marked the westward movement, that native burst of activity which was an "expressive" emblem "for the invention and development of a new national civilization" (Goetzmann, p. 305; Fussell, p. 13).

An examination of eastern attitudes toward the West on both sides of the Civil War reveals that Smith and Welter are needlessly opposed. Pre-Civil-War Easterners of high social status did react to the western experience with a mixture of patrician distaste and patriotic fervor, and the man of the West did for a time become the American hero. But the transition from the former attitude to the latter was by no means as smooth as Welter implies. As this chapter points out, the ambivalent nature of eastern responses to the West underwent a twofold transformation in the post-Civil-War period. In his fascination with raw industrialism, the fashionable Easterner of the 1870s and 80s scorned and disregarded the "westernness" of the West; out of his profound disillusionment with an industrial society, the Easterner of the 1890s and 1900s attempted to rehabilitate the enthusiasm for wide open spaces so characteristic of the pre-Civil-War point of view. Optimistic mid-century Americans delighted with Whitman in contradiction and alternative possibilities; their postbellum counterparts directed their energies toward industrial enterprise and then frantically attempted to restore the "balanced" civilization they had once supposedly attained. Inherent in that balance was the "idealization of western society as the model of our social aspirations" (Welter, in Saveth, *American History*, p. 322).

Specific studies of various nineteenth-century eastern travelers and commentators have been helpful in this chapter. On Cooper, Henry Nash Smith's chapters in *Virgin Land*, "Leatherstocking and the Problem of Social Order" and "Cooper and the Stages of Society," examine the interaction between a stable eastern social order and the western wilderness; while Donald Ringe, *James Fenimore Cooper* (New Haven, Twayne Publishers, 1962), and A. N. Kaul, *The American Vision* (New Haven, Yale University Press, 1963), discuss Cooper's simultaneous attraction for the most and least civilized aspects of nineteenth-century American society. Other books and articles which contributed to an understanding of Cooper include R. W. B. Lewis, *The American Adam* (Chicago, University of Chicago Press, 1955); Roy Harvey Pearce, "The Leatherstocking Tales Re-examined," *South Atlantic Quarterly, 46*

(1947), 524–37, and Charles B. Brady, "James Fenimore Cooper, Myth-Maker and Christian Romancer," in Harold C. Gardiner, ed., *American Classics Reconsidered* (New York, Scribners, 1958).

The recent literature on Washington Irving is not extensive. Stanley T. Williams' *Life of Washington Irving* (2 vols. New York, Oxford University Press, 1935) and Edward Wagenknecht's *Washington Irving, Moderation Displayed* (New York, Oxford University Press, 1962) discuss Irving's life and work as a unit, while William L. Hedges' *Washington Irving: An American Study* (Baltimore, Johns Hopkins Press, 1965) is a critical examination of Irving's career prior to his first visit West in 1832. Articles of interest on Irving and the West include Leonard B. Beach, "American Literature Re-Examined: Washington Irving, the Artist in a Changing World," *University of Kansas City Review, 14* (1948), 259–66; Samuel T. Williams, "Washington Irving and Andrew Jackson," *Yale University Library Gazette, 19* (1945), 67–69; Terence Martin, "Rip, Ichabod, and the American Imagination," *American Literature, 31* (1959), 137–49; Jason A. Russell, "Irving: Recorder of Indian Life," *Journal of American History, 25* (1931), 185–95; and Joseph P. Woburn, "Centennial of the Tour of the Prairies by Washington Irving (1832–1932)," *Chronicles of Oklahoma, 10* (1932), 426–33.

Francis Parkman's career has received considerable attention from modern scholars. The two most important full-length studies of Parkman are David Levin, *History As Romantic Art* (Stanford, Stanford University Press, 1959), which is an attempt to see Parkman in the context of the mid-nineteenth century Romantic movement, and Howard Doughty, *Francis Parkman* (New York, Macmillan, 1962), a brilliant parabiographic synthesis of Parkman's family background, neuroses, and literary achievements. Other recent treatments of Parkman include Mason Wade, *Francis Parkman: Heroic Historian* (New York, Viking, 1942), and Otis Pease, *Parkman's History: The Historian as Literary Artist* (New Haven, Yale University Press, 1953). Bernard DeVoto, in *Year of Decision* (Boston, Little, Brown, 1943), and Smith, in *Virgin Land*, have briefly treated Parkman's western travels, while William R. Taylor, "A Journey into the Human Mind: Motivation in Francis Parkman's La Salle," *William and Mary Quarterly, 19* (April 1962),

220–27, is an imaginative attempt to apply psychological techniques to the reading of one of Parkman's histories.

Eastern attitudes toward the West in the twenty-odd years following the Civil War have not been studied in detail. Earl Pomeroy's *In Search of the Golden West: The Tourist in Western America* (New York, Knopf, 1957), Robert Taft's *Artists and Illustrators of the Old West* (New York, Scribners, 1953) and Gene Gressley's *Bankers and Cattlemen* (New York, Knopf, 1966), have as their secondary concern the attitudes of eastern tourists, artists, and capitalists in the period.

Chapter 3

My analysis of the adolescence of Remington, Roosevelt, and Wister has been influenced by the writings of scholars in the field of social psychology, particularly those of Erik Erikson and Kenneth Keniston. Erikson's *Childhood and Society, Identity and the Life Cycle* (New York, International Universities Press, 1959) and *Young Man Luther* (New York, Norton, 1958) posit theories of human psychic growth, and the interrelations of psychoanalysis and history, and Keniston's *The Uncommitted: Alienated Youth and American Society* (New York, Harcourt, Brace and World, 1965) and "Social Change and Youth in America," *Daedalus, 91* (1962), 145–71, provide models for an examination of adolescence in a shifting cultural context.

The relationship of family structure to adolescent development has been studied in Talcott Parsons and Robert F. Bales, *Family, Socialization, and Interaction Process* (Glencoe, Ill., Free Press, 1955), and in Theodore Lidz, *The Family and Human Adaption* (New York, International Universities Press, 1963). Each of the above has been helpful in increasing my understanding of occupational role-playing, an important aspect of the adolescence of Roosevelt, Remington, and Wister. A number of suggestive articles on adolescence have been collected in Erik Erikson, ed., *The Challenge of Youth* (New York, Anchor, 1965); see especially Erikson's "Youth: Fidelity and Diversity," pp. 1–29.

Remington's youth has been dealt with in two biographical studies: Harold McCracken's *Frederic Remington: Artist of the Old West* (Philadelphia, Lippincott, 1947) and Robin McKown's

Painter of the Wild West: Frederic Remington (New York, Messner, 1959). McKown's account, though in part fictionalized, is more
reliable. McCracken has relied heavily on personal interviews with
Emma L. Caten, the sister-in-law of Remington, and John C.
Howard of Ogdensburg. These interviews took place long years
after the fact and cannot be regarded as authoritative; comparisons
with the *St. Lawrence Plaindealer* files for the years of Remington's youth reveal several inaccuracies, such as the contention that
Seth Remington returned to Canton from the Civil War in 1865
(he actually returned in 1867). McCracken's bibliographic check-
list of Remingtoniana is also spotty.

Several shorter works have shed more light on Remington's
youth. Atwood Manley, *Some of Frederic Remington's North
Country Associations* (pamphlet, Canton, N.Y., 1961), is a valuable
source of Remington's boyhood exploits, including several remarkable photographs. Robert Taft's chapter on Remington in his
Artists and Illustrators of the Old West, although specifically concerned with Remington's life in Kansas from 1883 to 1884, contains
a number of suggestive items on Remington's adolescence. Oris
Edison Crooker, "A Page from the Boyhood of Frederic Remington," *Collier's, 14* (September 17, 1900), and Nellie Hough, "Remington at Twenty-Three," *International Studio, 76* (February
1923), relate anecdotes of Remington's experiences at Highland
Military Academy and Kansas City respectively.

Roosevelt's adolescence has been studied in more detail, though
in most cases without the benefits of recent developments in the
social sciences. William T. Cobb, *The Strenuous Life: A History
of the Oyster Bay Roosevelts* (New York, Ridge, 1946), and Hermann Hagedorn, *The Roosevelt Family of Sagamore Hill* (New
York, Macmillan, 1954), accounts of Theodore Roosevelt's family
background, bog down in gossip and anecdote. The most complete
study of Roosevelt's youth is found in Carleton Putnam, *Theodore
Roosevelt: Volume One, The Formative Years* (New York, Scribners, 1958), which covers in detail Roosevelt's life from 1858 until
1886. Putnam, despite his title, does not pursue psychological
themes in Roosevelt's adolescence; he rather stresses the social
aspects of Roosevelt's family situation and his early athletic and
academic training. Henry Pringle, in his *Theodore Roosevelt: A
Biography* (New York, Harcourt, Brace, 1931), gives more atten-

tion to the psychic structure of Roosevelt. Pringle, who sees T. R. as a perpetual adolescent, is sometimes guilty of grinding an axe rather than allowing the many sides of Roosevelt's character to emerge.

Owen Wister's adolescence, like the remainder of his life, has received the scantiest of attention from scholars. Some of Wister's boyhood experiences are commented upon in Mrs. Frances K. W. Stokes' *My Father, Owen Wister* (Laramie, Wyo., University of Wyoming Library Associates, 1952) and *Owen Wister Out West* (Chicago, University of Chicago Press, 1958), while George T. Watkins, who was denied access to the Wister papers, has an unconvincing chapter on what he terms Wister's "formulative Years" in his "Owen Wister and the American West," unpublished doctoral dissertation (University of Illinois, 1959). Brief treatments of Wister's adolescent years in Philadelphia appear in George T. Watkins, "Wister and the Virginian," *Pacific Northwesterner*, 2 (Fall 1958), 49–52; Walter V. Clark, "Philadelphia Gentleman in Wyoming," *New York Times Book Review* (March 30, 1958), p. 1 (a review of *Owen Wister Out West*); and E. Digby Baltzell, in his *Philadelphia Gentlemen*. Each of these reflects the lack of source material available on Wister prior to June 1963, when the Wister Papers were opened to the public.

Chapter 4

The major studies of Roosevelt's Dakota experiences are Putnam, *Theodore Roosevelt*, pp. 198–595, and Hermann Hagedorn, *Roosevelt in the Bad Lands* (Boston, Houghton Mifflin, 1921). Putnam, as previously noted, is more thorough and reliable, although inclined to narrate rather than analyze. Three of Roosevelt's contemporaries have published their own accounts: Lincoln Lang, *Ranching with Roosevelt* (Philadelphia, Lippincott, 1926); William W. Sewall, *Bill Sewall's Story of T. R.* (New York, Harpers, 1919); and Jack Willis with Howard Smith, *Roosevelt in the Rough* (New York, Washburn, 1931). Each is a lively and impressionable account of the author's encounters with Roosevelt, less revealing of T. R. than of the author.

Several articles have illuminated portions of Roosevelt's Badlands experiences and commented on his western writings. Two by Ray H. Mattison on "Roosevelt and the Stockmen's Association"

(*North Dakota History*, *17* [April 1950], 73–95, and *17* [July 1950], 177–207) discuss T. R.'s presidency of the Little Missouri Stockgrowers Association in terms of his later career. Mattison had also contributed two other articles on Roosevelt's years in Dakota: "Ranching in the Dakota Badlands: A Study of Roosevelt's Contemporaries," *North Dakota History*, *19* (April 1952), 92–128, and, with Olaf T. Hagen, "Pyramid Park—Where Roosevelt Came to Hunt," *North Dakota History*, *21* (October 1952), 215–39. Much of the information found in the above is summarized in Ray H. Mattison and Chester L. Brooks, *Theodore Roosevelt and the Dakota Badlands* (Washington National Park Service, 1958), a sixty-page pamphlet issued on the hundredth anniversary of Roosevelt's birth. On Roosevelt's western writings, see George B. Utley, "Theodore Roosevelt's *Winning of the West:* Some Unpublished Letters," *Mississippi Valley Historical Review, 30* (March 1944), 495–506; Elwyn B. Robinson, "Theodore Roosevelt: Amateur Historian," *North Dakota History*, 25 (January 1958), 5–13; and Robert W. Sellen, "Theodore Roosevelt: Historian with a Moral," *Mid-America, 41* (October 1959), 223–40.

Chapter 5
Besides the very brief accounts of Remington's journeys to Dakota and the Southwest in McCracken's and McKown's biographies, and Robert Taft's chapter, "Remington in Kansas," in *Artists and Illustrators of the Old West*, pp. 194–211, there have been no studies of his western years. Nor have there been any recent examinations of Remington's writings on the West, with the exception of E. Douglas Allen's brief "Frederic Remington—Author and Illustrator," *New York Public Library Bulletin, 49* (October 1945), 895ff—a guide to Remington's periodical writings and illustrations; and Helen L. Cord, *The Collector's Remington* (privately printed, Woonsocket, R.I., 1946)—a terse but informative pamphlet. Remington as an artist and illustrator has also been treated in John I. H. Bauer, *Revolution and Tradition in Modern American Art* (Cambridge, Mass., Harvard University Press, 1958); Alexander Eliot, *Three Hundred Years of American Painting* (New York, Time, Inc., 1957); Oliver W. Larkin, *Art and Life in America* (New York, Rinehart, 1957); Lewis Mumford, *The Brown*

Decades (New York, Dover, 1955); and E. P. Richardson, *Painting in America* (New York, Crowell, 1956).

Chapter 6

Wister's western travels have been touched upon in Stokes, *Owen Wister Out West,* and treated in fuller detail in Watkins, "Owen Wister and the American West." Unfortunately, Watkins was not able to consult the typescripts of Wister's western journals in the Library of Congress, and had difficulty in gaining access to those journals which Mrs. Stokes did not include in her edition; hence his treatment of Wister's years in Wyoming is curiously incomplete in some places. For background material on the politics and economics of Wyoming in the 1880s and 90s and on the Johnson County War itself, the following studies have proved valuable: Lewis Atherton, *The Cattle Kings* (Bloomington, University of Indiana Press, 1961); John Clay, *My Life on the Range* (Norman, University of Oklahoma Press, 1963); Lewis L. Gould, "Willis Van Devanter in Wyoming Politics, 1884–1897" (unpublished doctoral dissertation, Yale University, 1966); Gressley, *Bankers and Cattlemen;* A. S. Mercer, *The Banditti of the Plains* (Norman, University of Oklahoma Press, 1949); and E. S. Osgood, *The Day of the Cattlemen* (Minneapolis, University of Minnesota Press, 1929). Helena Huntington Smith, *The War on Powder River* (New York, McGraw-Hill, 1966) should be used with care. Important articles include Lewis L. Gould, "A. S. Mercer and the Johnson County War: A Reappraisal," *Arizona and the West, 7* (Spring 1965), 5–20; Gene M. Gressley, "Teschemacher and deBillier Cattle Company," *Business History Review, 33* (Summer 1959), 121–37; "Harvard Man Out West: The Letters of Richard Trimble," *Montana, 10* (January 1960), 14–23; and "The American Cattle Trust: A Study in Protest," *Pacific Historical Review, 30* (February 1961), 61–77; as well as George T. Watkins, "Johnson County War," *Pacific Northwesterner, 5* (Spring 1961), 17–28, a bibliographical guide.

Secondary works on Wister's writings include E. Douglas Branch, *The Cowboy and His Interpreters* (New York, Appleton, 1928)—a savage treatment of Wister's lack of authenticity in his western tales; Joe B. Frantz and J. Ernest Choate, Jr., *The American Cowboy: The Myth and the Reality* (Norman, University of Oklahoma

Press, 1955)—a wry commentary on fiction and fact in legends of the Old West; S. M. Agnew, "Destry Goes on Riding: The Virginian," *Publisher's Weekly, 157* (August 23, 1952), 746–51, and Bennett Cerf, "Trade Winds: Fiftieth Anniversary of the Publication of the Virginian," *Saturday Review, 35* (July 1953), 4—tributes to the longevity of Wister's cowboy hero; George T. Watkins, "Wister and the Virginian," *Pacific Northwesterner, 2,* 49–52—a note on the composition of the novel; and Mody Boatright, "The American Myth Rides the Range," *Southwest Review, 36* (Summer 1951), 163–65, a provocative discussion of Anglo-Saxon supremacist notions reflected in the figure of the Virginian. Leslie Fiedler has some illuminating references to *The Virginian* and to the theme of East-West interactions in his *Love and Death in the American Novel* (New York, Stein & Day, 1966). Fiedler sees the West as in American literature, "a world of male companions and sport, an anti-civilization, simple and joyous," and finds *The Virginian* "a fable, cloying and false, which projects at once the self hatred of the genteel eastern sophisticate confronted with the primitive, and his dream of a world where 'men are men,'" (pp. 260, 355).

Chapter 7

The only full-length study of the Rough Riders is Clifford P. Westermeier's *Who Rush to Glory: The Cowboy Volunteers of 1898* (Caldwell, Ida., Caxton Printers, 1958). Westermeier's account, which also includes brief histories of the two other cowboy volunteer cavalry units of 1898, Grigsby's Cowboys and Torrey's Rocky Mountain Riders, is informative but of uneven quality. Briefer treatments of the Rough Riders include John Alley, "Oklahoma in the Spanish-American War," *Chronicles of Oklahoma, 20* (March 1942), 43–50; J. R. Johnson, "Nebraska's Rough Riders in the Spanish-American War," *Nebraska History, 29* (June 1948), 105–12; as well as Westermeier's "The Dodge City Cowboy Band," *Kansas State Historical Quarterly, 19* (February 1951), 1–11, and "Teddy's Terrors: The New Mexican Volunteers of 1898," *Kansas State Historical Quarterly, 27* (April 1952), 107–36. For background material on the Cuban crisis of 1896 and the events leading to the Spanish-American war, see Walter Lafeber, *The New Empire* (Ithaca, Cornell University Press, 1963), and Ernest R. May, *Imperial Democracy* (New York, Harcourt, Brace, 1961).

Chapter 8

The Roosevelt conservation movement, like many other reflections of administration policy in the Progressive Era, has under-
gone reexamination since the 1950s. Previous interpretations of
the Roosevelt conservationists had identified them with a long
American tradition of economic and social justice, and had suggested, to oversimplify, that the advocates of conservation were
"progressives" or "liberals" in terms of their social attitudes. Such
works as Roy M. Robbins, *Our Landed Heritage* (Princeton,
Princeton University Press, 1942), pp. 301–79, and E. Louise Peffer,
The Closing of the Public Domain (Stanford, Stanford University
Press, 1951), reflect this view. Building on original research as well
as a series of reinterpretations of the goals of the Progressive leaders and the locus of power in the Progressive Era, emanating perhaps from John M. Blum's *The Republican Roosevelt* (Cambridge,
Mass., Harvard University Press, 1954), Samuel Hays has challenged the earlier interpretation. Blum has pictured Roosevelt as a
pragmatic conservative utilizing power and political skills to
preserve a time-honored system of values; similarly, Hays sees conservation as an efficiency-minded movement concerned with
strengthening and modernizing certain established features of the
governmental structure (Hays, *Conservation and the Gospel of
Efficiency* [Cambridge, Mass., Harvard University Press, 1959]).

The implications of Hays' study for Progressive historiography
have been spelled out in two articles, "The Social Analysis of
American Political History, 1880–1920," *Political Science Quarterly, 80* (September 1965), 373–94, and "The Politics of Reform in
Municipal Government in the Progressive Era," *Pacific Northwest
Quarterly, 55* (October 1964), 157–69. Hays concludes that "available evidence indicates that the source of support for reform in municipal government did not come from the lower or middle classes,
but from the upper class. The leading business group in each city
and professional men closely allied with them initiated and dominated municipal movements." Although reformers "used the ideology of popular government," according to Hays, "they in no sense
meant that all segments of society should be involved equally in municipal decision making. . . . Municipal reform in the early twentieth
century involves a paradox: the ideology of an extension of political
control and the practice of its concentration." In the final analysis,

according to Hays, "the political leadership of the industrial elite depended as much upon its identification with particular culture patterns as upon its economic achievements." (Hays, *Pacific Northwest Quarterly*, *55*, 159, 160, 167; *Political Science Quarterly*, *80*, 381.)

Hays is suggesting that not only the conservation movement but perhaps the whole cluster of early twentieth-century reforms that historians have grouped under the term "Progressivism" had as their main sources of support "the leading business groups and professional men in each city": the "upper class." This is a radical departure from the interpretations offered by Hofstadter and Mowry, which picture the ideal Progressive as either an alienated professional or a middle-class white-collar worker. Hays' view tends to suggest, as Gabriel Kolko has maintained in *The Triumph of Conservatism* (New York, Free Press of Glencoe, 1963), that Progressivism was a movement to protect the interests of individuals at the apex of the industrial power structure. Yet Hays fails to stress strongly enough his awareness that the Roosevelt conservationists, like other Progressives, "adopted the ideology of an extension of political control" at the same time that they attempted to put its concentration into practice. What I have seen as a major objective of the Roosevelt conservationists can be held applicable to many Progressives: the restoration or maintenance of a "conventional consensus on a particular view of the universe, a particular set of values, and a particular constellation of behavioral modes in the country's commerce, its business, its social relations, and its politics. Progressivism sought to save the old view and the old values and modes, by seeking to educate the immigrants and the poor so as to facilitate their acceptance of and absorption into the Anglo-American mode of life." (Richard M. Abrams, "The Failure of Progressivism," unpublished manuscript read at the Organization of American Historians, Cincinnati, Ohio, April 28, 1966.)

For additional reexaminations of the Progressive Era, see the following articles: Robert H. Wiebe, "Business Disunity and the Progressive Movement, 1901–1914," *Mississippi Valley Historical Review*, *44* (March 1958), 664–85, and "The House of Morgan and the Executive, 1905–1913," *American Historical Review*, *65* (October 1959), 49–60; John M. Blum, "The Presidential Leadership of Theodore Roosevelt," *Michigan Alumni Quarterly Review*, *65*

(December 1958), 1–9; and the following appendixes to Elting E. Morison's edition of the *Letters of Theodore Roosevelt* (8 vols. Cambridge, Mass., Harvard University Press, 1951): Vol. 6, Apps. 1 and 2 (John M. Blum), and Vol. 8, App. 3 (Alfred D. Chandler, Jr.), as well as Elting E. Morison's introduction to Vol. 5.

Suggestive articles on the conservation movement include Whitney R. Cross, "Ideas in Politics: The Conservation Policies of the Two Roosevelts," *Journal of the History of Ideas, 14* (June 1953), 421–38; E. C. Blackory, "Theodore Roosevelt's Conservation Policies and Their Impact upon America and the American West," *North Dakota History,* 25 (October 1958), 107–17; Lawrence Bakestraw, "Uncle Sam's Forest Reserves," *Pacific Northwest Quarterly, 44* (October 1953); and especially J. Leonard Bates, "Fulfilling American Democracy: The Conservation Movement, 1907 to 1921," *Mississippi Valley Historical Review, 44* (June 1957), 29–57. Bates reaffirms older interpretations of the social attitudes of the Roosevelt conservationists. Studies of two of the major advocates of conservation policy are M. Nelson McGeary, *Gifford Pinchot: Forester-Politician* (Princeton, Princeton University Press, 1960), and Martin L. Fausold, *Gifford Pinchot, Bull Moose Progressive* (Syracuse, Syracuse University Press, 1961), on Pinchot; and William Lilley, III, "The Early Career of Francis G. Newlands, 1848–1897" (unpublished doctoral dissertation, Yale University, 1966), on Newlands.

Chapter 9

Little has been written on contemporary reaction to the writings of Roosevelt, Remington, and Wister or on the various relationships between the men themselves. Don D. Walker, "Wister, Roosevelt, and James: A Note on the Western," *American Quarterly, 12* (Fall 1960), 358–66, raises some interesting notions about the relationship of masculinity-worship to the western novel, while Carl Bode, "Henry James and Owen Wister," *American Literature, 26* (May 1954), 251–52, contains an astonishing letter from James to Wister, which reaffirms the notion of a cluster of shared attitudes in the decade of consensus. Said James, who is often thought of as a critic of all that was crudely and boisterously American: "What I like best in [*The Virginian*] is exactly the fact of the *subject* itself, so clearly and finely felt by you, I think, and so firmly carried out as the exhibition, to the last intimacy, of the man's character, the personal and moral complexion and evolution, in short, of your hero. On this I heartily congratulate you; you have made him *live* . . . you have reached with him an admirable objectivity, and I found the whole thing a rare and remarkable feat . . . write me another W[ild] W[est] novel all the same . . . write me something equally American on this scale or with this seriousness—for it's a great pleasure to see you bringing off so the large and the sustained. How I envy you the personal knowledge of the Wild West, the possession of the memories that *The V[irginian]* must be built on, and the right to a competent romantic feeling about them." (James to Wister, August 7, 1902 [italics James'].) A final article is N. Orwin Rush's "Frederic Remington and Owen Wister: The Story of a Friendship," in K. Ross Toole et al., eds., *Probing the American West* (Santa Fe, Museum of New Mexico Press, 1962), pp. 154–57, which reprints several letters exchanged between Wister and Remington from 1896 until 1909.

Index